Erotic
Photography

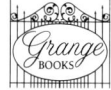

Grange
BOOKS

Text: Alexandre Dupouy

Page 4 :
N° 51
c. 1925
A. Noyer Editions
Gelatin silver print, 24 x 18 cm

Layout:
Baseline Co Ltd
127-129A Nguyen Hue
Fiditourist 3rd Floor
District 1, Ho Chi Minh City
Vietnam

© 2007, Sirrocco, London, UK
© 2007, Confidential Concepts, Worldwide, USA
© Alexandre Dupouy Collection

Published in 2007 by Grange Books
an imprint of Grange Books Plc
The Grange Kingsnorth Industrial Estate
Hoo, nr Rochester, Kent ME3 9ND
www.grangebooks.co.uk

ISBN: 978-1-84013-852-8

Printed in China

"Eroticism lies in the possibility of a movement. It belongs to the realm of the dream."

Jean-François Somain

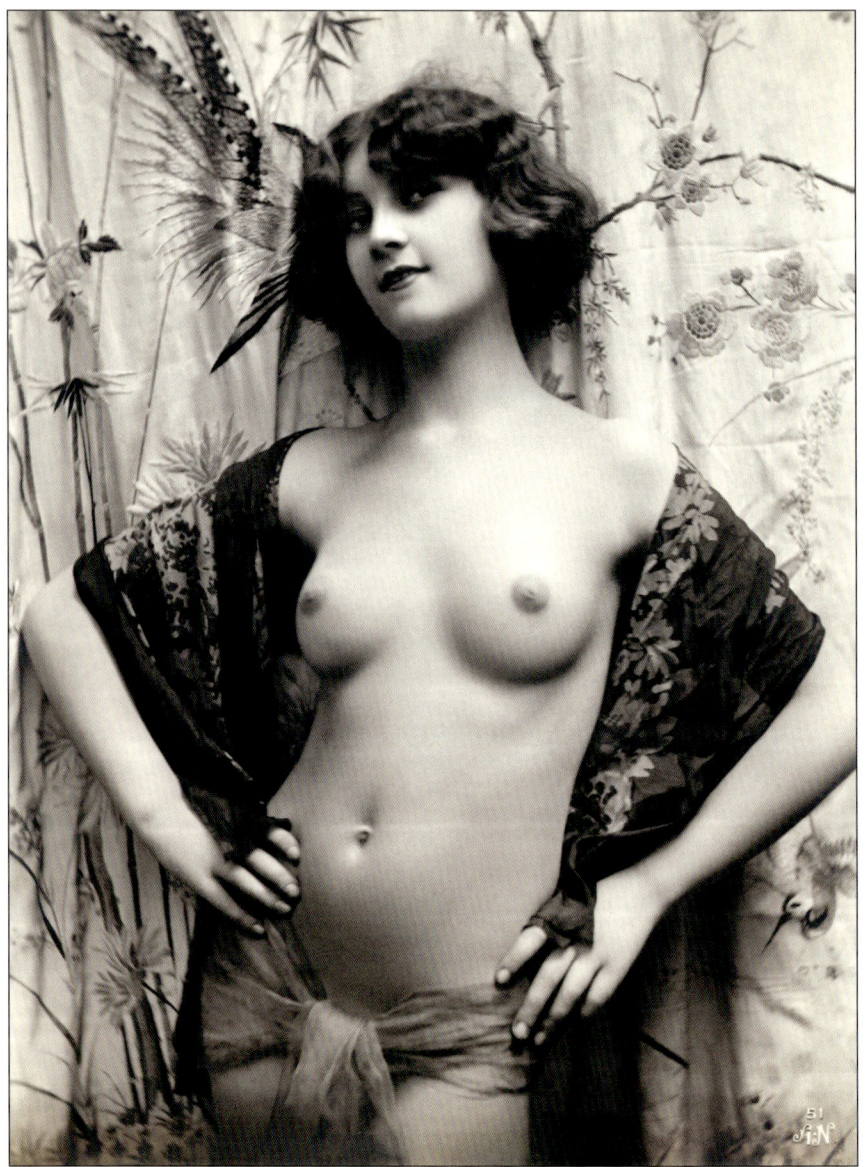

4

History of Erotic Photography

1850-1860

The daguerreotypes available were intended for a wealthy clientele. Afterwards, different photographic procedures, especially on paper, enabled the duplication of images.

1861-1913

Imperial and republican censorship obliged photographers to work in an academic atmosphere, hypocritically aimed at helping the traditional fine arts of painting and sculpture, or in total anonymity, indulging in sheer abandon when intended for lovers of pornography. This anonymity was unavoidable in order to escape the wrath of justice and the discomfort of prisons, but was profitable when it came to illustrating the most shocking subjects.

A. Bert

Yrélaw

Å (monogram)

J. R.

Boulanger

M.F.

1914-1918

With postcards, nude photography became a common sight. Hundreds of thousands of these little cards depicted the comforting image of a desirable woman on the front with the tacit approval of the authorities.

1919-1939

With the war over, women, having suffered a number of difficulties and sorrows in remaining at home by themselves, became emancipated. They discovered, among other things, that they were fully capable of doing a man's job. Their attitudes changed. For the photographer, they no longer posed in an academic manner in order to serve as models for hypothetical artists. They were free and this feeling showed in their images.

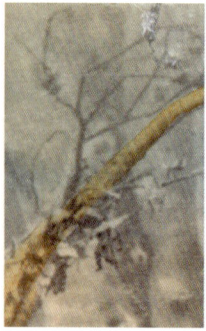

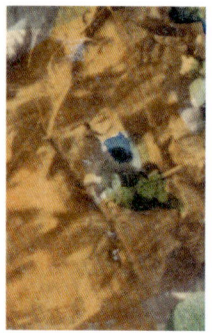

Introduction

The aim of this History of Erotic Photography is to present previously unpublished images, taking care to avoid those well known images taken by famous photographers which have already been the subject of monographs or numerous publications. The selection made here has no encyclopaedic value, and is based on entirely suggestive criteria.

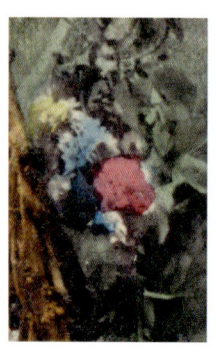

Untitled

c. 1855
Auguste Belloc
Hand-painted albumen print mounted on canvas,
Stereoscopic View, 8.5 x 16.5 cm

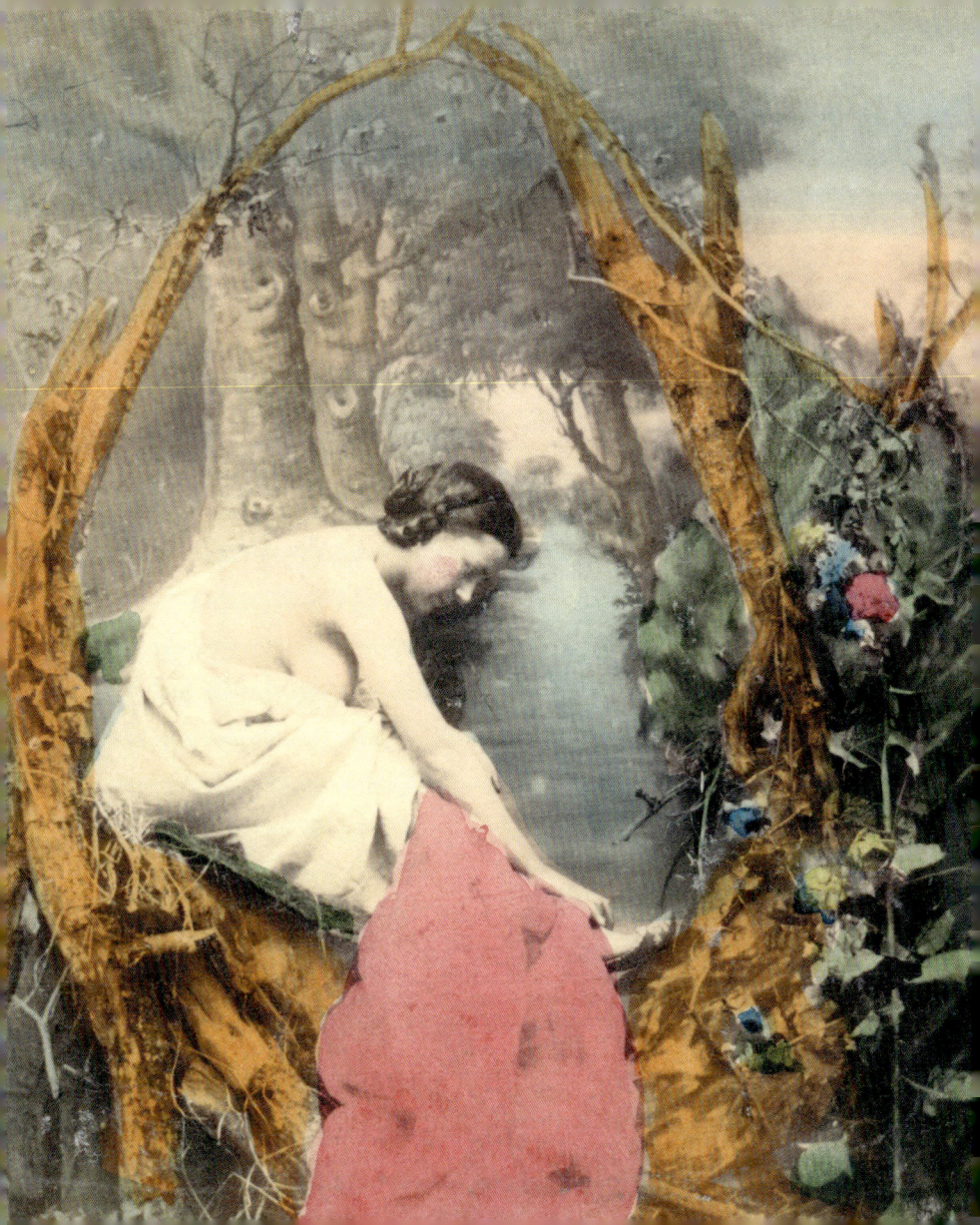

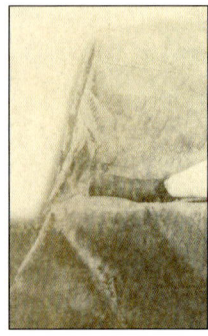

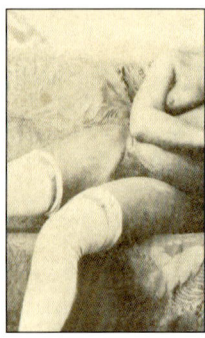

It is neither about presenting an exhaustive inventory, nor a specific objective. Choosing images is, above all, an expression of one's own personal tastes - one's infatuation for those women of old-fashioned charms, who, thanks to the wonder of the photographic miracle, have been preserved from the ravages of age and time.

It should be pointed out that the first decades of erotic photography were essentially French.

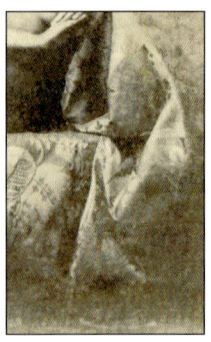

Visiting Card
———————

c. 1855
Anonymous
Print on salted paper mounted on board,
6.5 x 10.3 cm

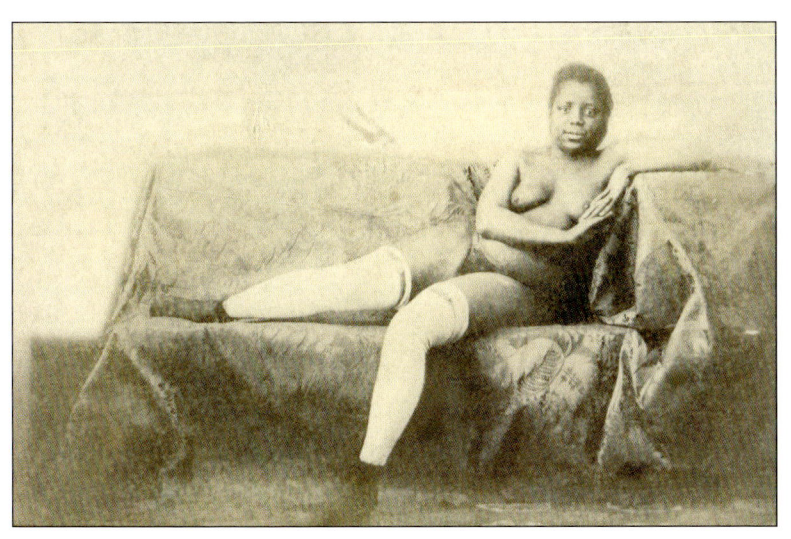

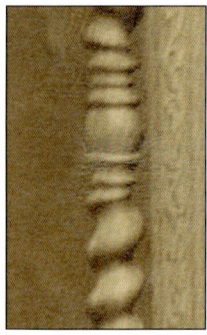

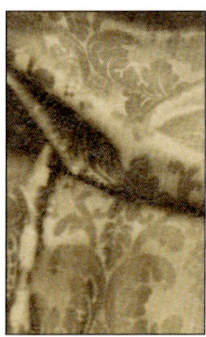

The main reason for this is that photography was first developed in France, where research into new procedures of iconographic reproduction began in the 18th century. In the 19th century, liberalism was more widespread in France than elsewhere. Licentious French images were imported into Italy, Spain, the United States, Germany and Great Britain, as production in these countries was limited, due to the fact that these works were more severely repressed.

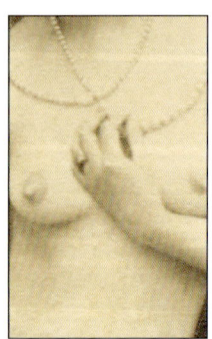

Untitled

---

c. 1855
Auguste Belloc
Print on salted paper from collodion humid negative,
20.7 x 15.5 cm

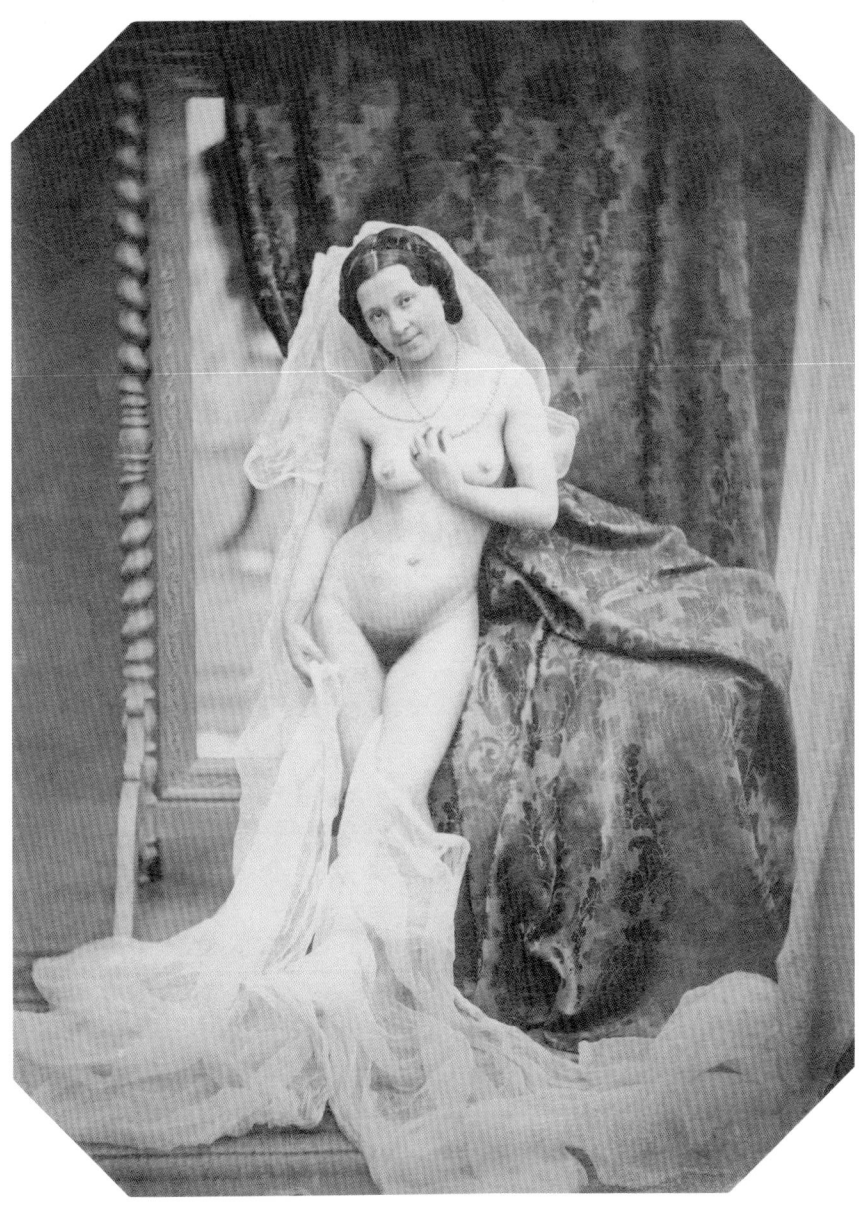

13

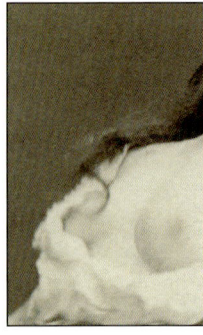

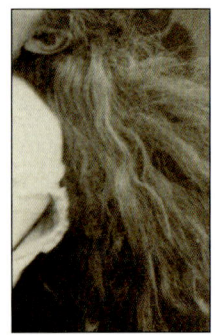

As far as the first century of the history of photography is concerned (1839-1939), all the international collections - both old and contemporary - comprise mainly French images. When the English authors Graham Ovenden and Peter Mendes entitled their work *Victorian Erotic Photography*, it was, in fact, largely made up of works of Parisian origin from Belloc, Braquehais, Durieu, Vallou and Villeneuve.

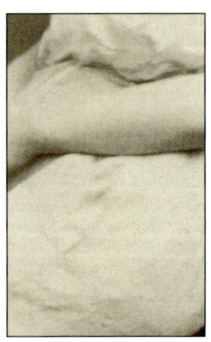

Annex 652, Visiting Card
***

c. 1860
André Disdéri
Albumen print mounted on board, 10.3 x 6.5 cm

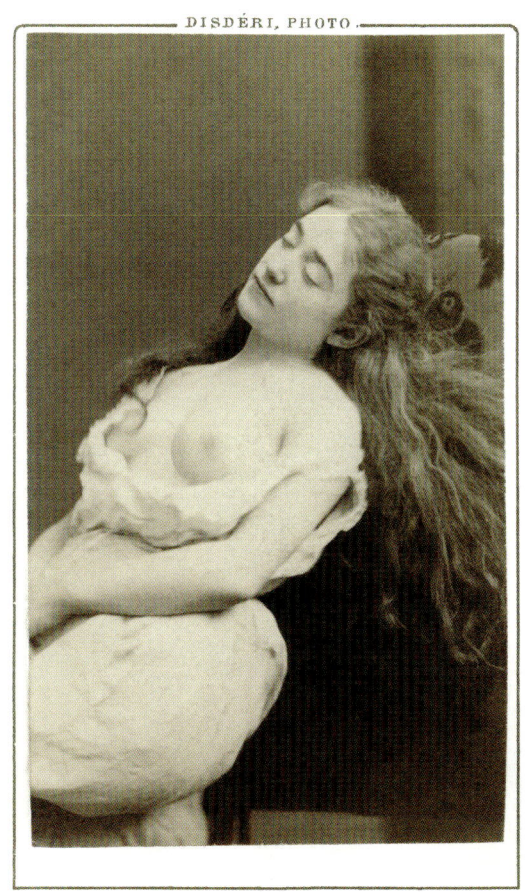

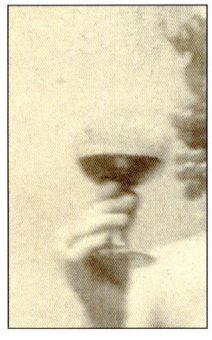

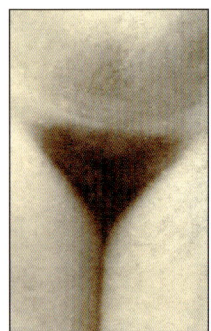

When the American Richard Merkin, professor at the Rhode Island School of Design, presented his collection in the work entitled *Velvet Eden*, the majority of the images were French. The first American images that he selected date from 1920, the first German ones from 1930, and together they only represent a tiny fraction of the total number. One of the leading reference works in the field of erotic

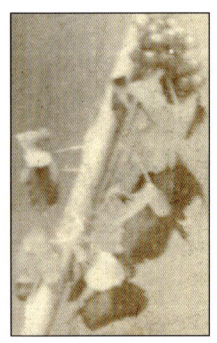

Bacchante
_____

c. 1860
Ch. Naudet
Print on salted paper toned with gold,
21.5 x 10 cm

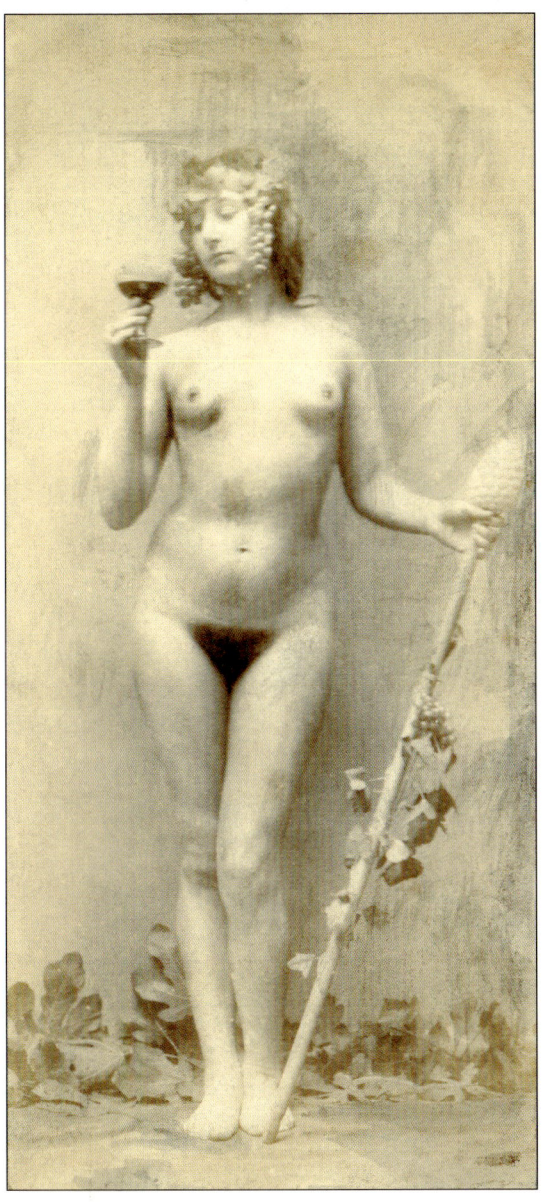

17

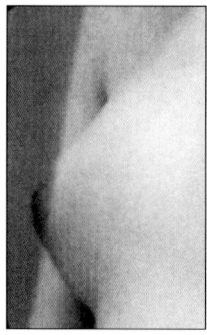

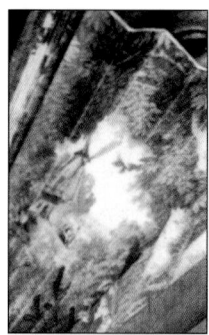

photography *Die Erotik in der Photographie* (three volumes published by half a dozen eminent doctors in Vienna in 1931) brings together the best of the German collections of the period and includes several hundred reproductions, the minority being German and Austrian, whereas the French production accounts for the majority of the period preceding the First World War.

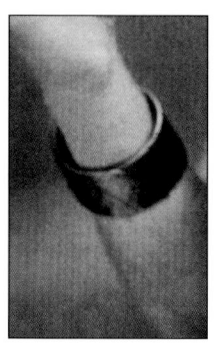

Sarah Bernhardt
_____

c. 1868
Anonymous
Only known portrait of Sarah Bernhardt with nude torso,
14.5 x 10.5 cm

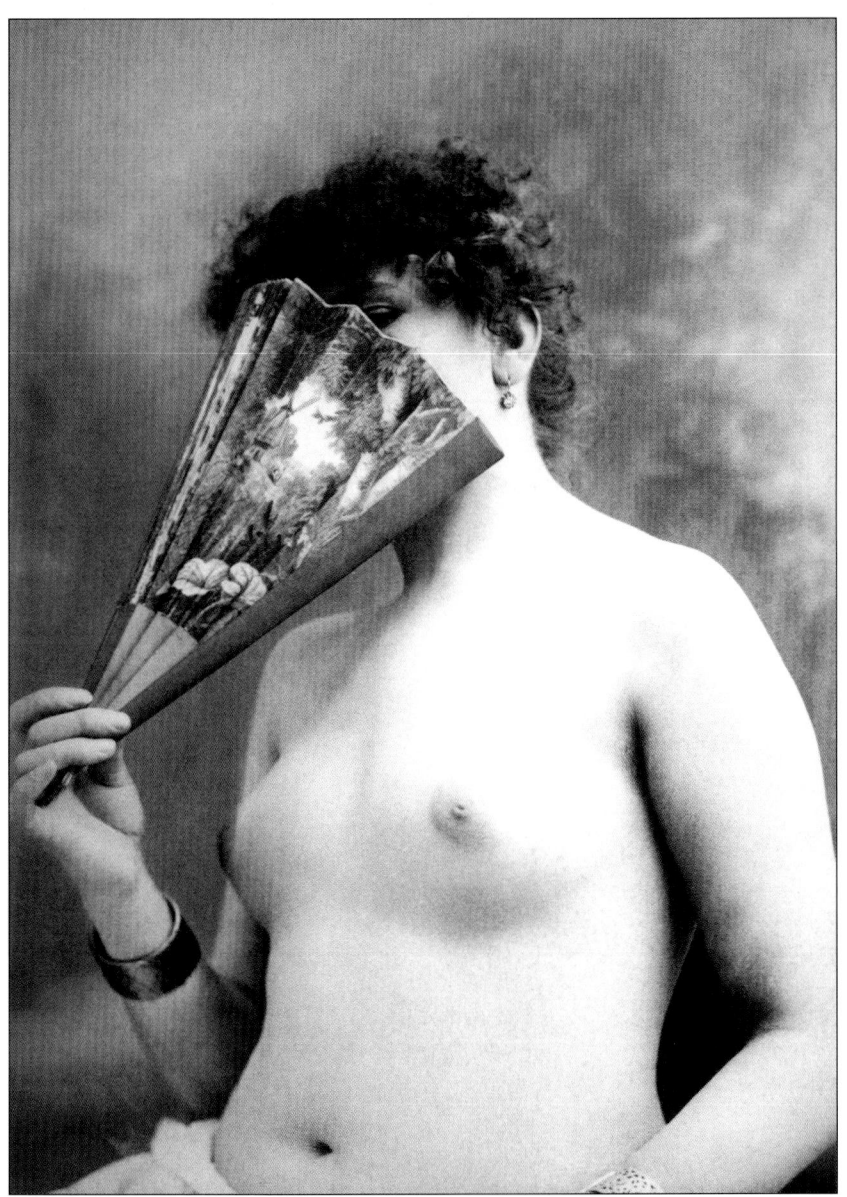

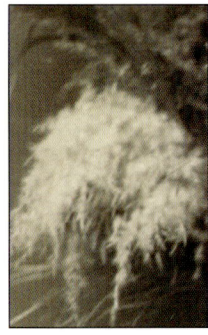

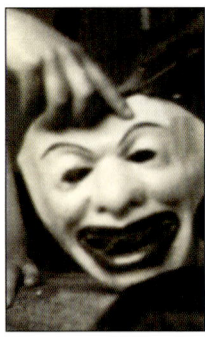

However, this French particularity and specificity lessened throughout the 20th century and has now completely disappeared. The same goes for all themes covered by photography. Whatever the reason, the history of this French specificity could not have been told without the protection of this heritage by a number of passionate collectors. It may be a lewd and playful heritage, but it is representative of the morals and mentality of each period.

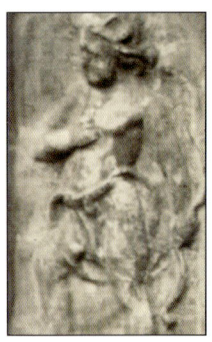

N° K 65
———
c. 1870
Anonymous
Albumen print, 26.6 x 19.5 cm

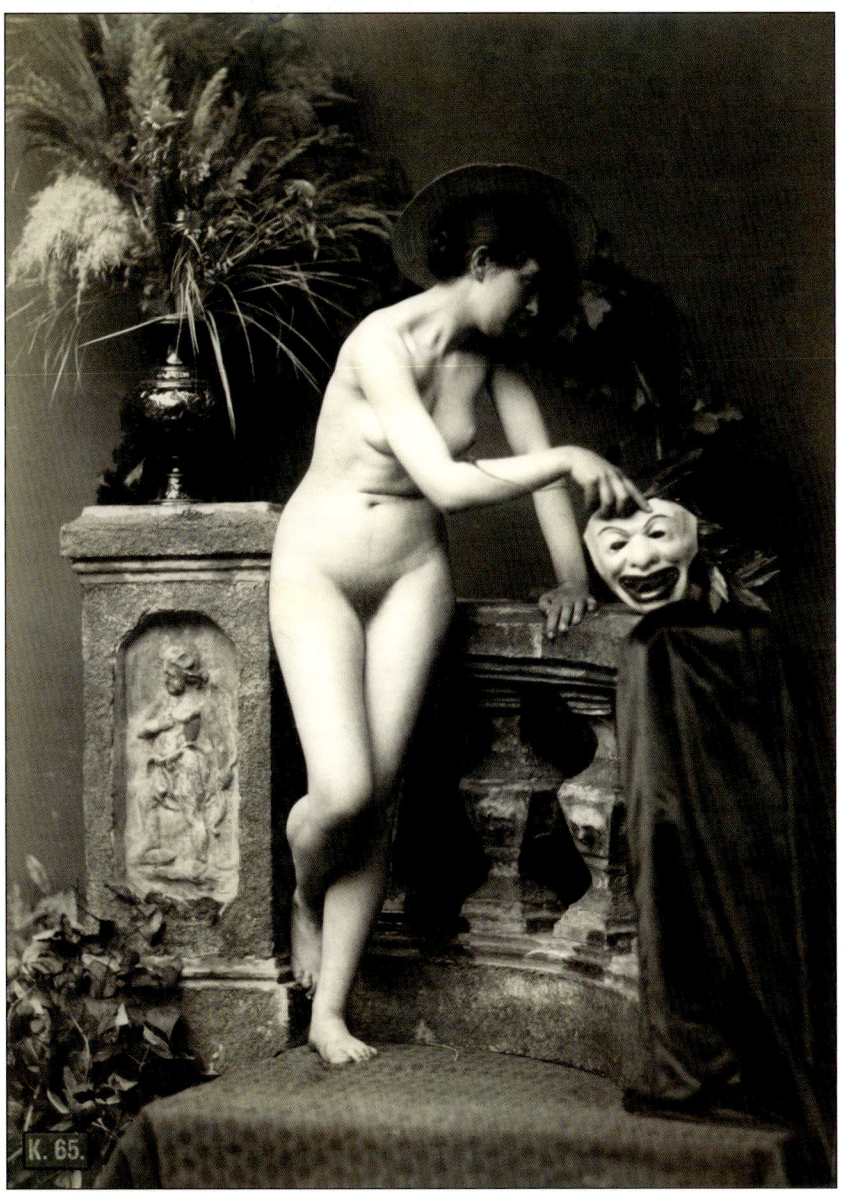

K. 65.

21

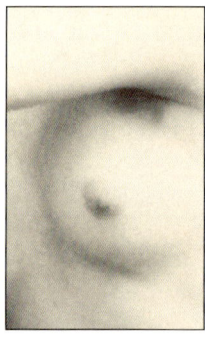

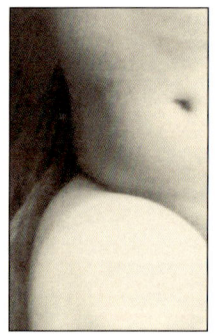

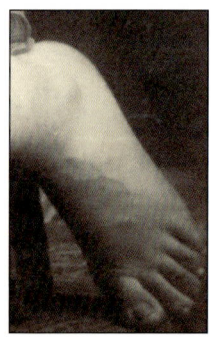

Photography Conquering Nudity

Whether it be painting, sculpture, engraving or lithography, all forms of art have been at the service of eroticism from the beginning. Photography is no exception to this rule. The first photographic processes, the daguerreotypes, were enriched from conception by nudes, which offered an imagery reminiscent of the painting of the time, albeit in a more realistic, though simultaneously cruder, manner.

N° 563

———

c. 1870
Gaudenzio Marconi
Albumen print, 21.8 x 16 cm

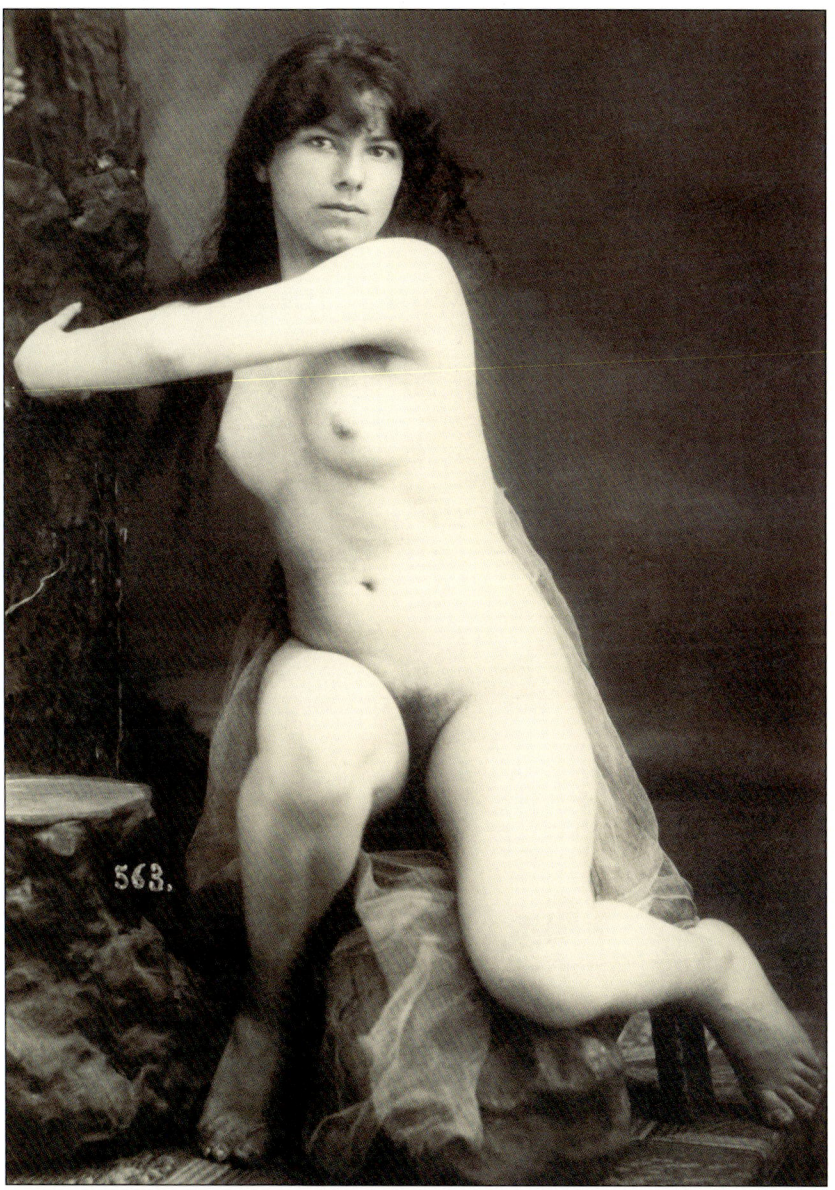

563.

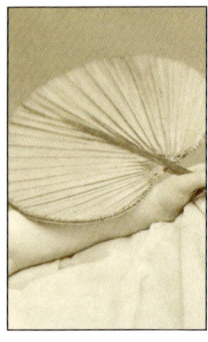

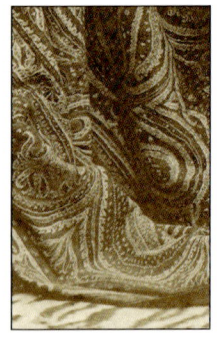

On 19th of August 1839, Louis-Jacques Mandé Daguerre, having given up his activities as a painter and set decorator, presented his invention during a public meeting of the Science Academy. It was a huge success and he was granted a pension, which he shared with Isidore Niepce, the son of his partner Nicéphore, who died in 1833.

In exchange, in a display of generosity never to be seen again, the French State acquired the rights of the process and placed

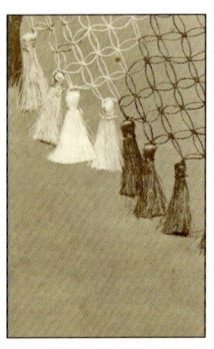

N° 33

———

c. 1870
Anonymous
Albumen print, 21 x 27 cm

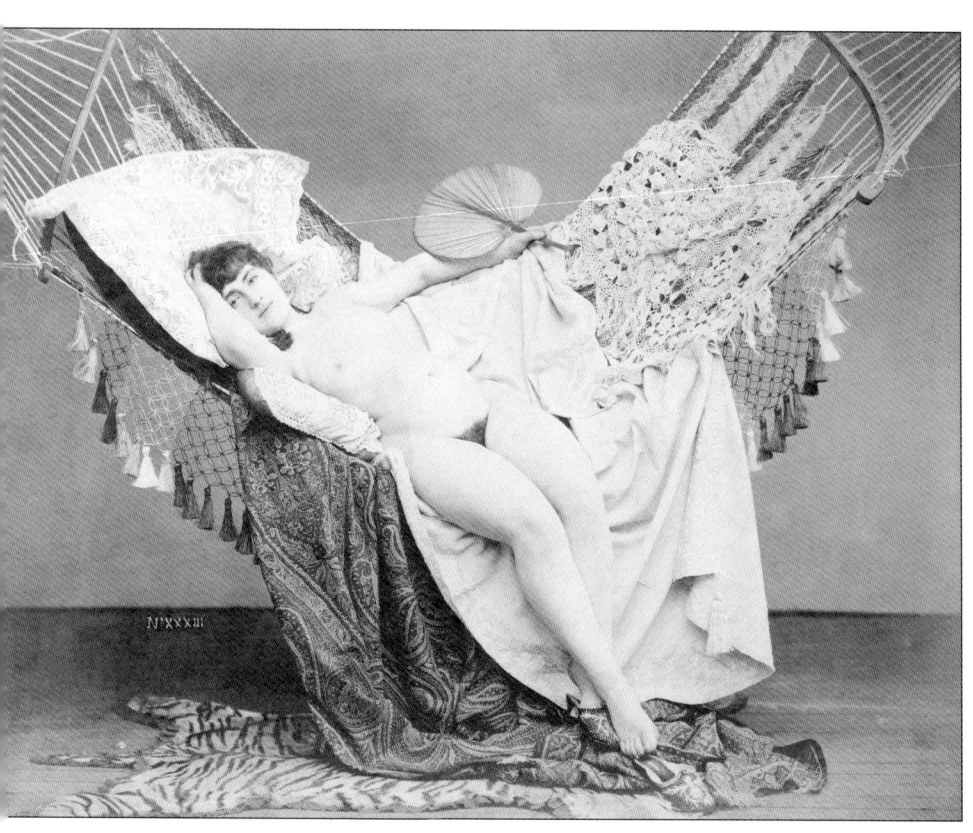

N°XXXIII

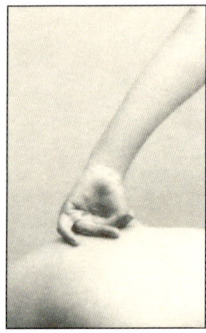

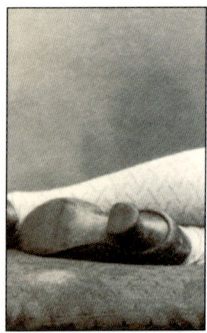

them graciously at the disposal of apprentice photographers the world over. Describing the conception of the first photographic images leaves one a little lost for words. How were researchers able to come up with a formula so hard on the sense of smell; that magic formula allowing the reproduction, in two dimensions, of what the naked eye offers on a daily basis? The operation is complicated and the number of manipulations and substances to complete it seems limitless.

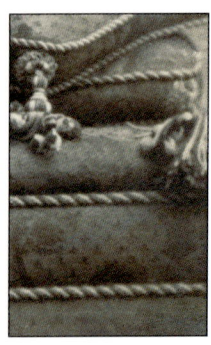

Untitled
———

c. 1880
Anonymous
Albumen print, 9.5 x 13.5 cm

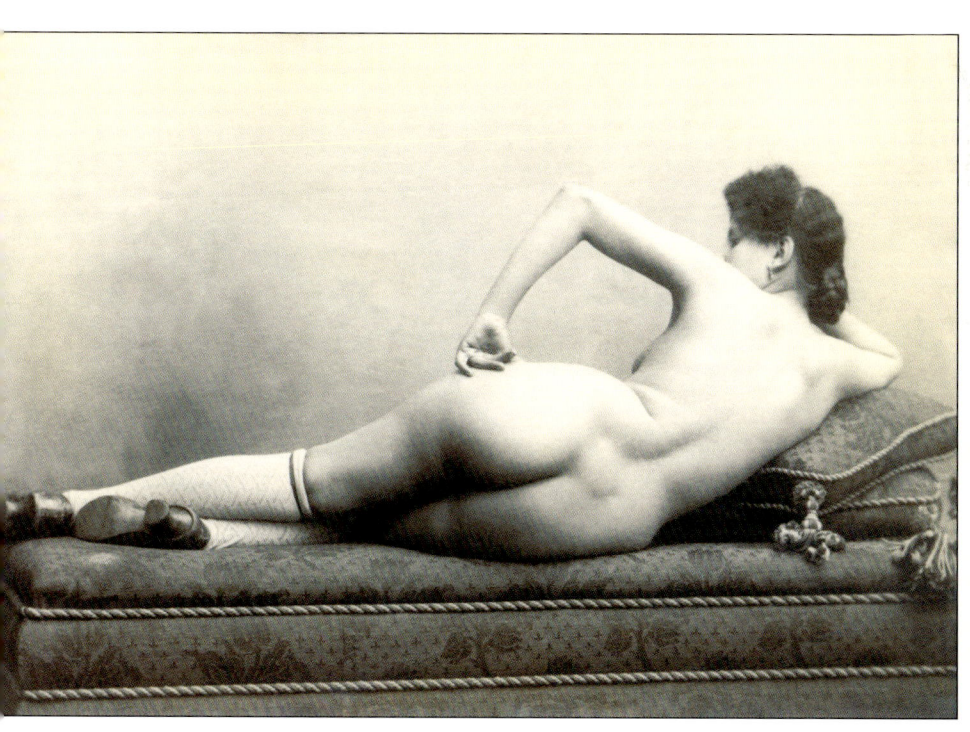

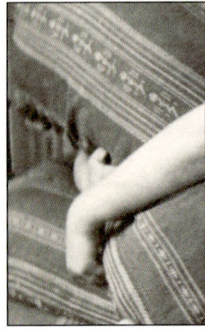

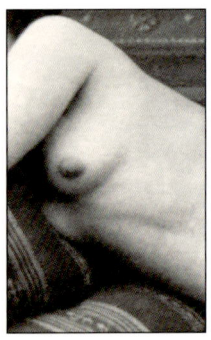

In order to produce a daguerreotype, you need a copper plate, which is then silver-plated and cleaned and polished meticulously with pumice stone powder. The plate is then covered with a thin coat of silver iodide in an iodising box. This has to be done by candlelight or with a slightly open door, in order to avoid any premature exposure to light. It is then placed in a dark room, to be exposed for an undetermined period of time, defined only

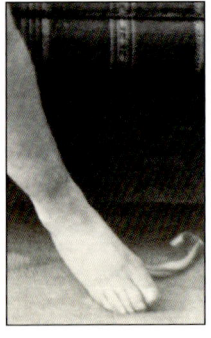

Untitled

c. 1880
Anonymous
Albumen print, 9.5 x 13.5 cm

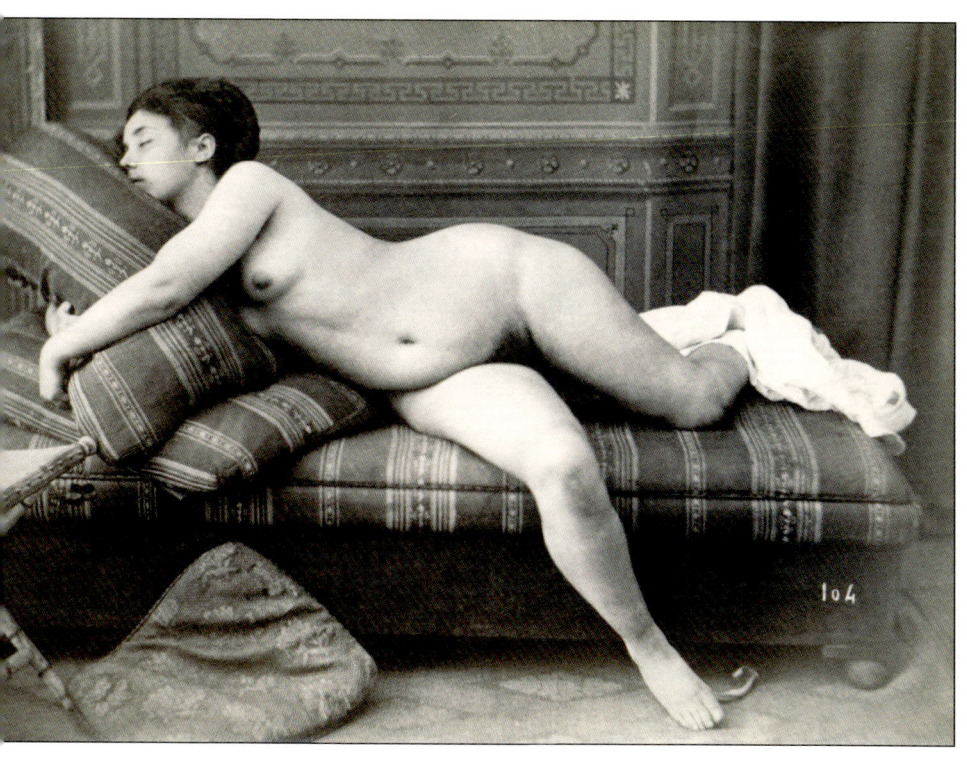

104

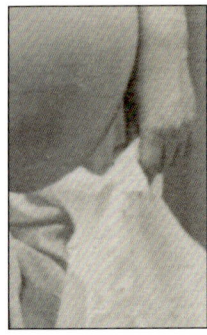

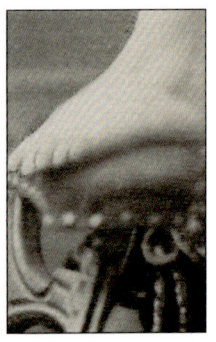

by the artist's instinct, the result depending on the temperature, humidity, the weather and the exposure time. The plate has still not changed. The image is revealed by holding it above a burner giving off mercury vapours (particularly nauseating and dangerous) that settle on the exposed parts.

The operation comes to an end by washing the plate with very hot salty water. Colour is added by sticking on dry pigments using liquid Arabic gum.

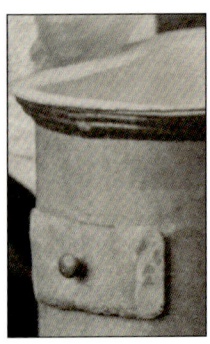

Untitled

c. 1890
Anonymous
Albumen print, 20.7 x 13.7 cm

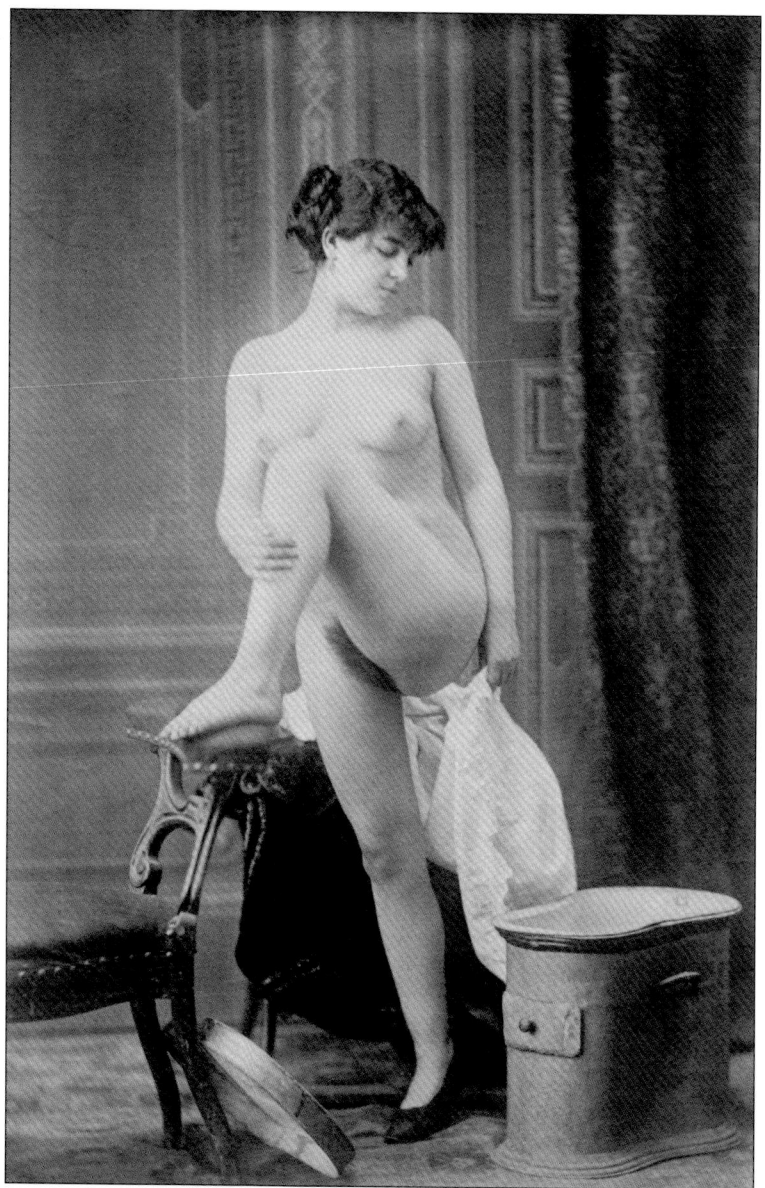

31

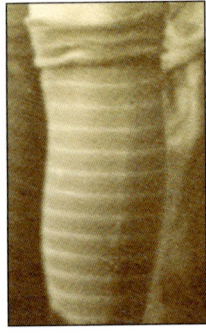

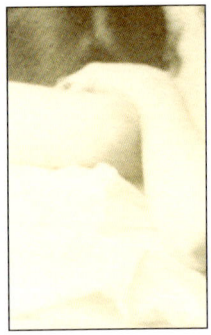

The daguerreotype was followed by the discovery of the ferrotype and ambrotype - positive processes with a one-off print, which, like their predecessor, were expensive to make, expensive to buy and accordingly only intended for a well-off clientele.

The very first images were of landscapes or reproductions of objects. It was very difficult to photograph nudes or take portraits, given that a posing time of several minutes was required.

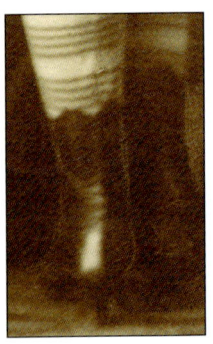

N° 499

c. 1890
Anonymous
Albumen print, 20.7 x 13.7 cm

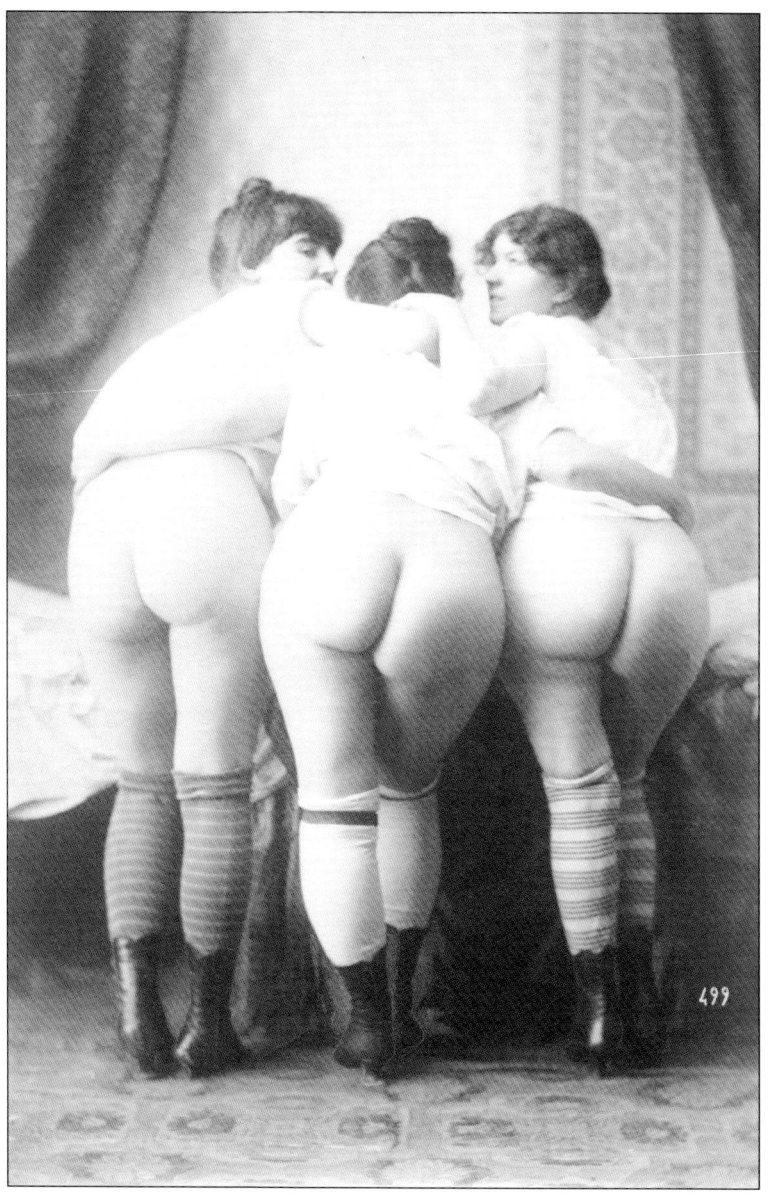

499

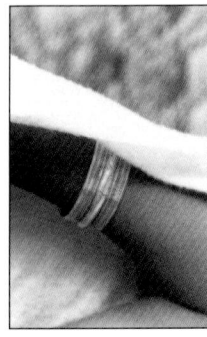

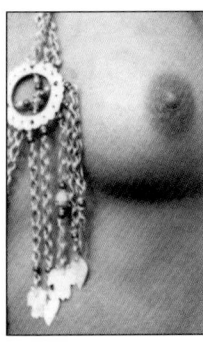

However, this duration was soon reduced to tens of seconds. While the process became international, France retained its hegemony over the form. This was particularly the case with regards to erotic photography, which appeared immediately.

The first nudes must have been taken as early as 1840. According to Sylvie Aubenas in her preface for *Obscenities*, a certain Noël-Marie Paimal Lebours, optician by trade, maintains he photographed a nude in 1841, while being very careful about appearing to be *the* precursor.

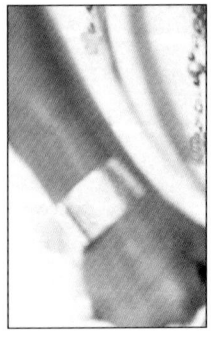

N° 996

———

c. 1890
Lehnert & Landrock, Tunis (?)
Albumen print, 17 x 12 cm

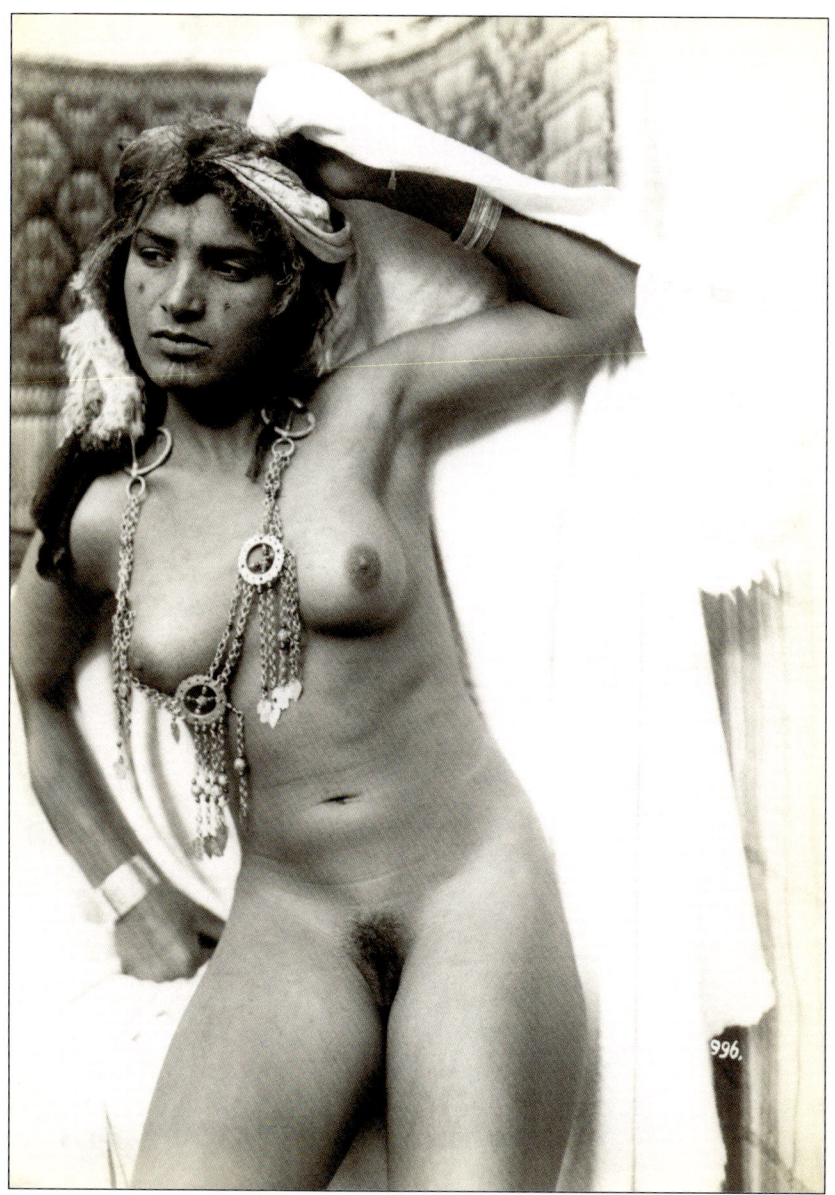

996.

35

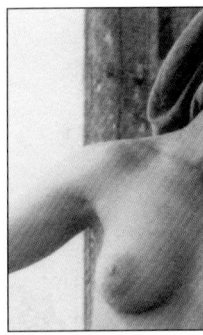

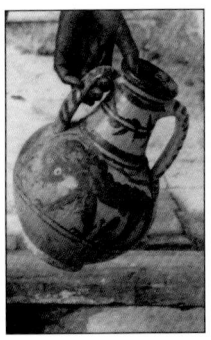

The same year, Talbot discovered the calotype. This was the first negative, forefather of our modern celluloid films. As the calotype was on paper, the process was complicated, not very reliable and not very practical.

It was not until 1853, however, that real progress was made when the Englishman Frederick Scott Archer invented the negative on glass, which permitted reproduction on paper in unlimited quantities. From this date on, certain photographers made nudes their speciality.

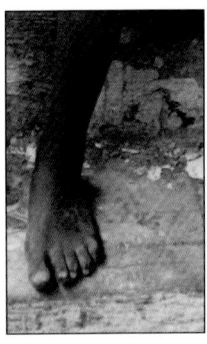

N° 1059

c. 1890
Lehnert & Landrock, Tunis (?)
Albumen print, 17 x 12 cm

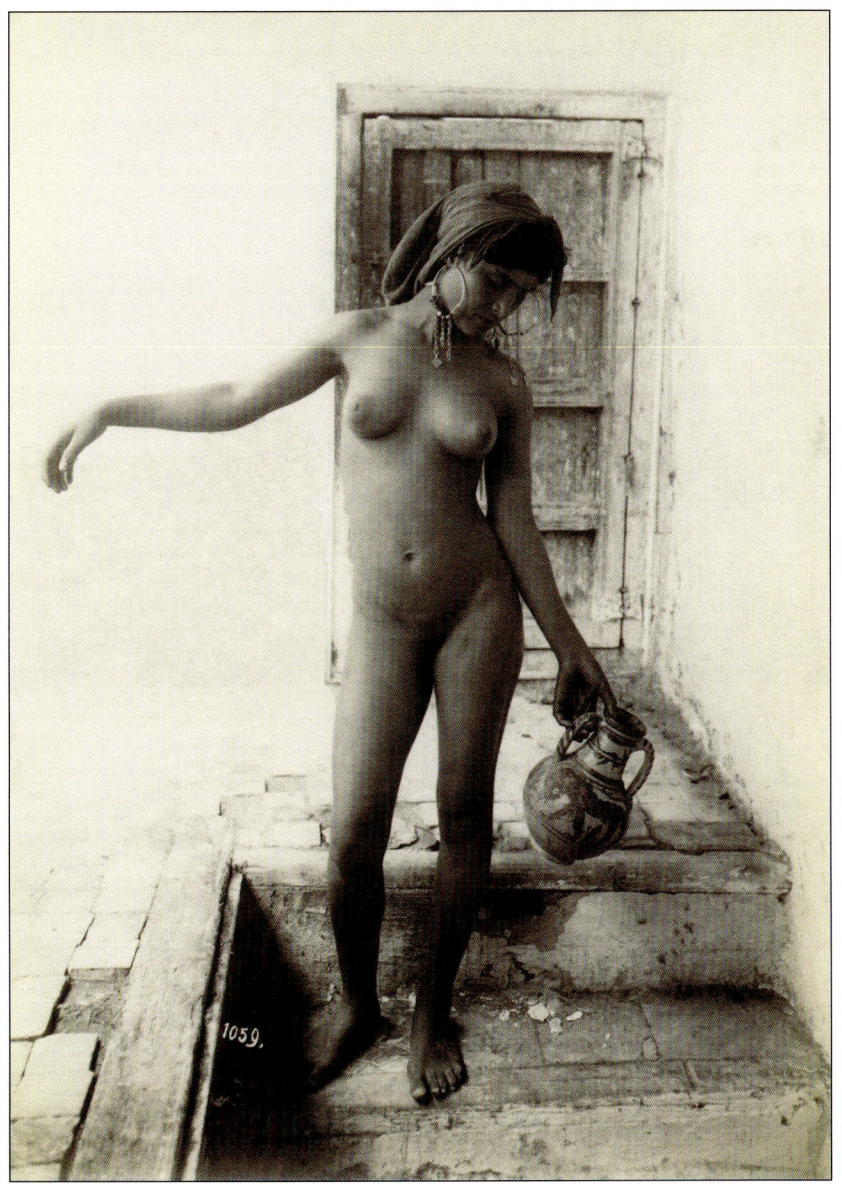

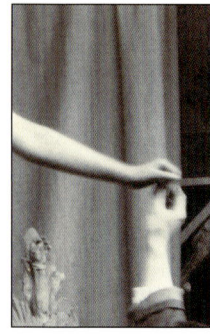

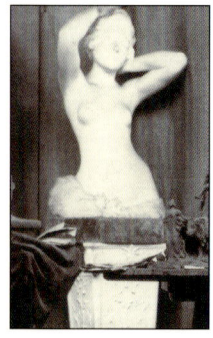

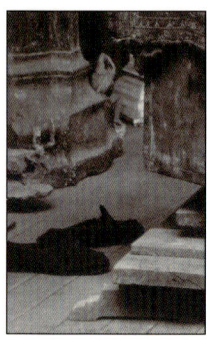

They mimicked artists and painters by making pastiches of their compositions and the use of accessories, including draping, columns and fabric. In fact, most of the precursors of photography came directly from painting.

The interconnection between the two processes seemed obvious: photographers were inspired by painters, and painters made use of photography. With photography, artists no longer had to put up with models who either did not turn up or were late.

Sculptor and Model at Work
_____

c. 1890
Anonymous
Gelatin silver print, 12.5 x 10.2 cm

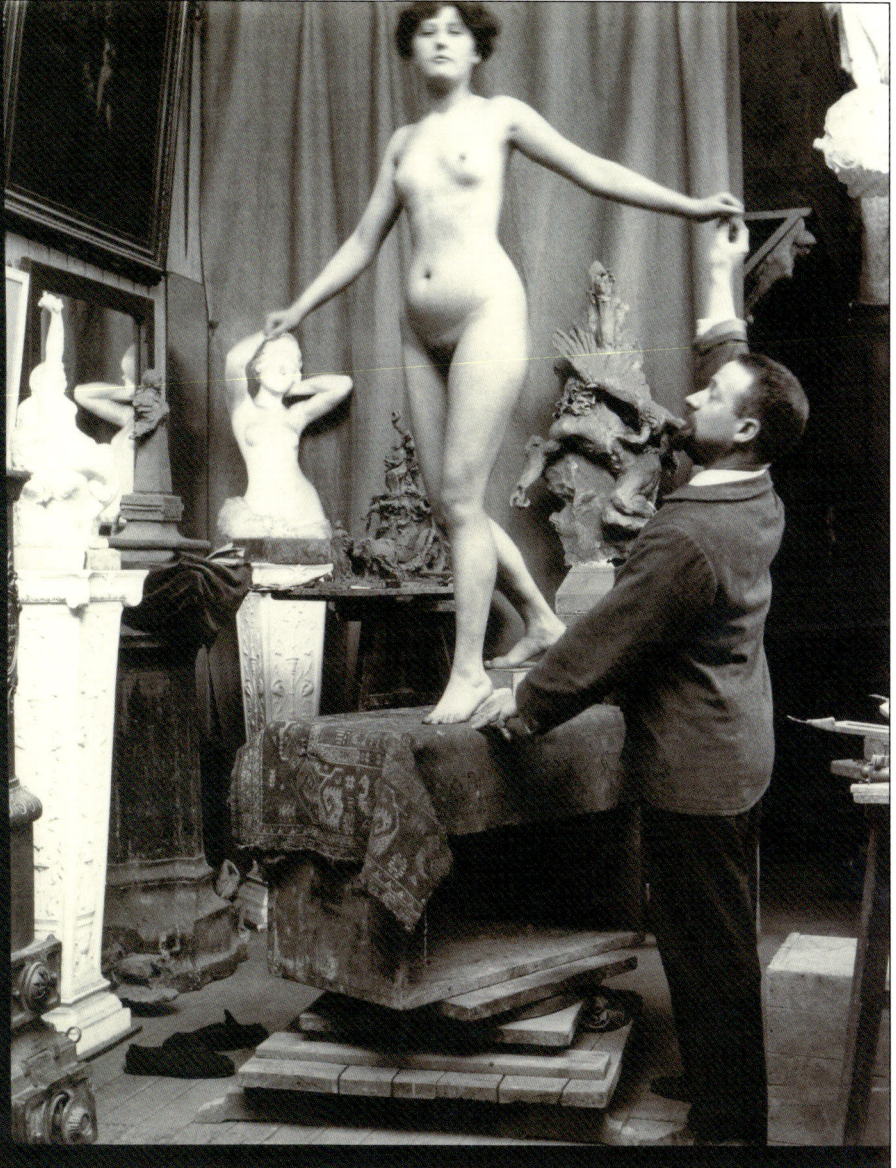

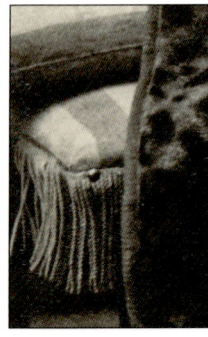

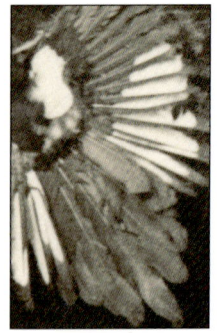

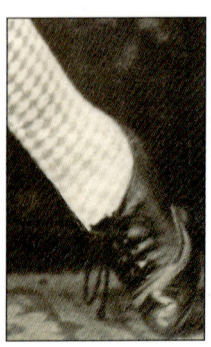

Unlike models, who can often be offhand, photographic images are always at your disposal and are hardly ever late. Delacroix, ardent champion of the new art, was inspired by the images of his friend, the photographer Eugène Durieu. Ingres appreciated "this automatic process".

"How beautiful, how beautiful!" he declared to his students when contemplating a large print of antique marble. "Photography is such an admirable thing! Look, Gentlemen, who among us would be capable of such

N° 505
———

c. 1890
Anonymous
Albumen print, 13.7 x 20.7 cm

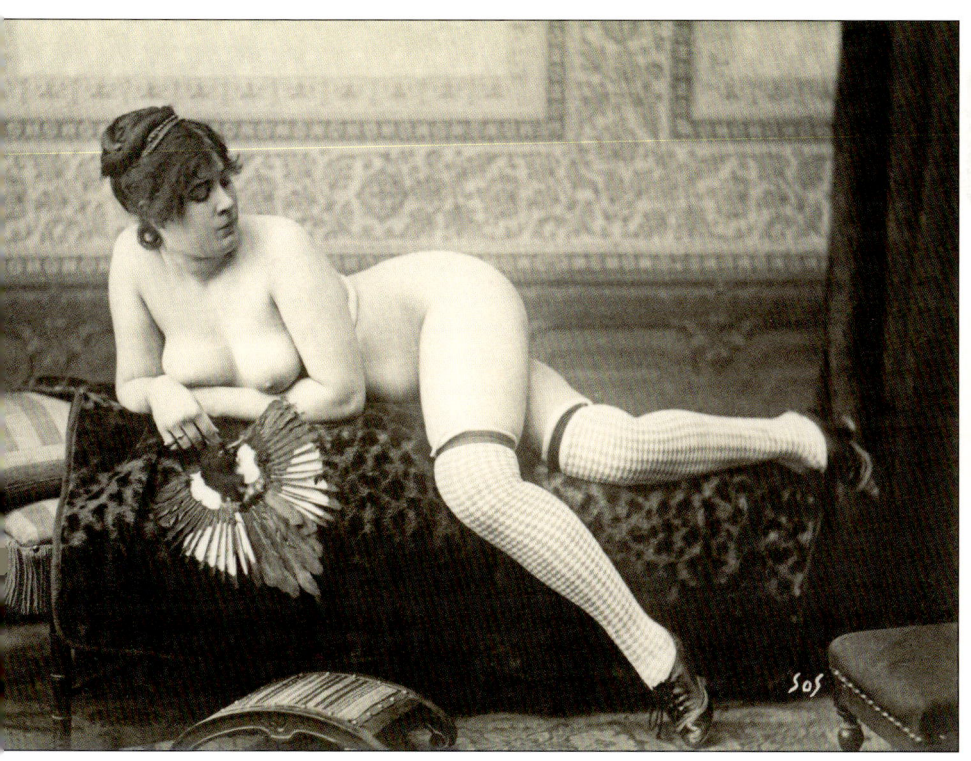

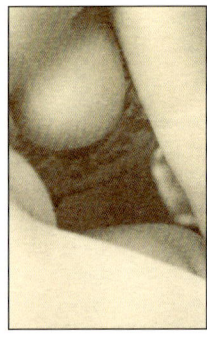

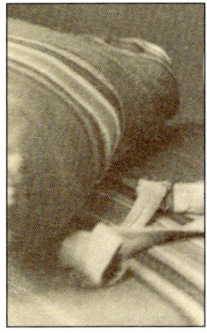

faithfulness, of that assurance in the interpretation of the lines, of that delicacy in the contours? Ah yes, to be sure Gentlemen, photography is very beautiful. It is very beautiful but we mustn't say so!" Unlike the other fine arts, the very nature of photography means that it cannot idealise its subject, and when faced with a naked body, the boundary between art, the nude, eroticism and pornography is very difficult to define, given that the differences are so much a question of culture and education.

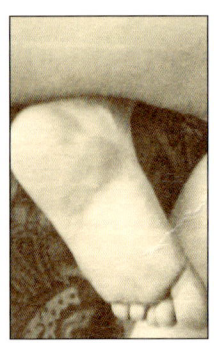

N° 68

———

c. 1890
Anonymous
Albumen print, 20.7 x 13.7 cm

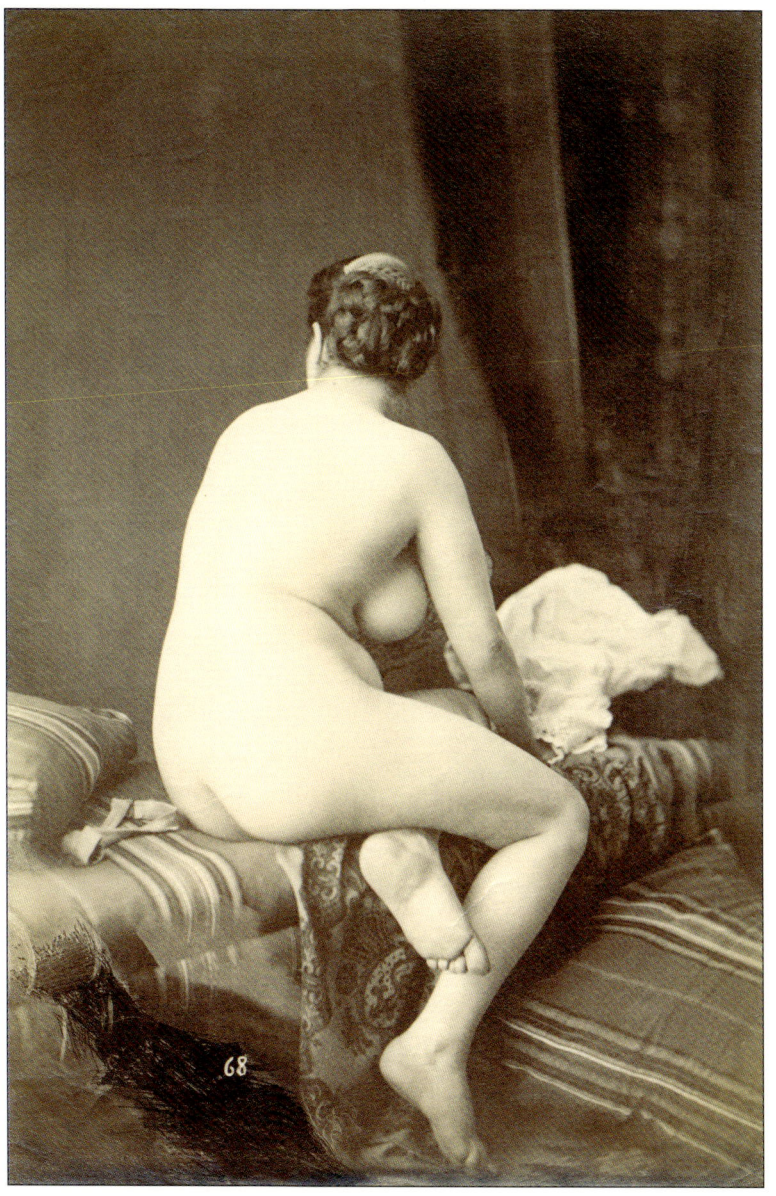

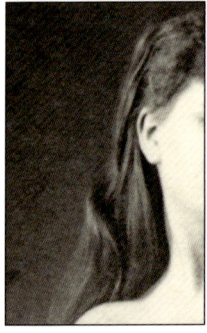

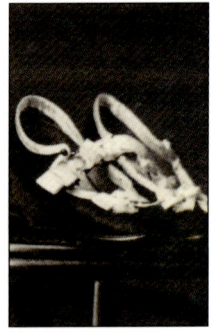

The Academic Alibi

I t is obvious that what is erotic for some will be considered pornographic by others. From the very beginning of photography there was, on the one hand, a pornographic production; and, on the other hand, there was production that was recorded and registered at the Print Room of the Imperial Library under Napoleon III. This was later to become the National Library from the third

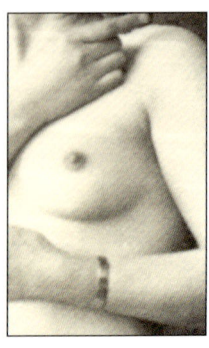

N° 555

———

c. 1890
Anonymous
Albumen print, 20.7 x 13.7 cm

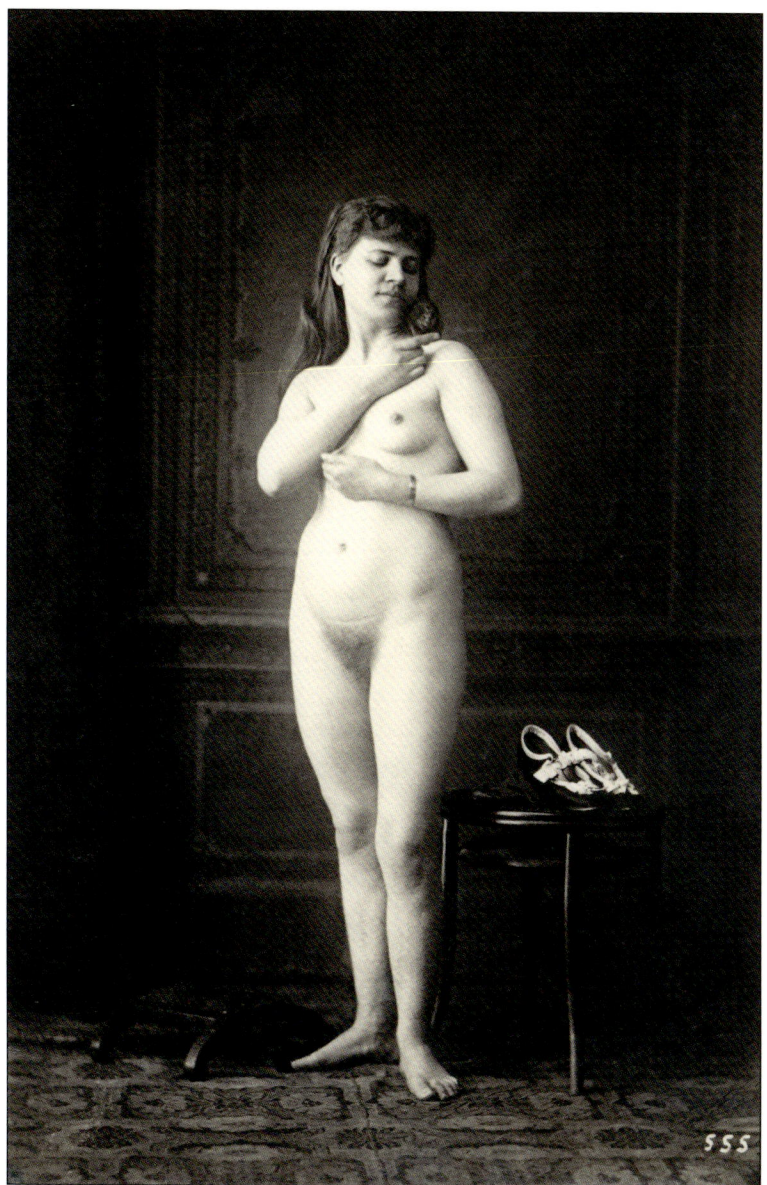

555

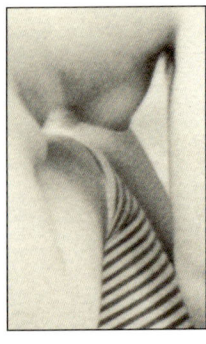

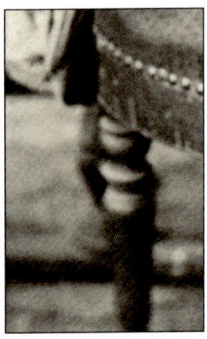

republic on, in order to obtain authorisation to commercially exploit the negatives as "studies for painters" or "nudes" ("nude" refers to an undraped human figure, used since antiquity in painting and sculpture). The master forerunners of nude photography were all French. They were the heirs of the miniaturists of the 18th century. Their names were Auguste Belloc, Vallou de Villeneuve, Félix-Jacques-Antoine Moulin, Bruno Braquehais and Alexis Gouin.

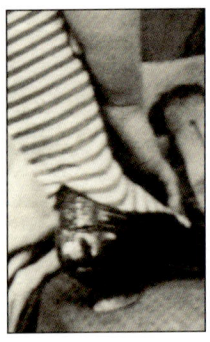

N° 105

c. 1890
Anonymous
Albumen print, 20.7 x 13.7 cm

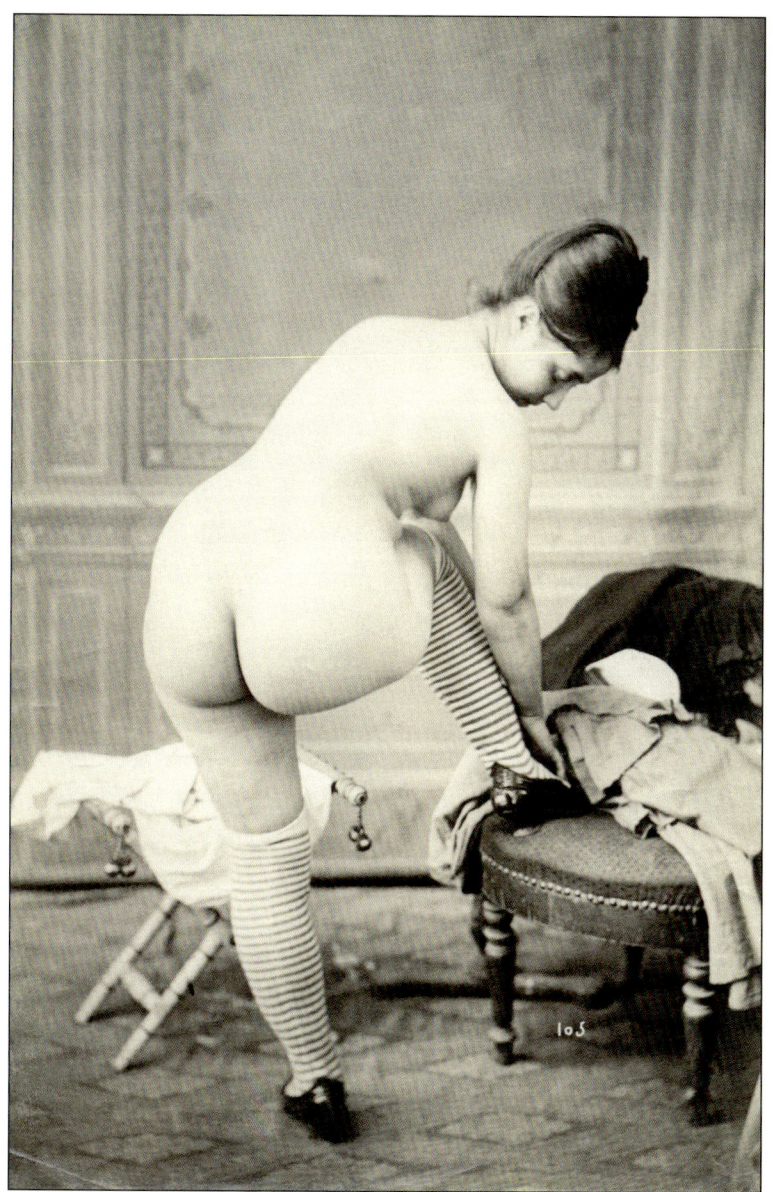

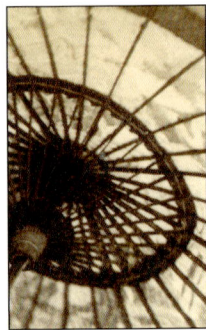

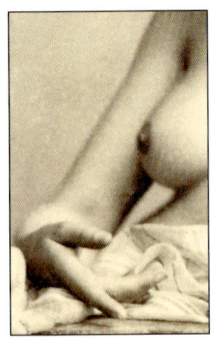

They worked in Paris, lived in the same district around the Grands Boulevards, knew each other and swapped their models, accessories and sometimes even their images, thus drawing a red herring across the trail of the police and making it difficult nowadays to attribute to one or the other these images that they wanted to be anonymous.

The appearance of the photographic nude, which was cruder than that of sculpture or painting, had difficulty in becoming a feature of artistic practice.

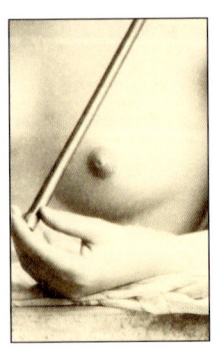

Visiting Card N° 1152

---

c. 1890
Anonymous
Albumen print mounted on board, 11 x 16.2 cm

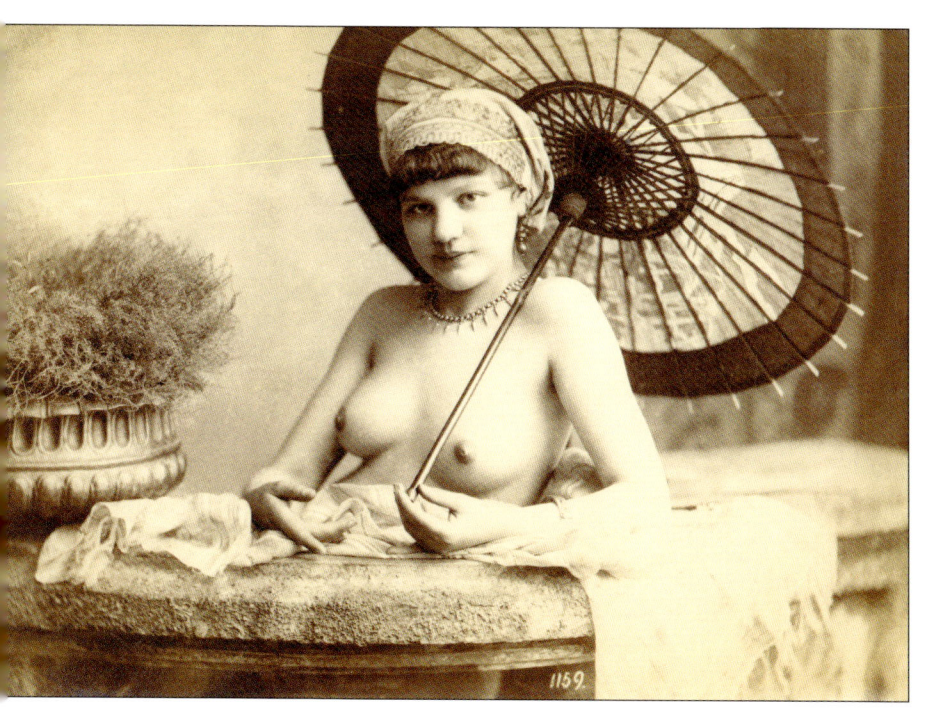

49

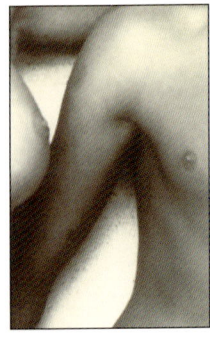

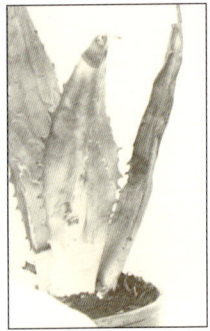

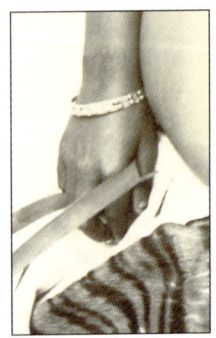

With photography, the body is the reflection of reality and could no longer be touched up. Each image freezes a moment of truth, and, sometimes, it is better not to know the truth. As proof of this, Félix Moulin was prosecuted and condemned by the authorities in 1851 to one month in prison and a fine of one hundred francs for affront to public decency for having taken "pornographic" daguerreotypes.

Untitled

c. 1895
Anonymous
Gelatin silver print, 23 x 16.5 cm

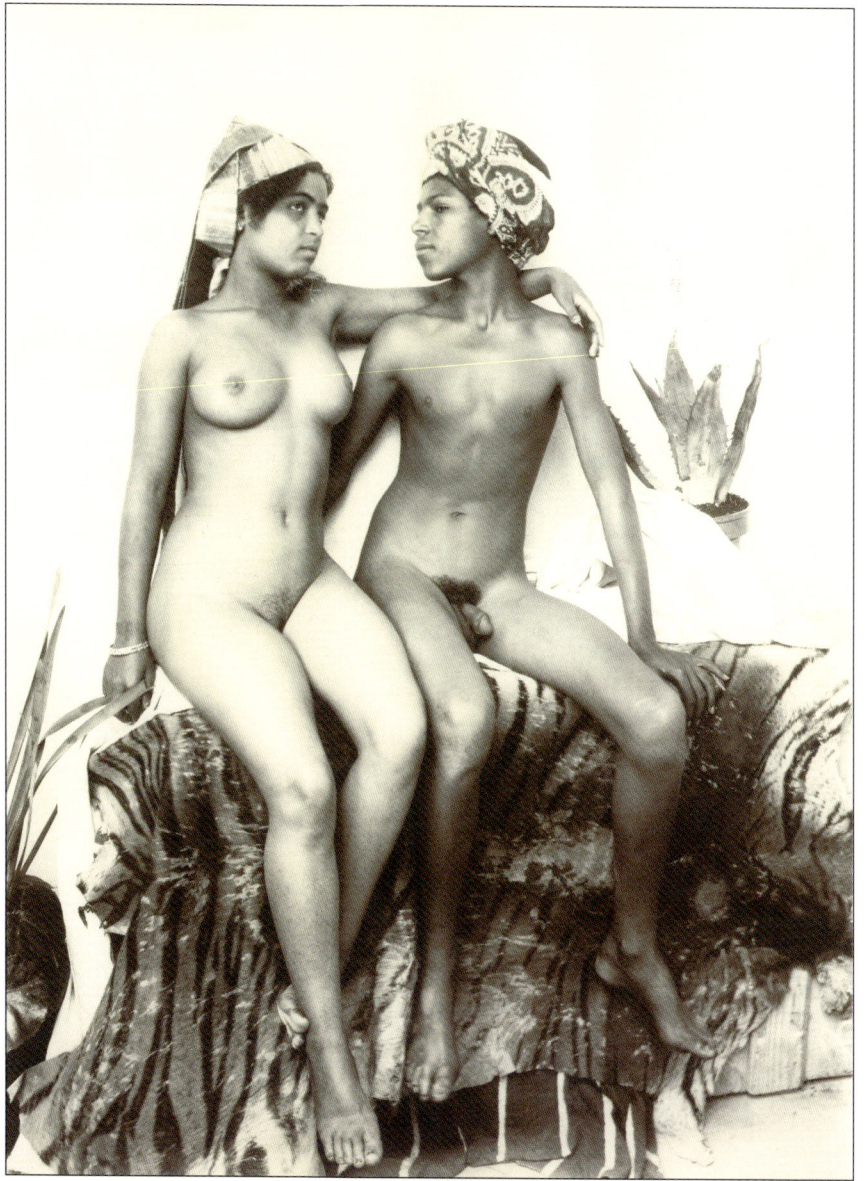

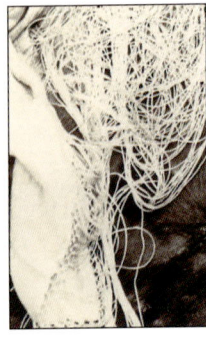

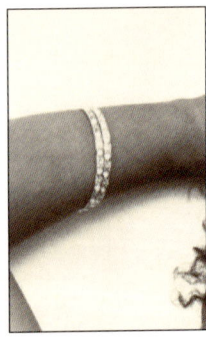

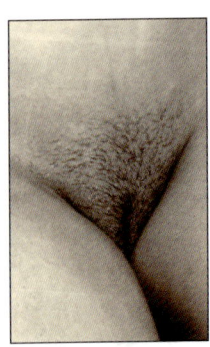

Pretending to tow the line, the following year he deposited some sixty odd works on paper at the Print Room of the Imperial Library, thus allowing him to exploit these images commercially. Artists were relatively protected, as creation was not considered a crime in itself. Models, and those selling images, were more often and more severely condemned.

Untitled
———
c. 1895
Anonymous
Gelatin silver print, 23 x 16.5 cm

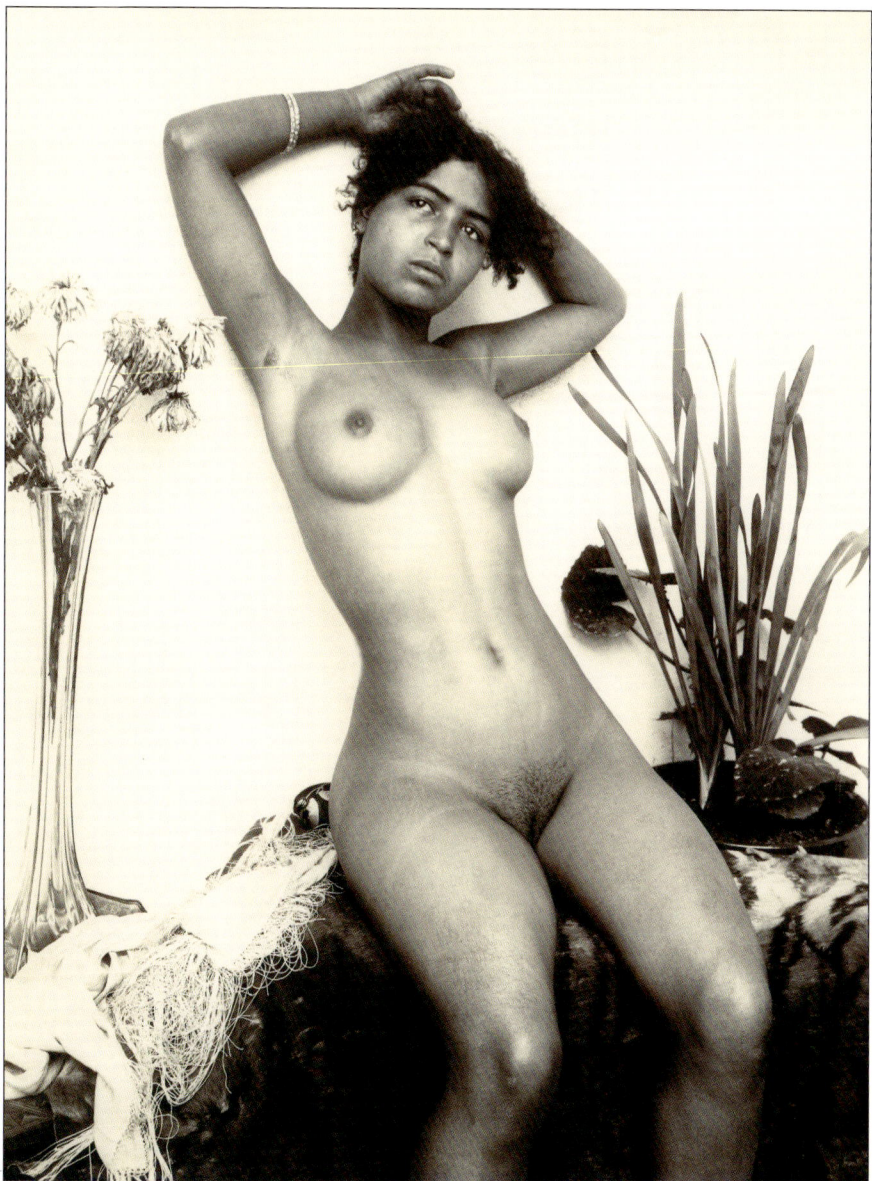

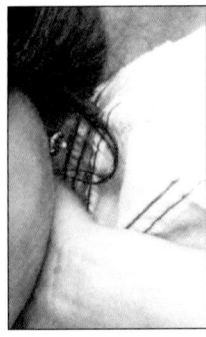

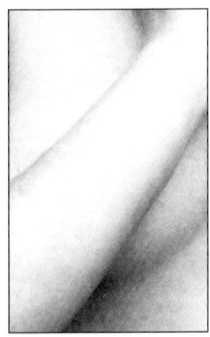

In 1857, four models were each sentenced to six months in prison and given a hundred franc fine.

In spite of these difficulties, images were produced in France where they were circulated more freely than in the rest of the world. These images were exported to the rest of Europe, in particular to Victorian England where the climate was still more puritan. Most erotic daguerreotypes were composed of two almost identical images which, when placed in a

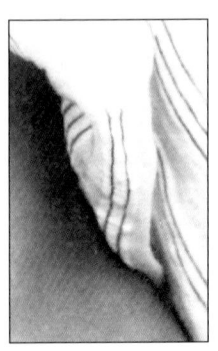

N° 2474

c. 1895
Vincenzo Galdi
Albumen print, 23 x 16.5 cm

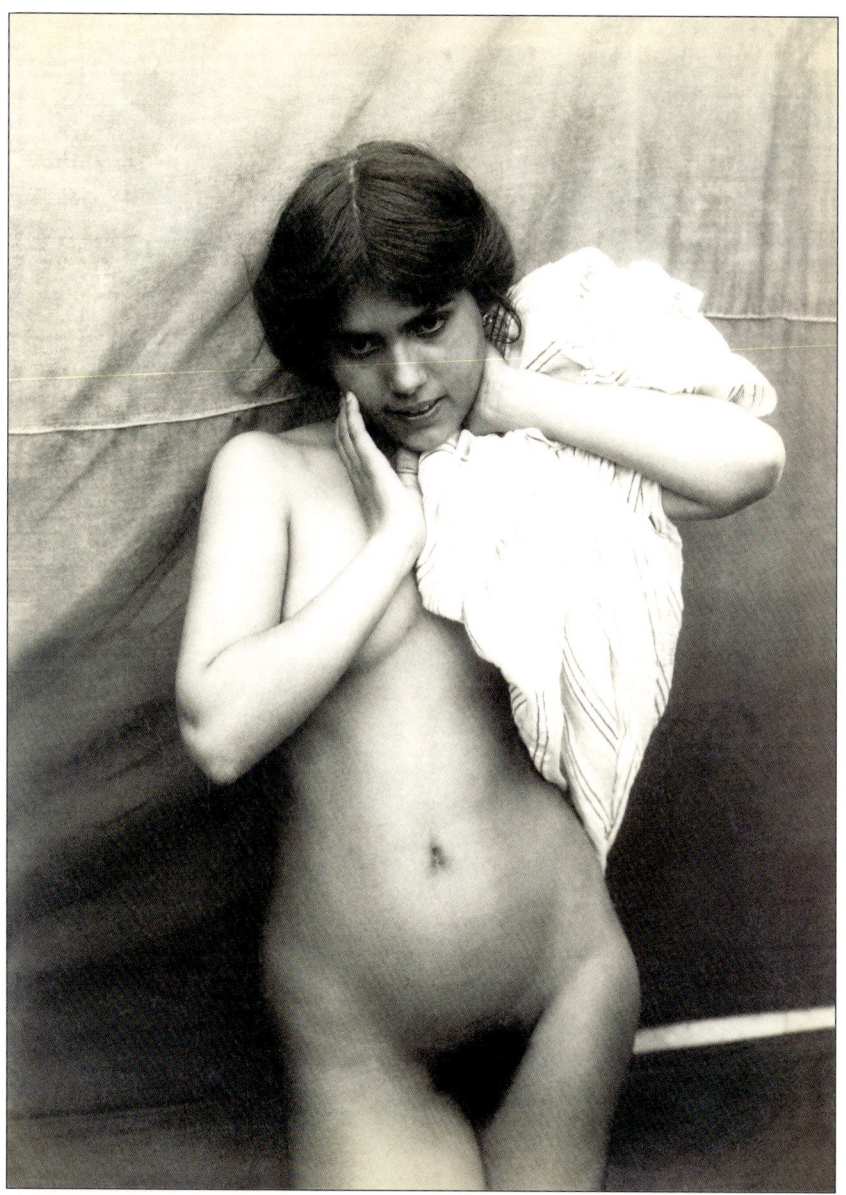

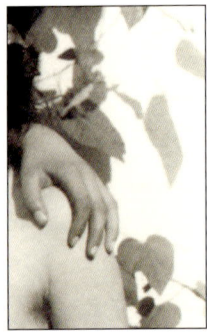

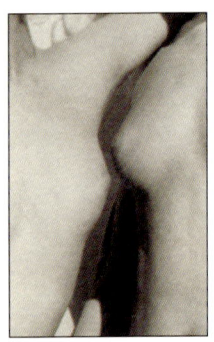

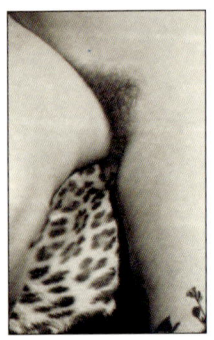

stereoscopic viewfinder gave the impression of contours. This procedure enhanced, among other things, the plump curves of the models and was a great success. With the arrival of paper as a medium, production and demand grew. The paper that was used changed with different discoveries. First there was salted paper, which was paper that was soaked in a solution of sodium chloride, a five percent solution of simple kitchen salt to which starch or gelatine was added.

N° 10404
———

c. 1895
Guglielmo Plüschow
Albumen print, 23 x 16.5 cm

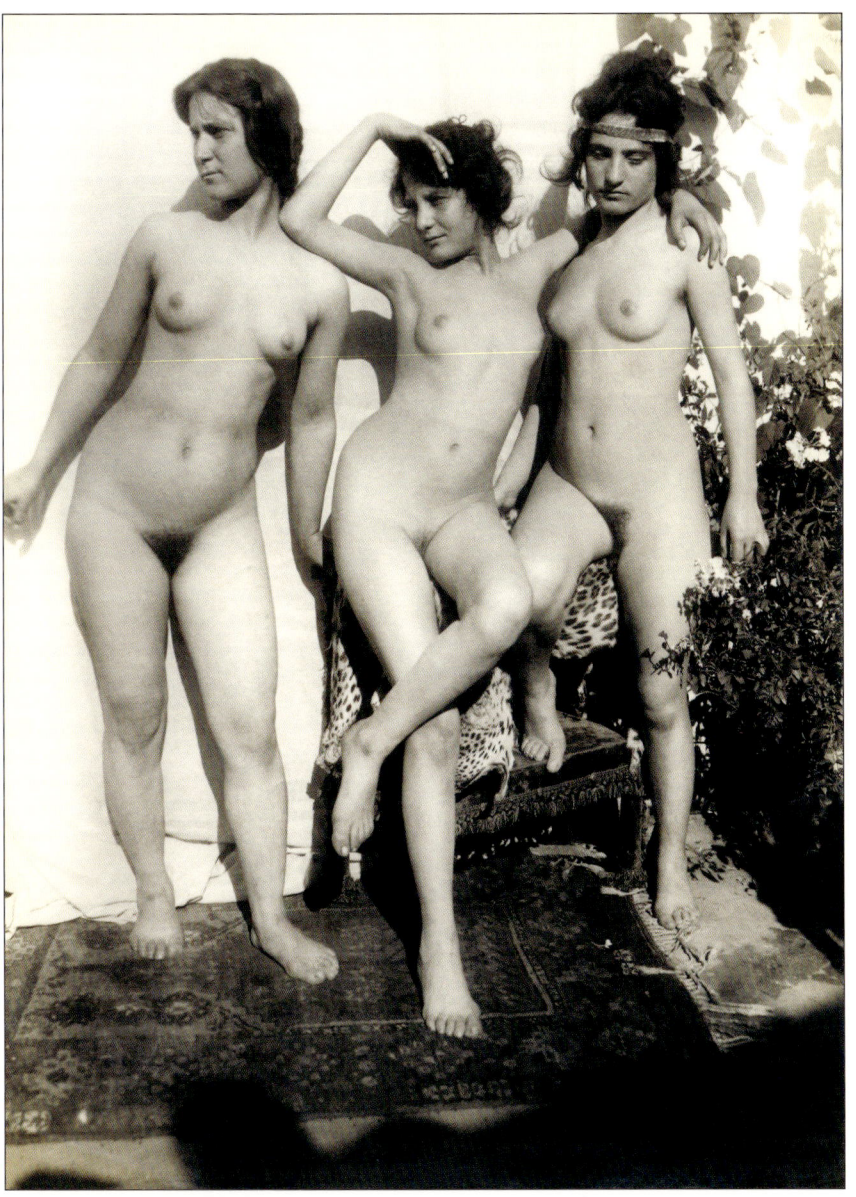

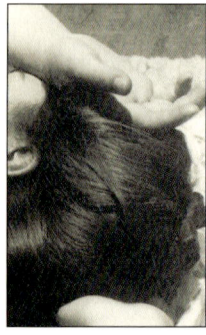

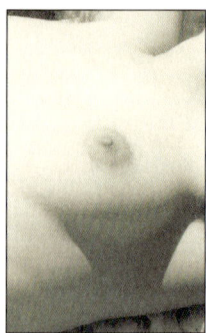

Then it was allowed to dry out before it was soaked in a fifteen percent solution of silver nitrate. It was then left to dry out again, and then darkened directly, that is to say, the sheet of paper was in direct contact with the negative and exposed to sunlight. The process could take several hours in overcast weather. The operation was completed by fixing the image in a bath of sodium hyposulphite.

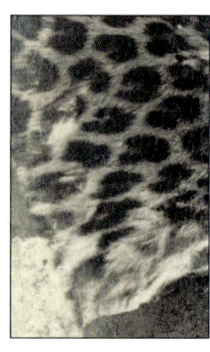

N° 3510
_____

c. 1895
Vincenzo Galdi
Albumen print, 16.5 x 23 cm

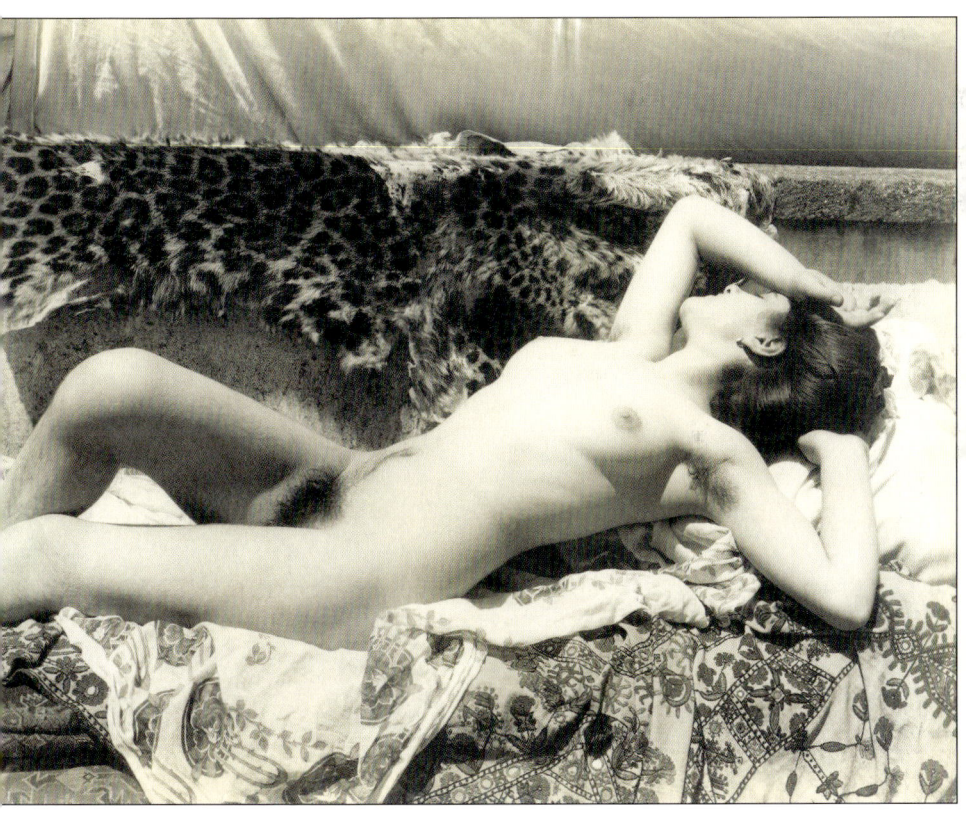

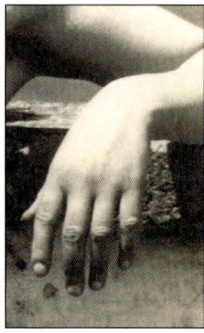

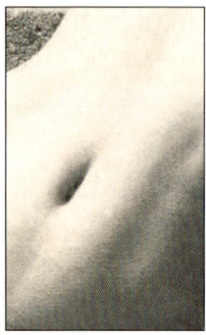

It was, sometimes, toned beforehand with the help of gold salts and then washed with running water, preferably with a low mineral content. This procedure did not permit enlargement, as the size of the print obtained was the exact replica of the negative. Photographers were obliged to resort to large format cameras if they wanted to obtain large negatives.

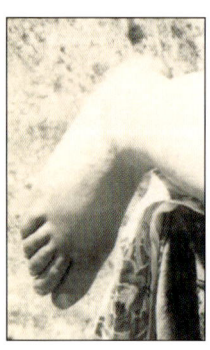

N° 3530

c. 1895
Vincenzo Galdi
Albumen print, 23 x 16.5 cm

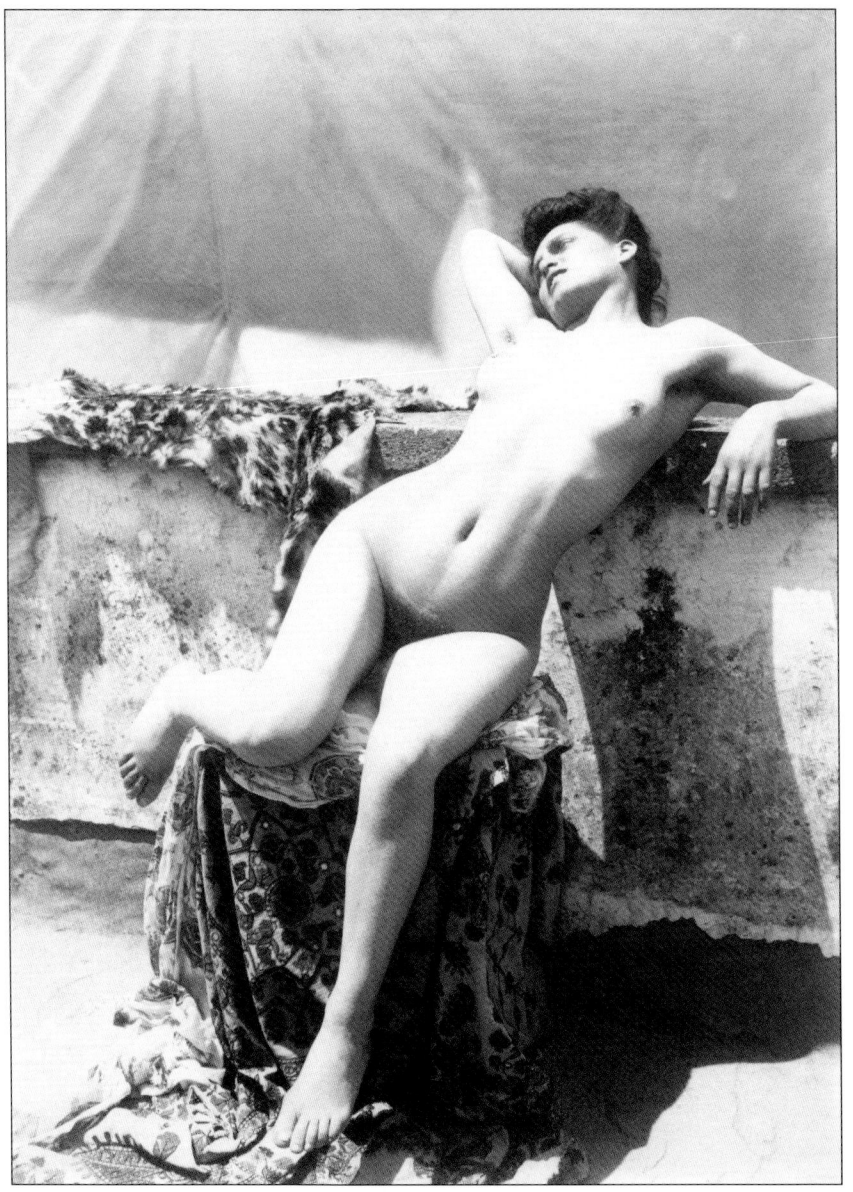

61

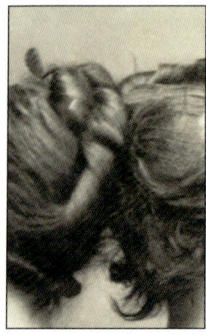

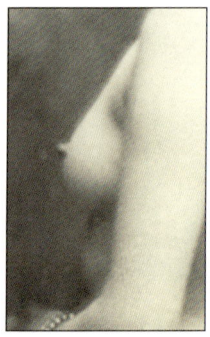

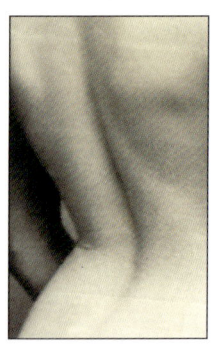

Louis-Désiré Blanquart-Evrard introduced albumenised paper at the Science Academy in 1850, and was a great success until the end of the 19ᵗʰ century. The procedure appears simple. The paper was simply covered with a coat of egg white, from where the paper got its name. The image obtained had a contrast, definition and brilliancy of a superior quality to that obtained until this point, and which did not exist with salted paper, where the image,

Untitled
———

c. 1900
Anonymous
Gelatin silver print, 14 x 9 cm

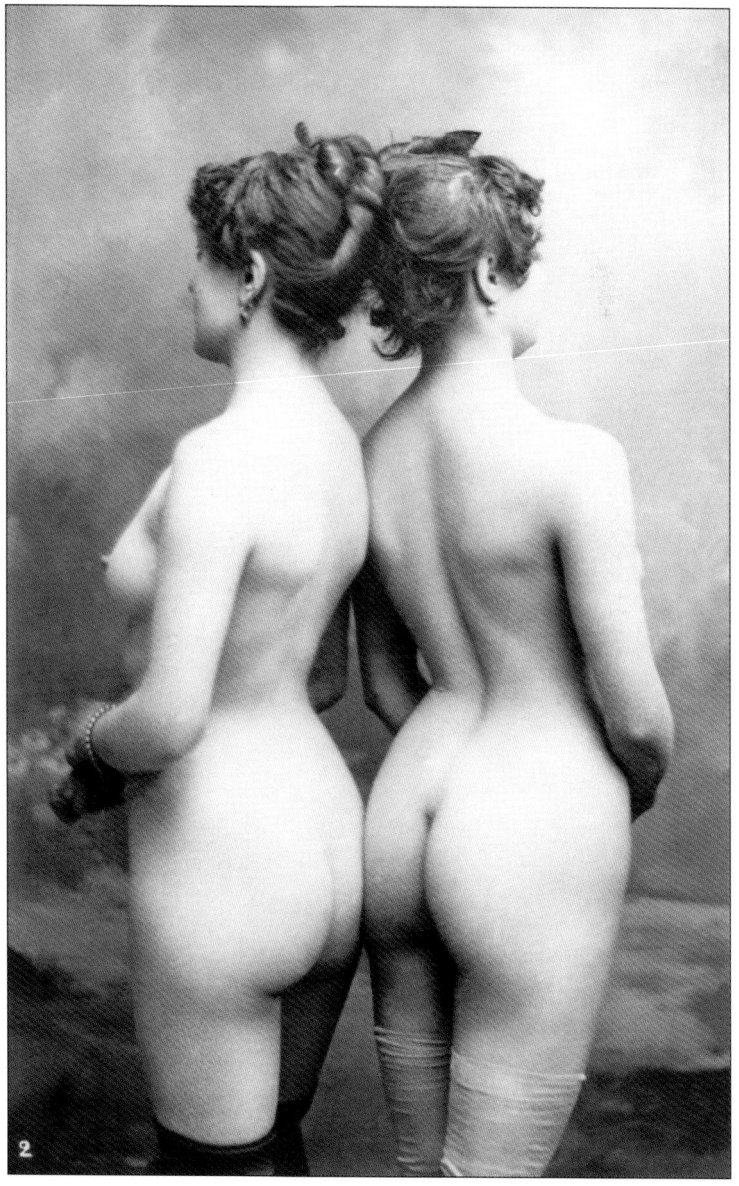

2

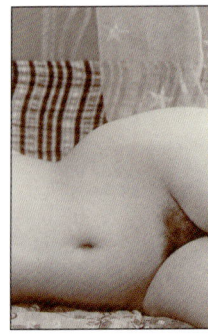

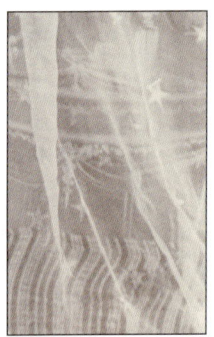

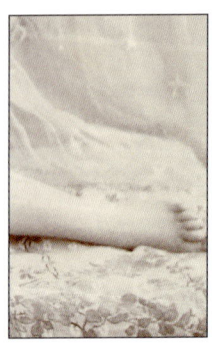

which was a little yellow, a little dull and badly defined, was on the paper itself, whereas with albumin it was in the coating. The clarity of the image was near that of the quality of the daguerreotype with the added bonus that it allowed an unlimited circulation.

In 1854, the photographer André Adolphe Eugène Disdéri made photography popular with the visiting card format. Using the same plate, he took several shots of small images

Untitled
————

c. 1900
Anonymous
Gelatin silver print, 12 x 16 cm

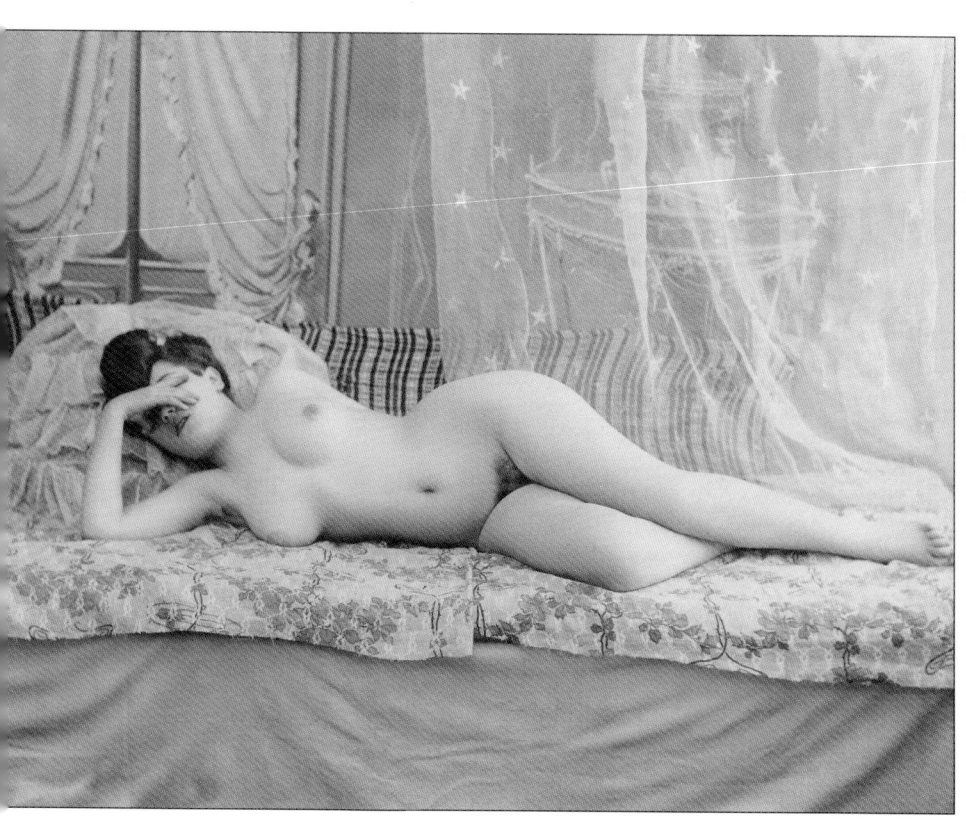

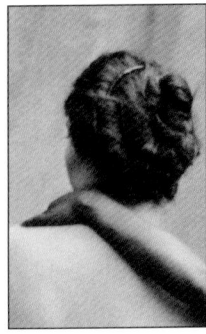

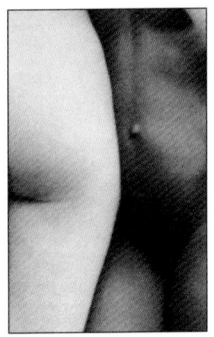

which were then stuck onto card (format 8 x 5.5 on card measuring 11.5 x 6.5). This procedure was mainly used for portraits on the same lines as the miniatures of the 18th century where people could go about their daily business carrying an image of their lady friend or relative on them. This size was ideal for nude photographs, as the photograph could be discreetly concealed in the wallet of anybody.

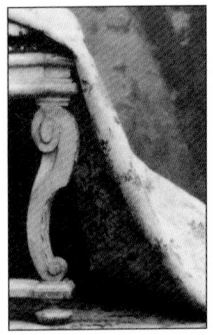

Untitled

c. 1900
Jean Agélou
Gelatin silver print, 17.2 x 11.7 cm

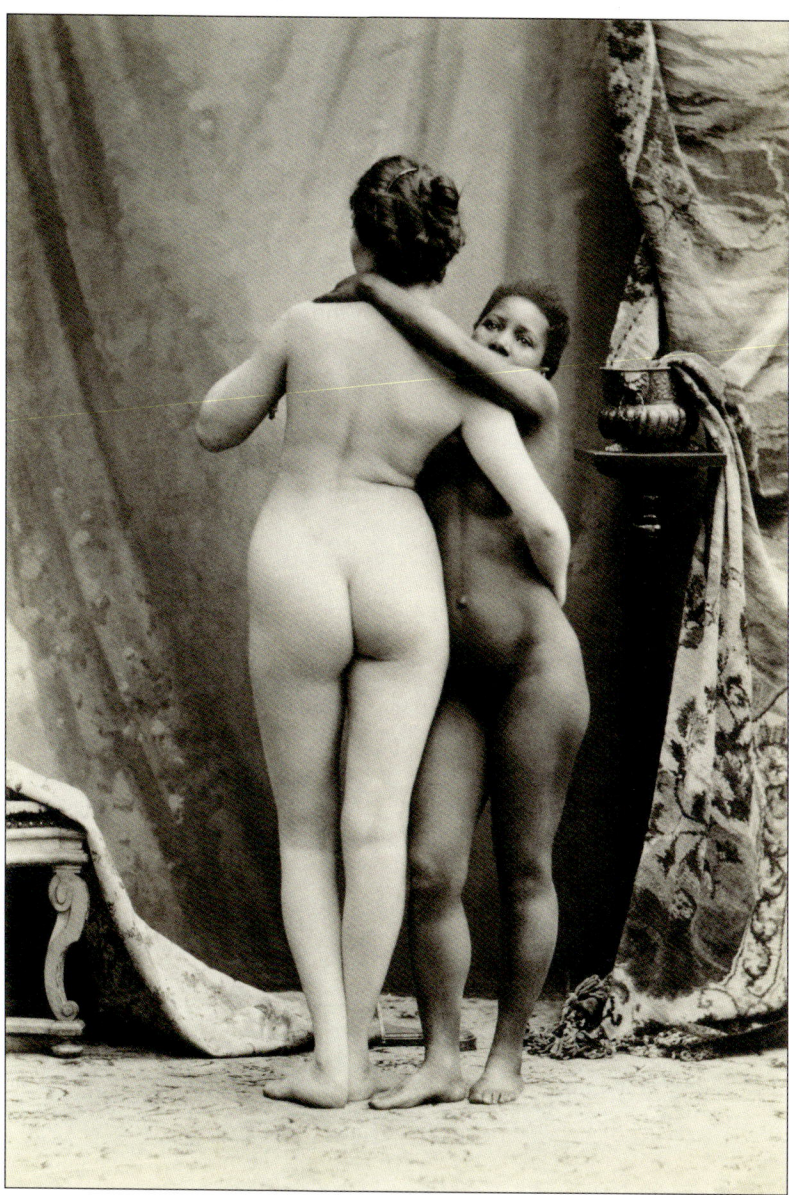

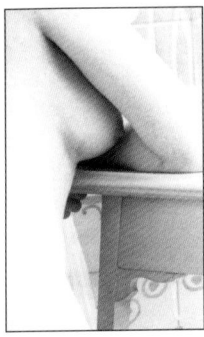

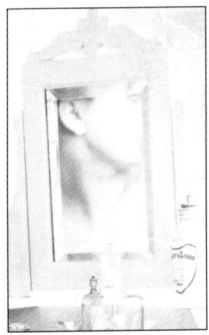

As with the daguerreotype, the size left little room for anecdotes, and the nude model appeared with the minimum of accessories. In the same year, Louis-Camille d'Olivier deposited sixty odd "academic studies" on salted paper and even more the following year. The larger formats of prints on paper, the anatomic and academic studies under the artistic alibi, gradually enabled more elaborate images, based on compositions often copied from pictorial and theatrical productions.

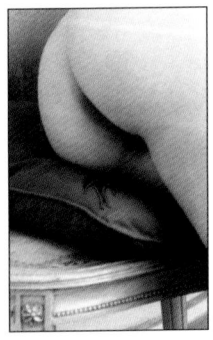

Untitled
_____

c. 1900
Anonymous
Gelatin silver print, 15.8 x 11.7 cm

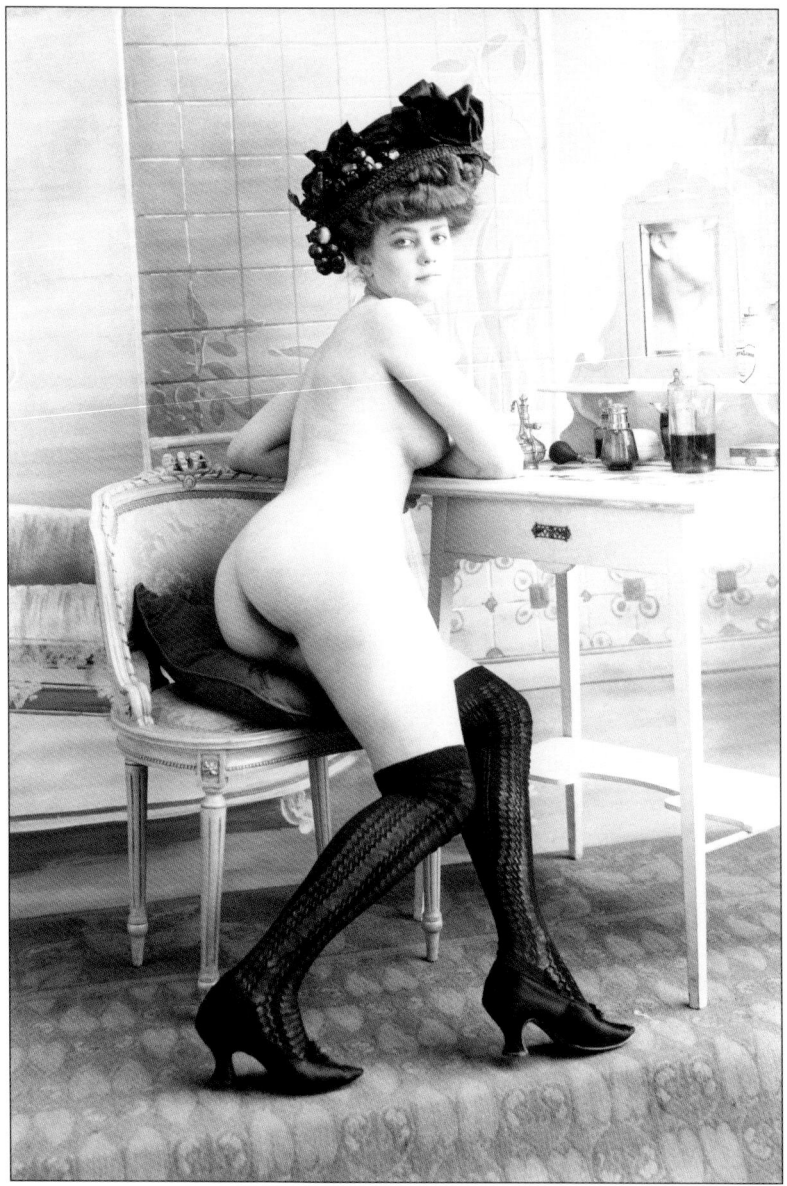

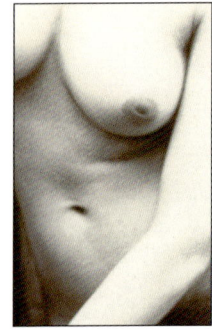

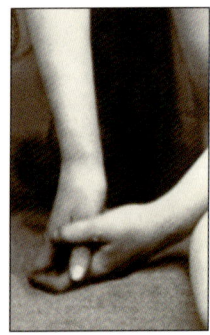

This is followed by reconstitutions evoking fantasies which would bewitch the end of the 19th century; antiquity with its mythological allegories and orientalism, exploited by both conventional and grandiloquent artists, the so called "Pompeian or Neo-Greek painters" such as Jean-Léon Gérôme or writers such as Pierre Louÿs or Félicien Champsaur.

In October 1860, the police searched the house of the photographer Belloc at no. 16 rue de Lancry, in the 10th district of Paris.

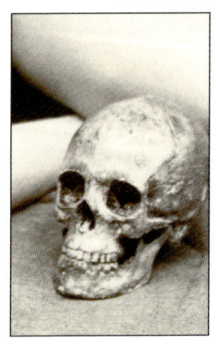

Untitled

c. 1900
Anonymous
Gelatin silver print, 17.7 x 9 cm

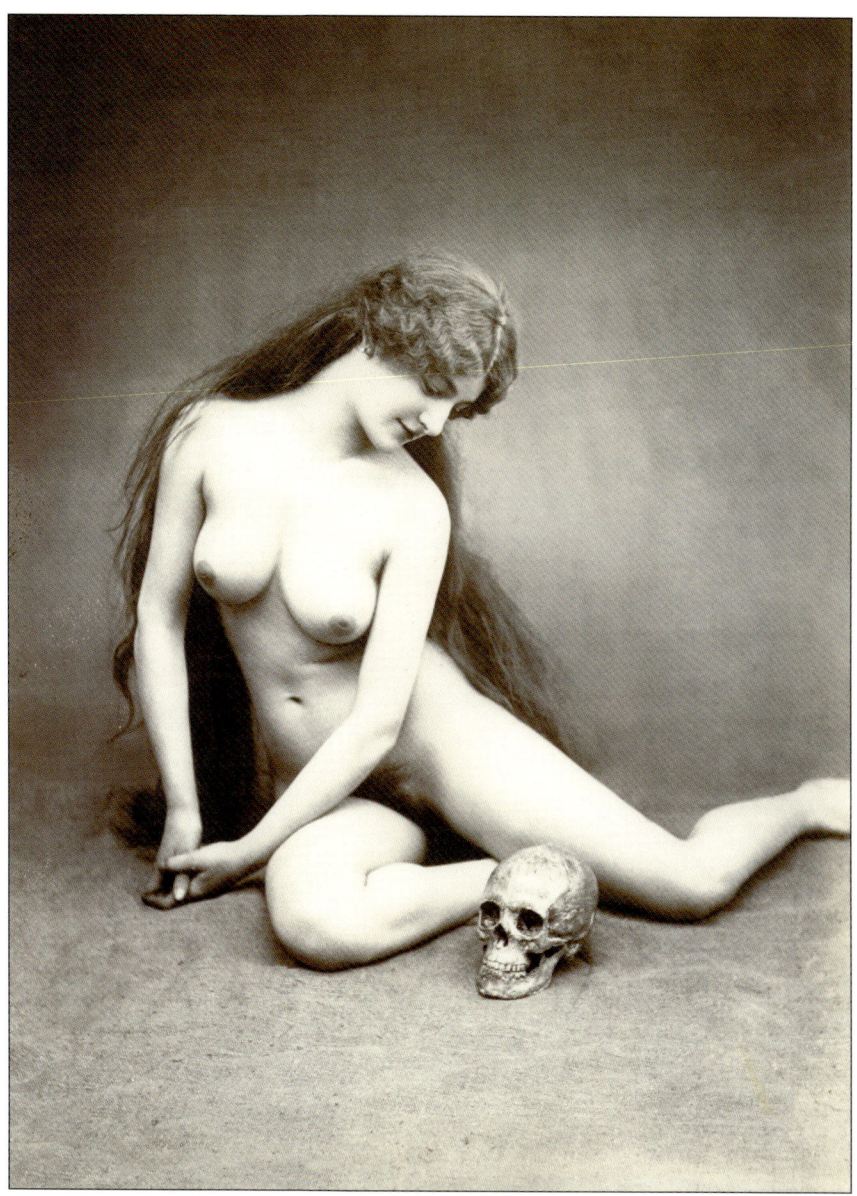

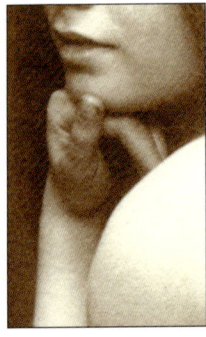

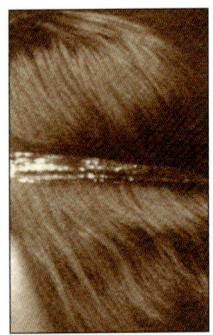

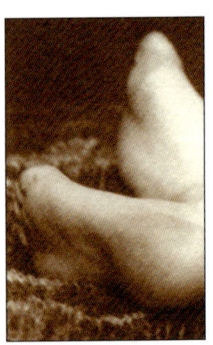

A certain Madame Ducellier was caught sitting at a table with nineteen pornographic pictures that she was in the process of colouring. More than four thousand photographs were seized from safes, writing desks and even in developing tanks, where some works were being processed. Most of them were described as being of an obscene nature. Although he practised the honourable activity of

N° 21

———

c. 1900
H.C.W., Paris
Gelatin silver print, 23.7 x 17.7 cm

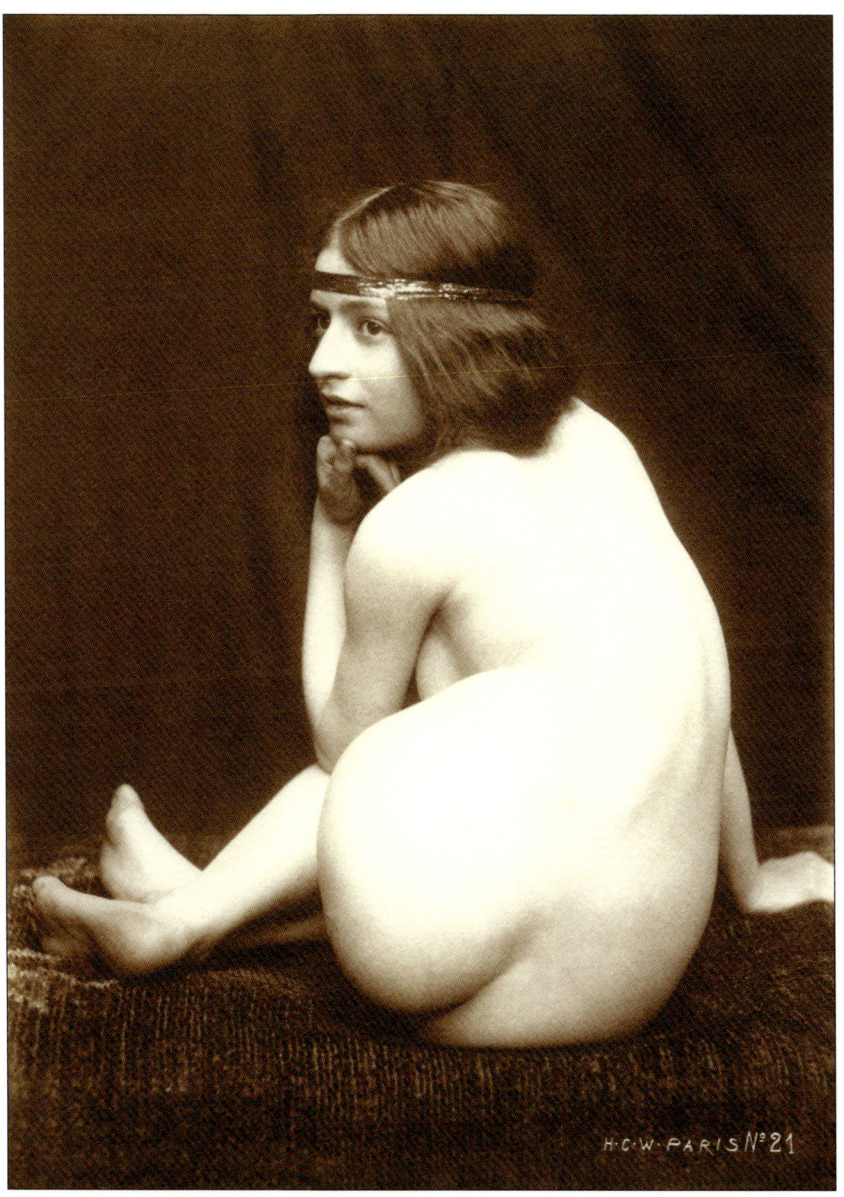

H C W PARIS Nº 21

73

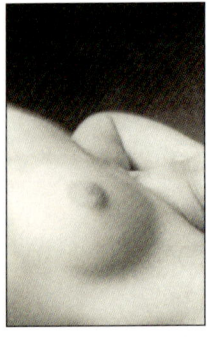

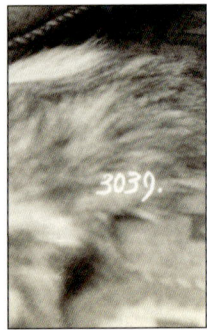

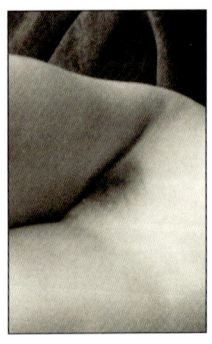

photography, was a teacher, was the founding member of the French Photographic Society and was the author of technical manuals, Belloc was a sort of Dr. Jekyll and Mr. Hyde of erotic photography. He had already been condemned in 1857 and fined one hundred francs for "publication of unauthorised photographs and affront to public decency".

N° P 194
———————

c. 1900
Anonymous
Gelatin silver print, 10 x 13.7 cm

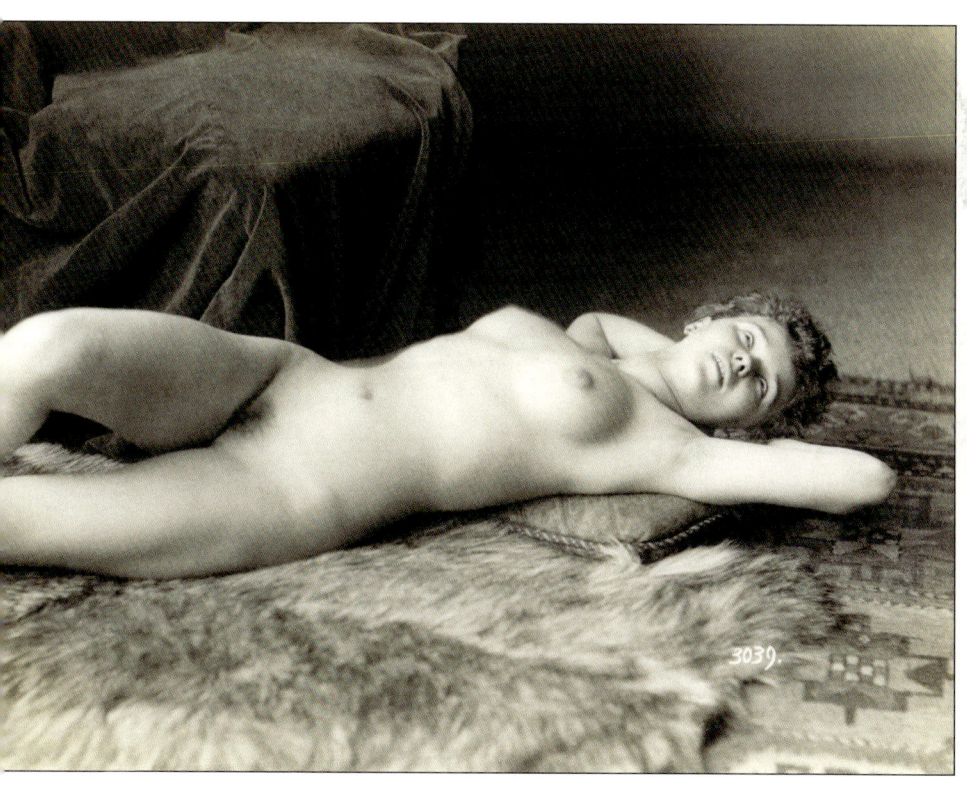

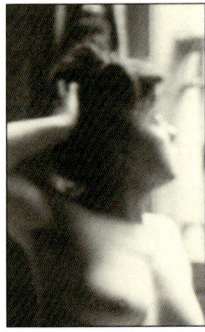

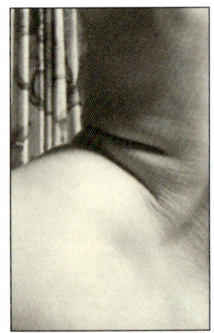

For his second appearance in court, he was sentenced to three months in prison and a three hundred-franc fine.

Six years later, less than two hundred prints were deposited at the Print Room of the Imperial Library, the other few thousand having mysteriously been mislaid between the offices of the police and the Imperial Prosecutor.

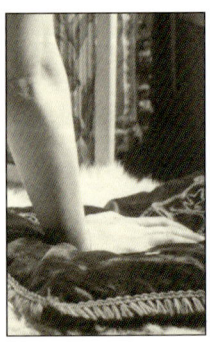

N° 18

———

c. 1900
H.C.W., Paris
Gelatin silver print, 11.3 x 16 cm

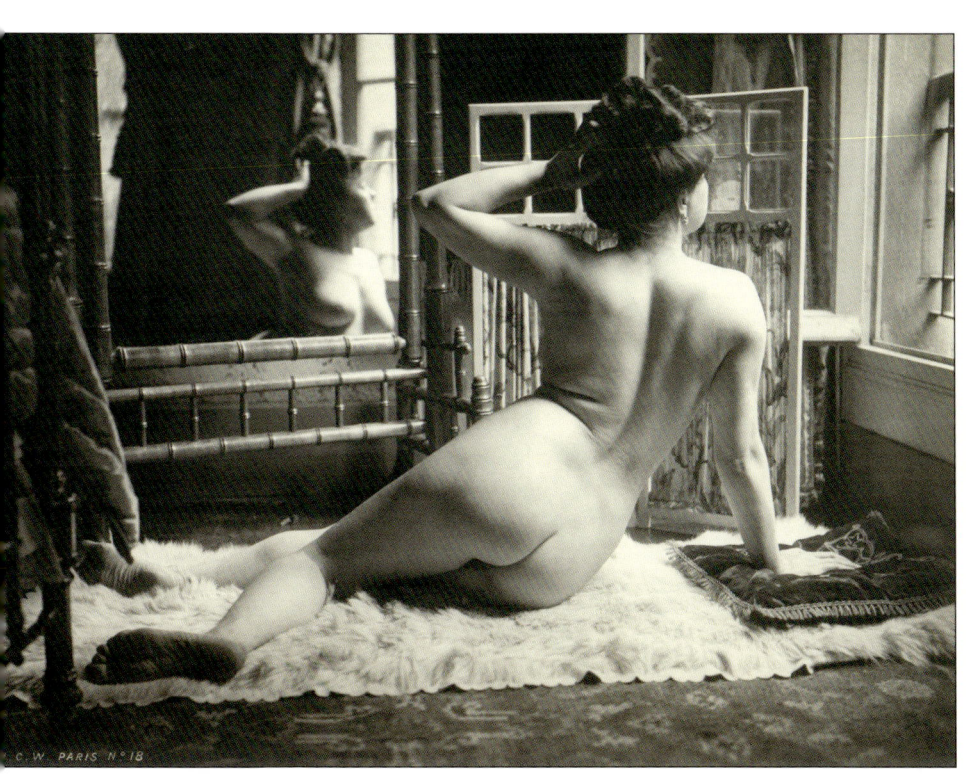

C.W. PARIS N°18.

77

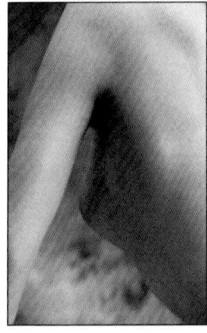

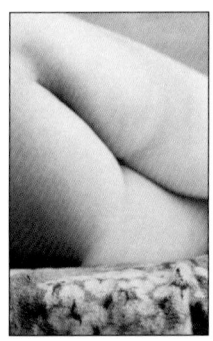

In 1860, manufacturers upturned the cottage industry in which photographers operated by providing them with pre-coated paper that they would no longer need to prepare themselves. Photography, in this manner, became an industrial process.

These new techniques shortened the posing time and allowed for the duplication of images, thus reducing costs. The Imperial Censor, followed by the Republican Censor, obliged photographers to work in an

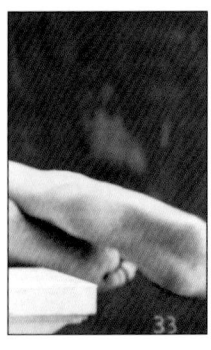

Untitled

c. 1900
Anonymous
Gelatin silver print, blank-backed postcard, 9 x 14 cm

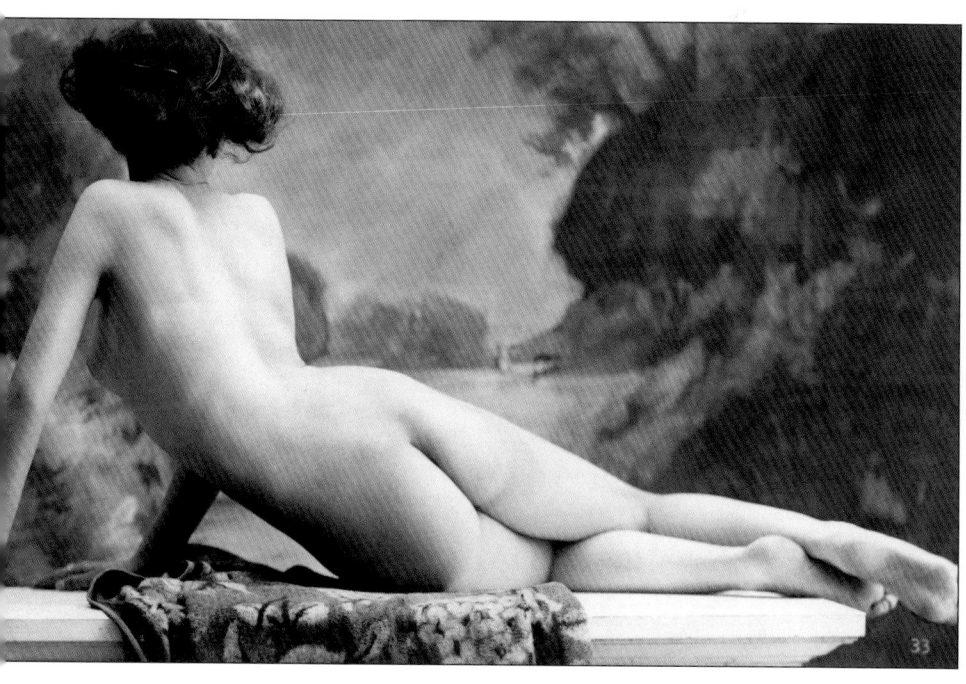

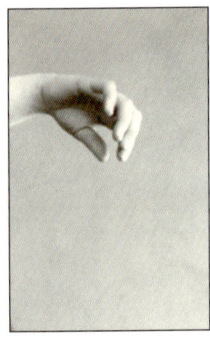

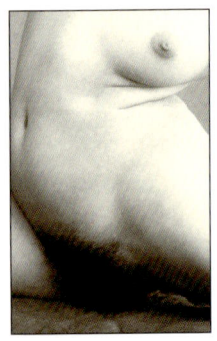

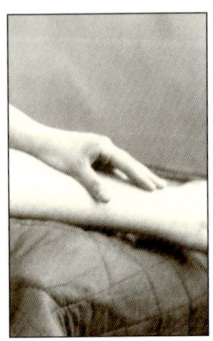

academic manner, a manner which was designed for inspiring painters and sculptors. However, even nude photographs of models designed for painters were of interest to those who were more concerned with the erotic connotation of the images and their suggestive content than their artistic qualities. The photographs were sold by hawkers or in bookshops in the Grands Boulevards district, often in arcades frequented by prostitutes.

N° 192

———

c. 1900
Henri Holtramare
Gelatin silver print, 11.7 x 15.7 cm

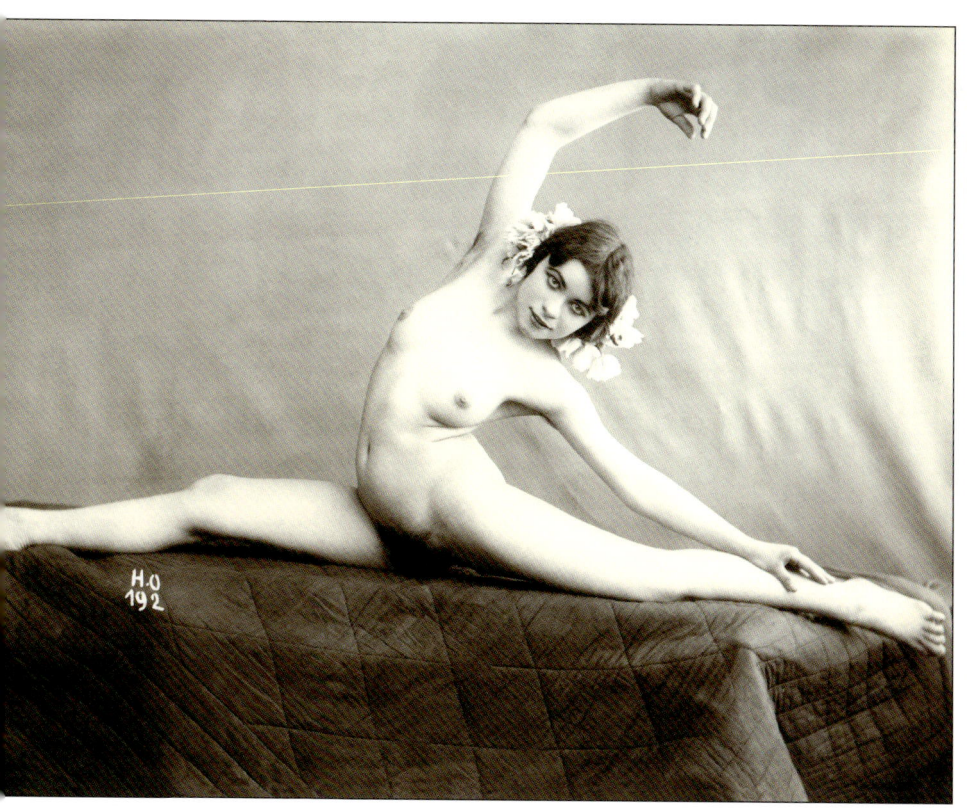

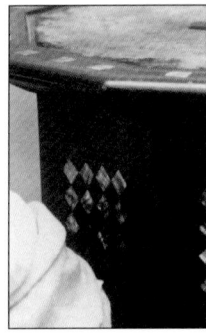

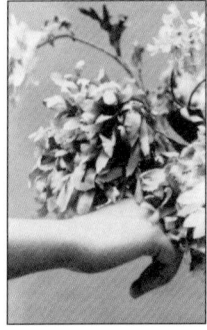

The moral question of circulation to the general public was not a problem when it only concerned the daguerreotypes, as the excessive cost ensured a limited distribution to the elite. It now became a problem, as it was possible for every soldier, schoolboy, young man or even young woman to acquire or have access to a licentious image, even if the image was academic. The mid-nineteenth century was a time of great confusion between moral order and artistic aestheticism.

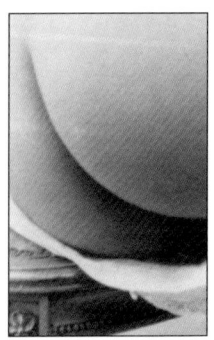

Untitled

c. 1900
Anonymous
Gelatin silver print, 16.6 x 11 cm

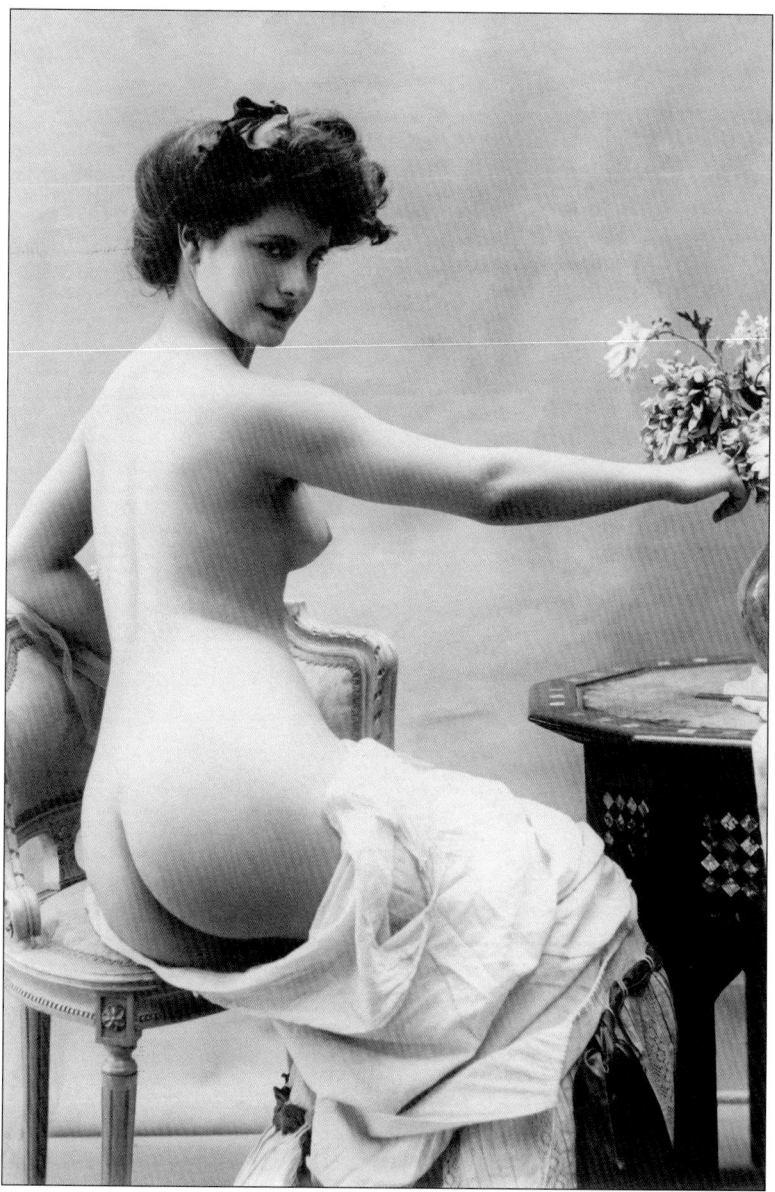

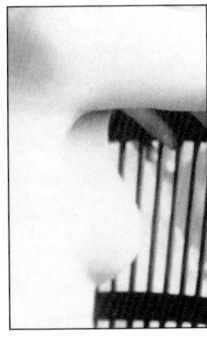

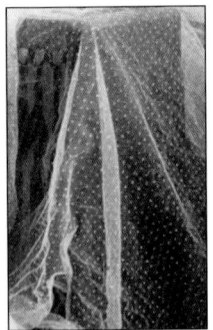

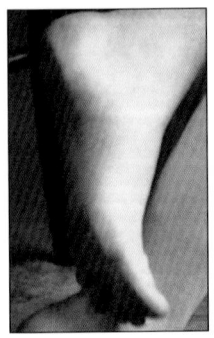

This was the time when Courbet would make a scene at every exhibition at the Salon, when Flaubert and Baudelaire, nowadays considered as classic writers, were accused of obscenity, when the paintings *Le Déjeuner sur l'herbe* and *Olympia* were condemned because Manet depicted nude women looking at the spectator. It was a period looking for an identity, caught between its Republican and Bonapartist convictions and those desirous of

Untitled

c. 1900
Anonymous
Gelatin silver print, 22 x 16.8 cm

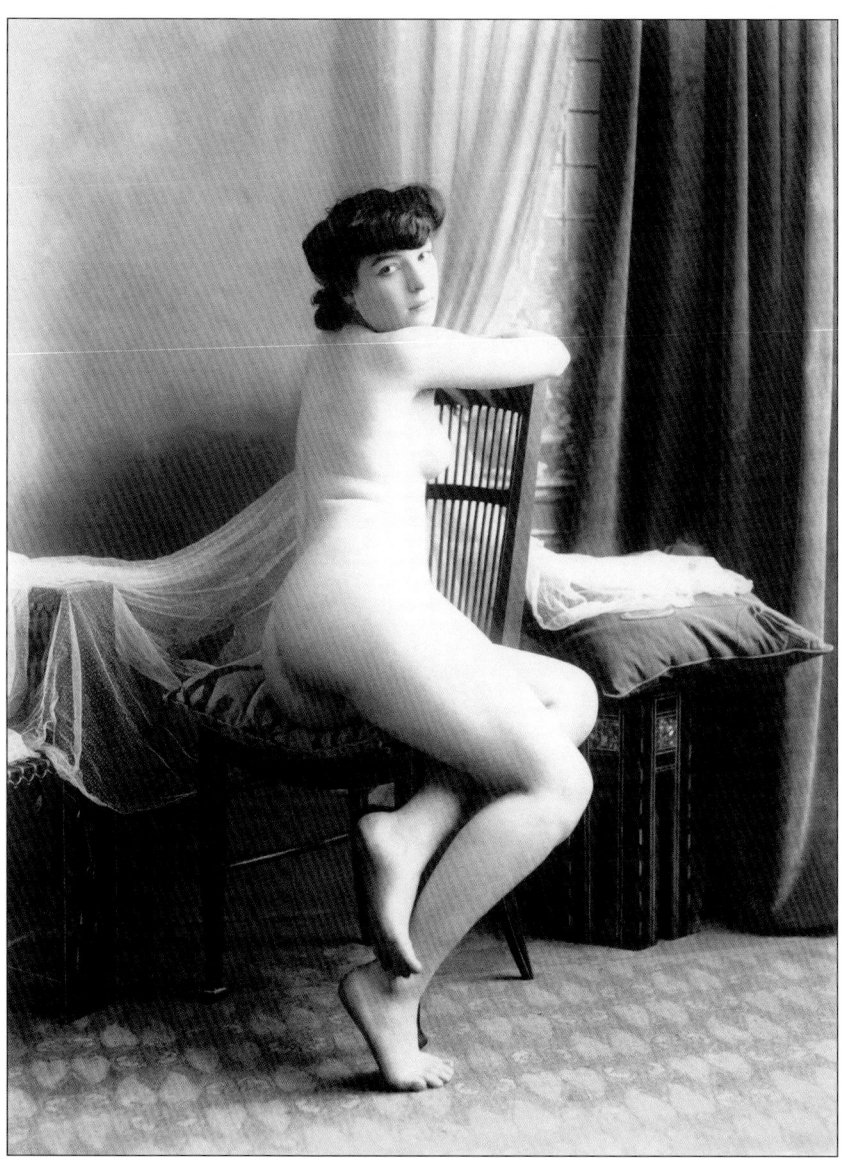

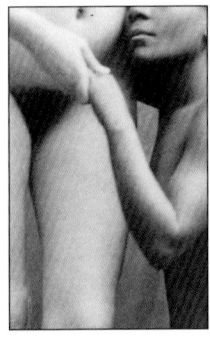

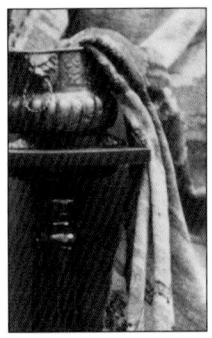

a return to the royalty and the Old Regime, a time when, thank God, there were virulent opponents to obscurantist fundamentalism in France. It was therefore difficult for the nude to find its place in society. What appeared obvious to the Greeks of antiquity as a figure of grace and beauty, at a time when nudity was synonymous with well-being in a civilisation without inhibition where athletes were nude, had become disgraceful, perverse and

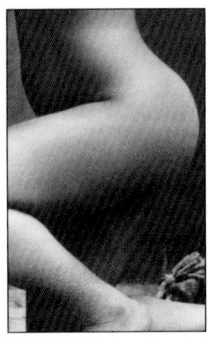

Untitled

c. 1900
Henri Oltramare (?)
Albumen print, 14.2 x 10 cm

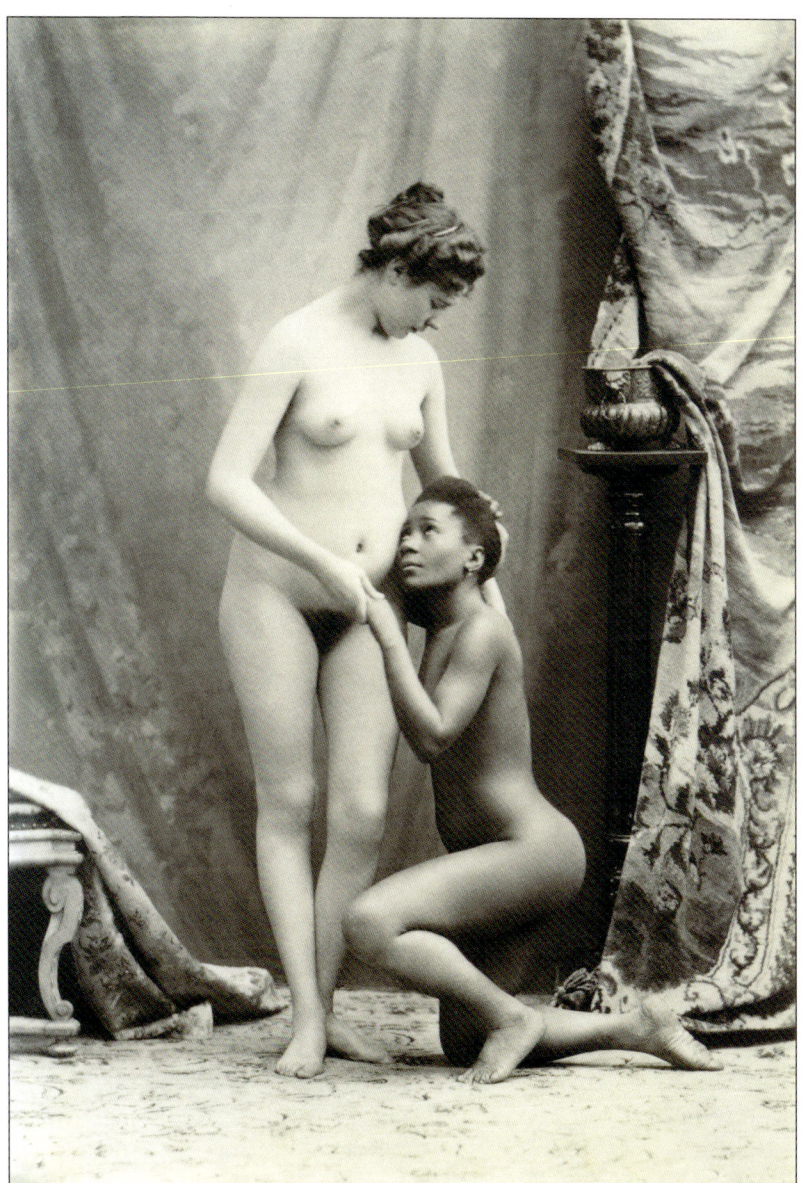

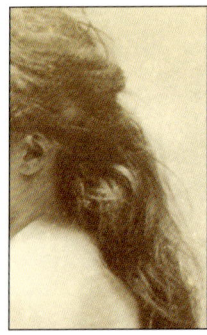

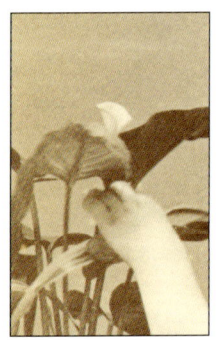

monstrous at certain periods by a civilisation stamped with Christian Puritanism. Dominated by the burgeoning middle classes, the 19th century, with its hatred of the body, appears to be the most representative period of this tragic effect. For the Christian, the mind must fight against carnal pleasures, and eternal orgasm will only be obtained after death, after having paid for the original sin which is linked to shame of the body.

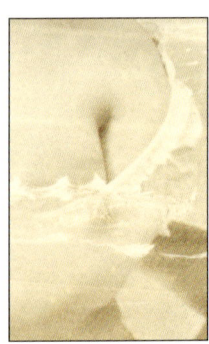

Summer Night
_____

c. 1900
J. E. Lecadre
Albumen print mounted on board, 16.5 x 10.7 cm

J. E. Lecadre

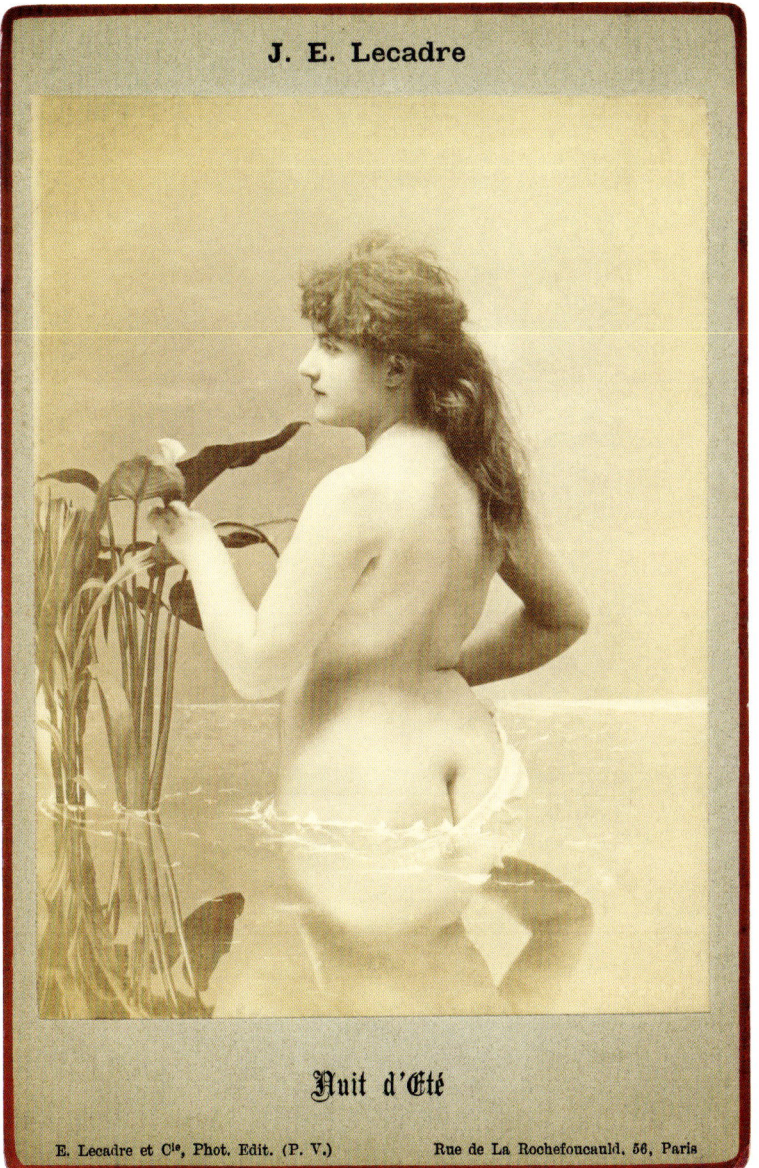

Nuit d'Été

E. Lecadre et Cⁱᵉ, Phot. Édit. (P. V.)   Rue de La Rochefoucauld, 56, Paris

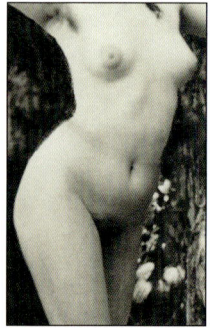

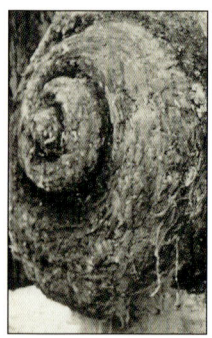

"Then the eyes of both of them were opened, and they realised they were naked; so they sewed fig leaves together and made coverings for themselves."

Then came the period of Napoleon III who reigned from 1852 to 1870 and who entrusted the transformation of Paris to Haussman. The Prefect Baron Haussman would transform the City of Lights into a glorious place. The whole world was dazzled by its elegance and lavish festivities.

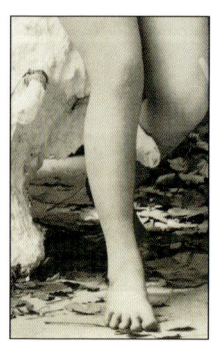

Untitled

c. 1905
Anonymous
Gelatin silver print, blank-backed postcard, 9 x 14 cm

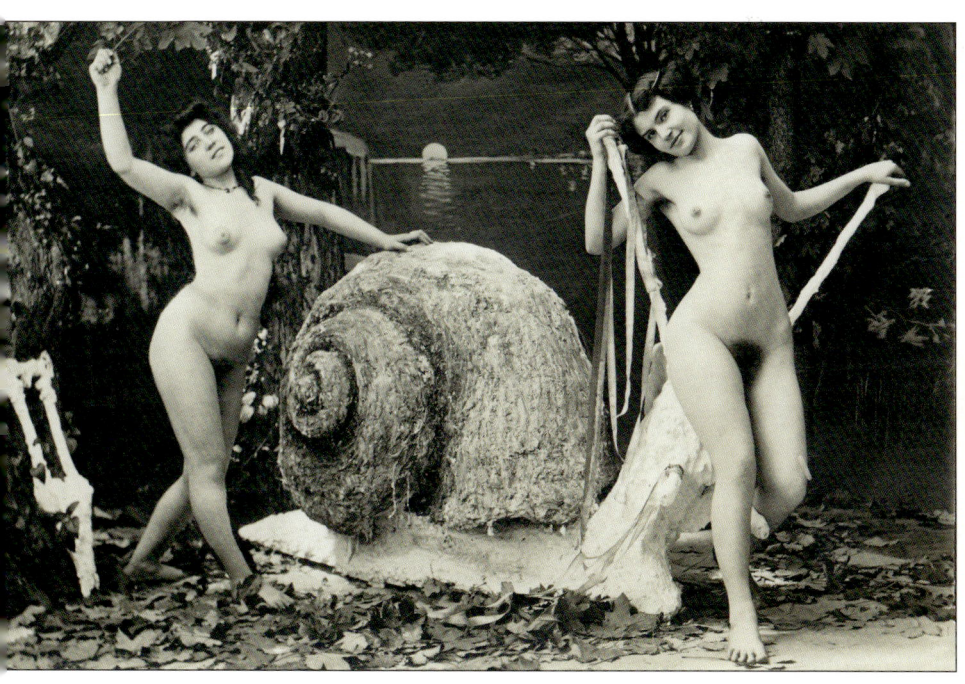

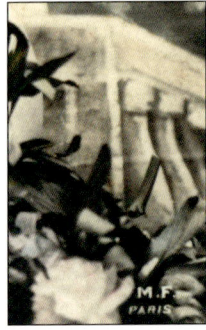

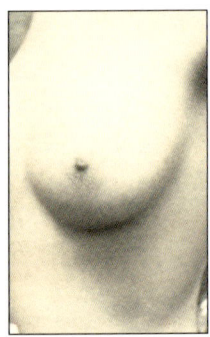

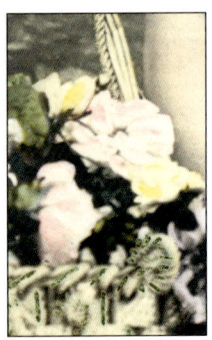

Cosmopolitan Paris, the undisputed pleasure capital, had no problems in providing ladies of the night for those interested, and artists with models. Thousands of young girls arrived every year from the provinces. They were escaping from poverty, sadness and the lack of any future in the countryside. However, nothing was free in Paris, everything had to be paid for. Given that a factory worker earned on average one

Untitled

c. 1908
M.F., Paris
Hand-painted printed-back postcard, 14 x 9 cm

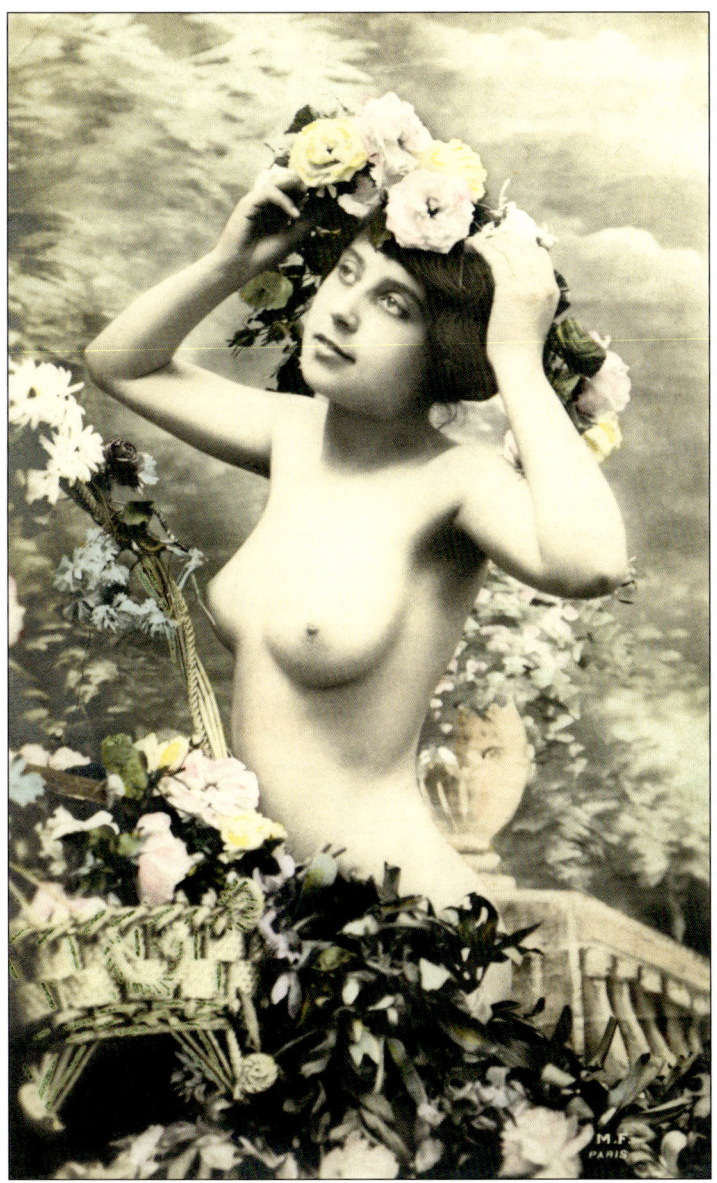

M.F.
PARIS

93

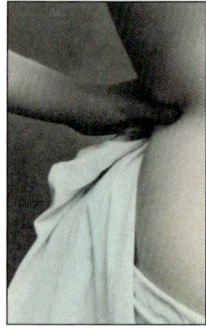

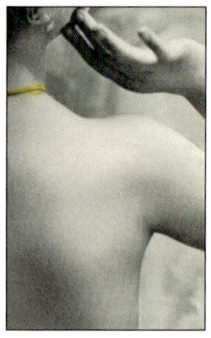

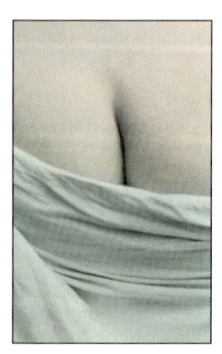

and a half francs a day around 1875, it is easy to understand those who, casting modesty aside, agreed to pose for artists for four hours in return for five francs. This amount would frequently be doubled if the model was able to pose for four hours in the morning and then for four hours again in the afternoon. Moreover, the life of an artist was very attractive.

N° 84

———

c. 1908
Anonymous
Hand-painted blank-backed postcard, 14 x 9 cm

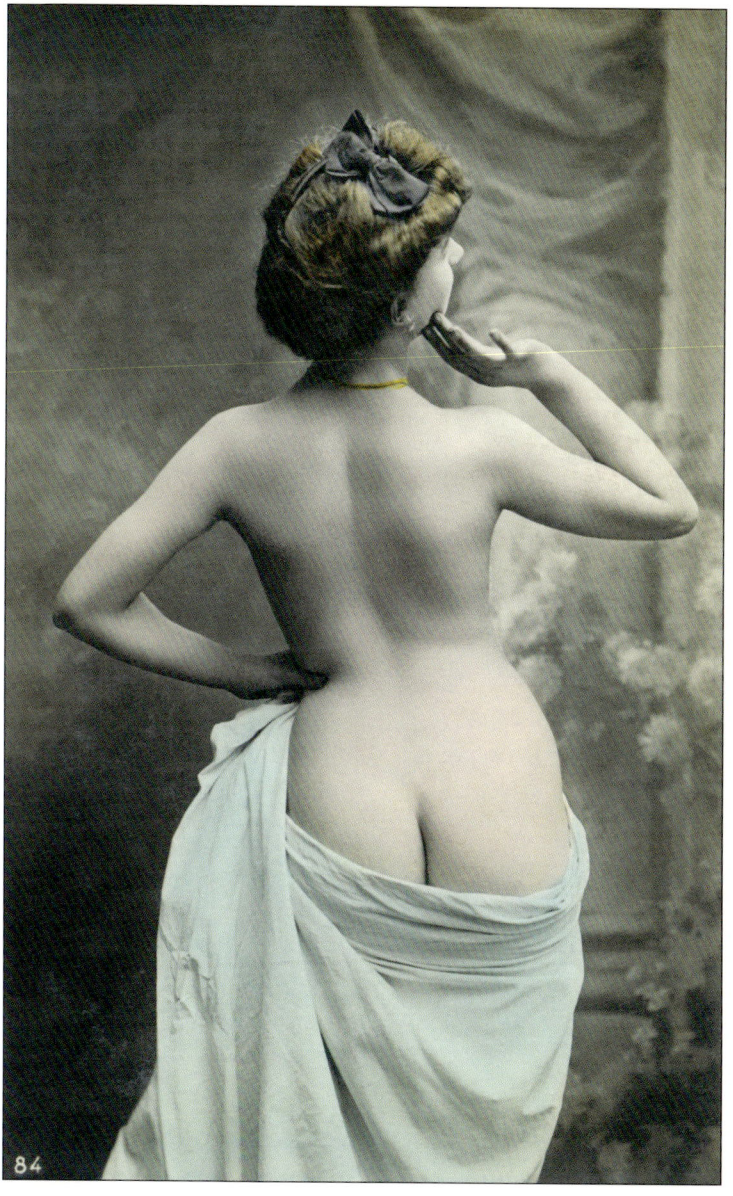

84

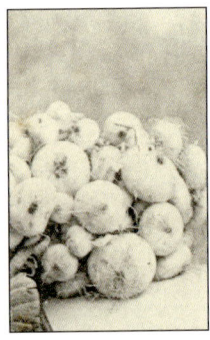

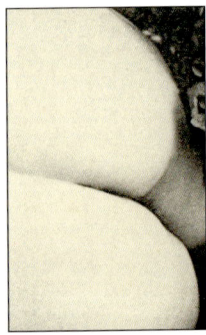

As well as casual models, photographers also had a large reserve of professional models at their disposal, who were also regularly used by Parisian painters. Their models for cherubs, St. John, Venus or baby Jesus were mostly of Italian origin and they lived with their families in the Latin quarter at in the rue Mouffetard, between the Saint-Victor square, ironically known as piazza Saint-Victor, and the Contrescarpe square, crammed into

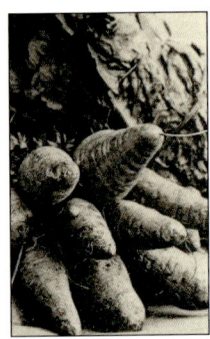

"Au Trèfle" Brand

c. 1908
Anonymous
Phototype, printed-back postcard, 9 x 14 cm

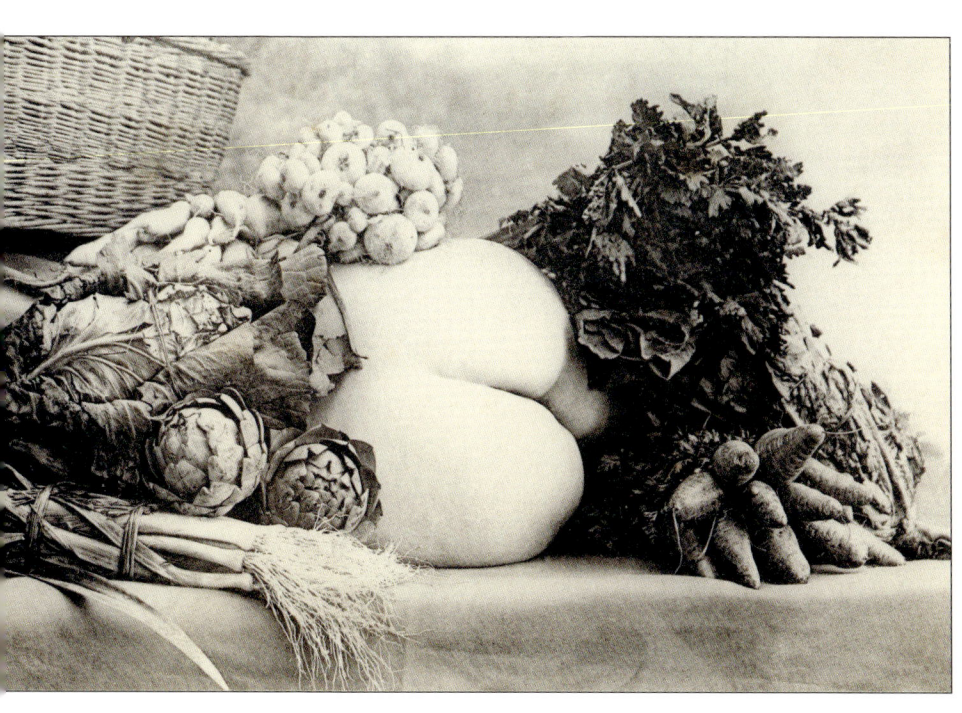

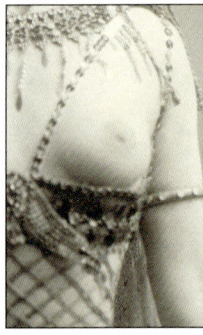

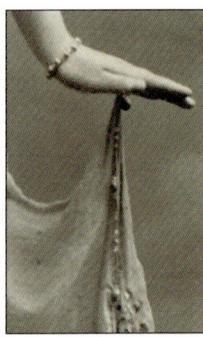

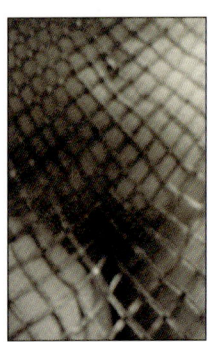

squalid buildings, where the artists who visited them were able to make their lives a little easier, financially speaking.

Some models were used for the beauty of a certain part of their body; for example, their hands, bosom, feet or for a particular quality required by the artist. For those models who posed in "academic costume," that is to say without any costume, it was modestly said that they "posed comprehensively".

Visiting Card
───────────

c. 1909
Bert Editions
Gelatin silver mounted on board, 16.5 x 10.7 cm

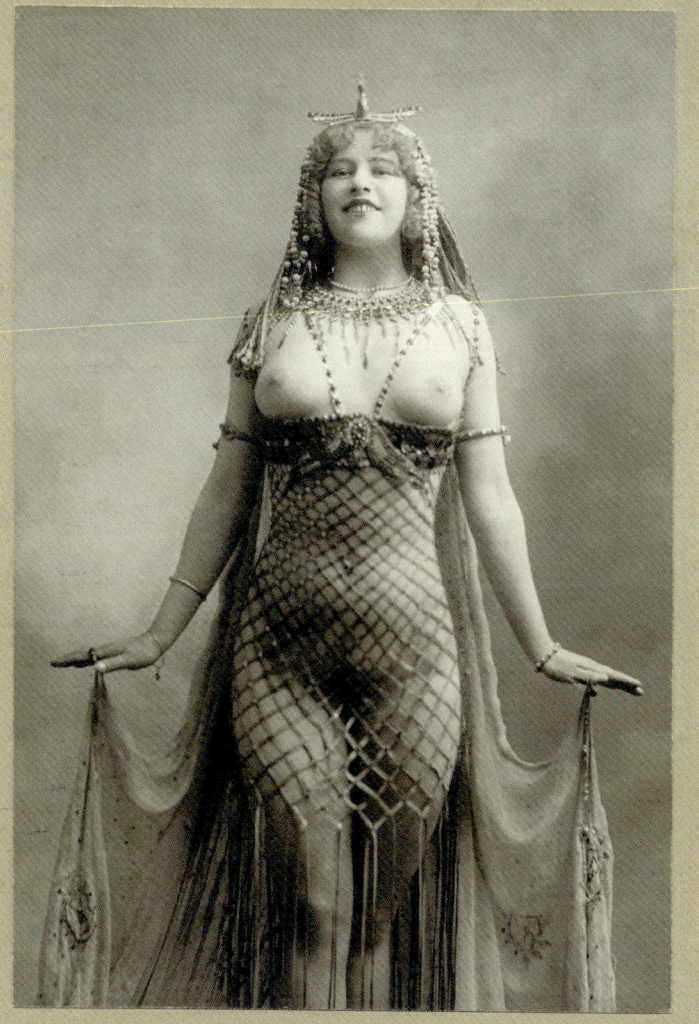

35, BOUL.ᵈ DES CAPUCINES
· PARIS ·

A. Bert

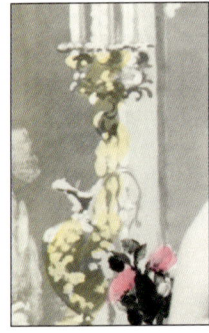

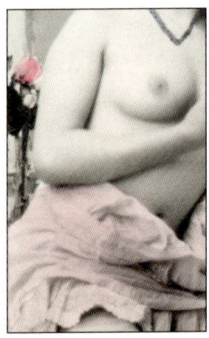

Total perfection of figure was mandatory conformity with the classical shape. In his work *Artists Models*, Paul Dollfus presents Italian models by use of odious and racist statements, though such statements were probably considered trivial at the time. However, he was obliged to take note of and acknowledge the choices of the artists of his time who were motivated by the radiant hereditary beauty of Italian men and women.

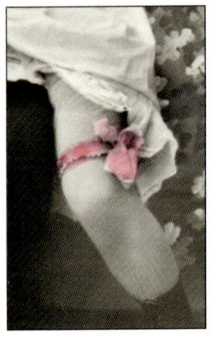

Untitled
—————

c. 1910
W. A., Paris
Hand-painted printed-back postcard, 14 x 9 cm

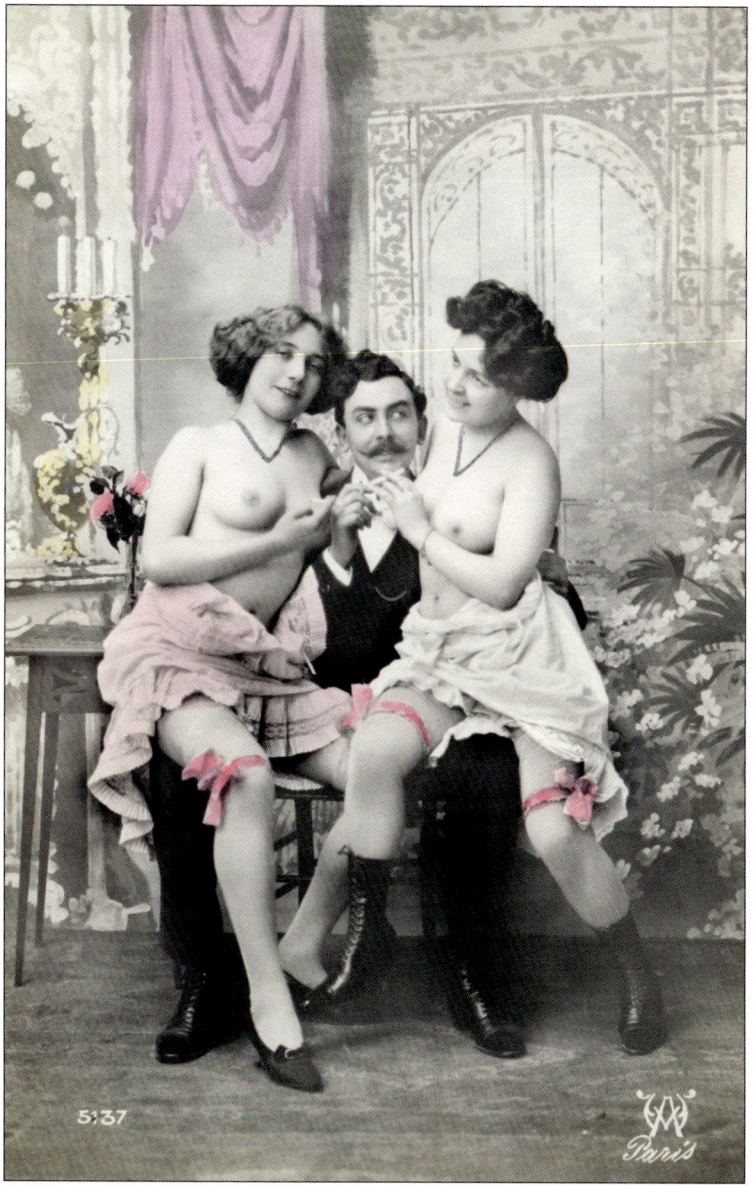

5:37

Paris

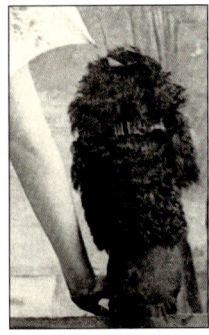

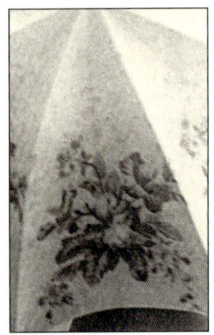

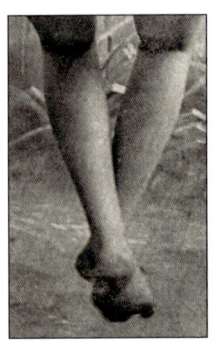

"The women have very classical and regular figures until the age of about twenty. The whole body is attractive. The lines of the shoulders and neck are harmonious. The breasts are, in the prime of youth before maternity, firm and well placed, lending elegance to the bosom. The outline of the hips, the stomach and the top of the thighs are regular and pure. The head often that of a model from antiquity,

"Au Trèfle" Brand

c. 1910
Anonymous
Phototype, printed-back postcard, 14 x 9 cm

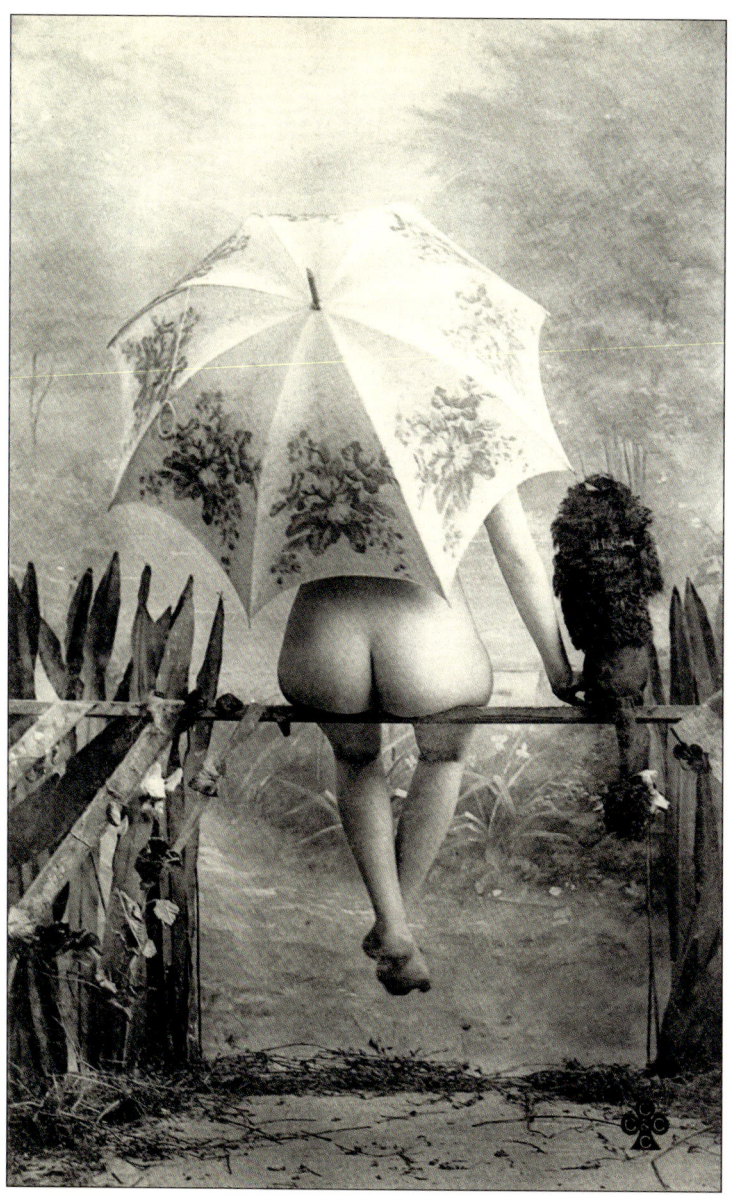

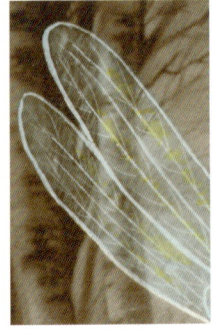

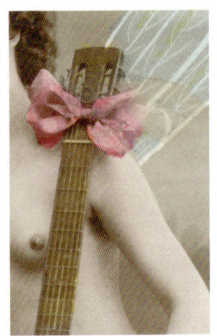

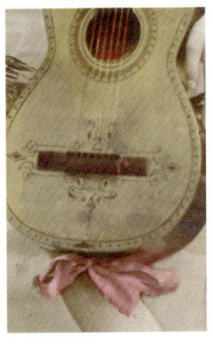

is very beautiful of line, reminding one of a virgin or a goddess without the need to idealise. The old men have tapered hands, long hair and the splendid beards of Heavenly Fathers. Most of the models have been working from a very young age." Dollfus relates this amusing dialogue. "An Italian model was asked, 'How old are you?'"

"Fourteen years old."

"And how long have you been posing?"

Idea 228

c. 1915
M. Boulanger
Printed-back postcard, 14 x 9 cm

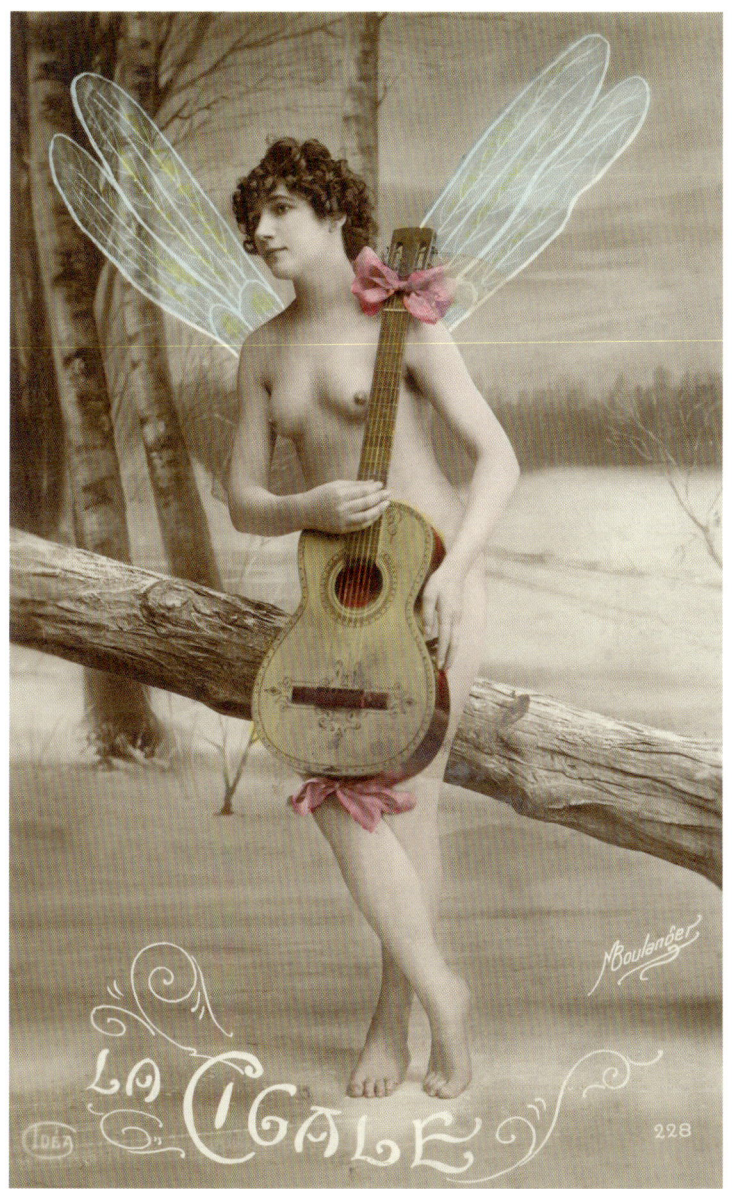

LA CIGALE

M.Boulanger

228

105

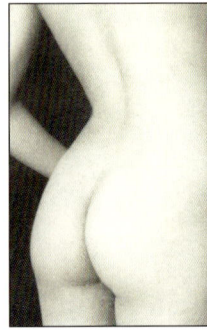

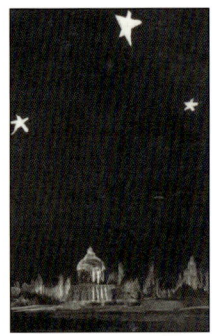

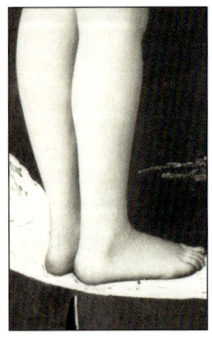

"For thirteen years."

Newborn babies were used to portray the baby Jesus, suckling the breast of their mother, the Virgin Mary. From the age of two, infants were used to portray cherubs, the Putti that were necessary for the imagery of the painters influenced by Pompeii such as Bouguereau. Around the age of seven or eight, they would be used as part of a composition of allegories, for crowd scenes or religious subjects.

Nº 171
———

c. 1915
Anonymous
Blank-backed postcard, 14 x 9 cm

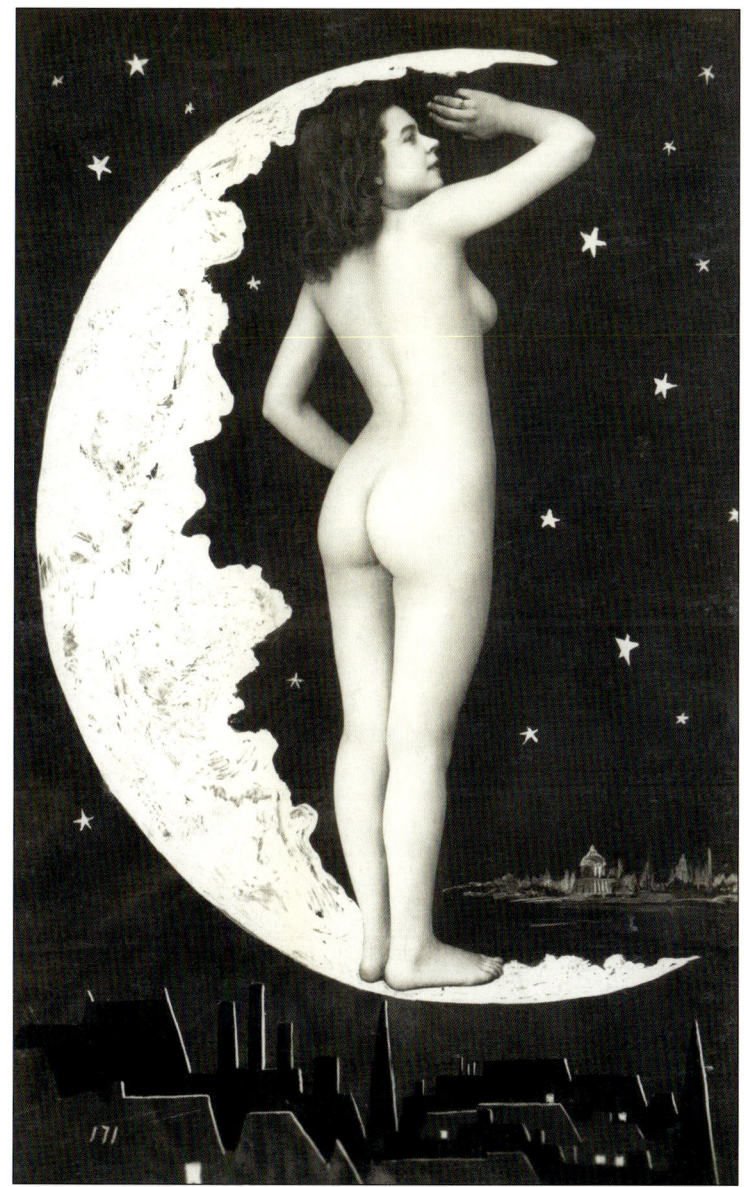

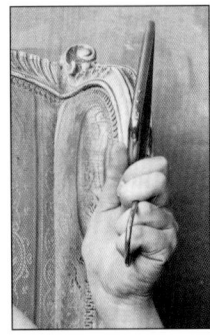

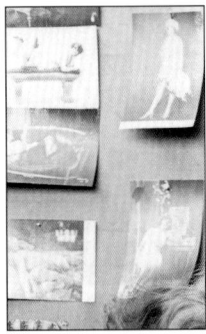

At the age of fourteen, the boys and girls were fully developed and could, therefore, be used for any representation for the painter or the photographer.

In 1871, Maddox invented the gelatine-silver-bromide, that is to say a suspension of silver bromide in the gelatine of the paper itself, a procedure that is still used to this day, thus completing the evolution of the principal procedures used in photography.

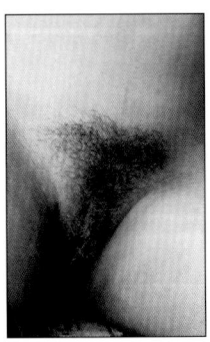

Untitled

c. 1915
Anonymous
Gelatin silver print, 18 x 13 cm

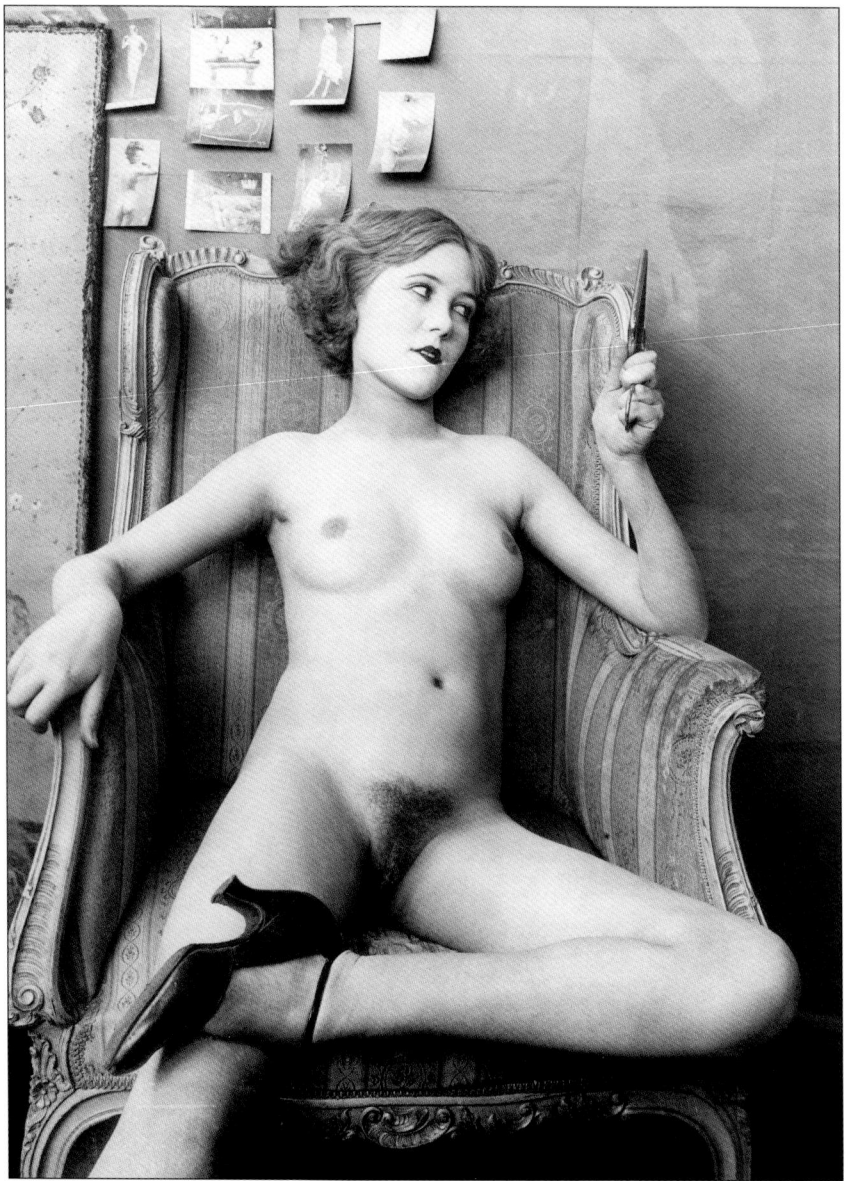

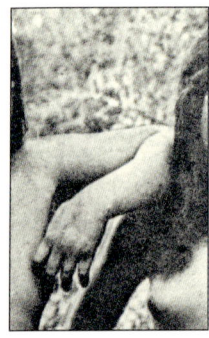

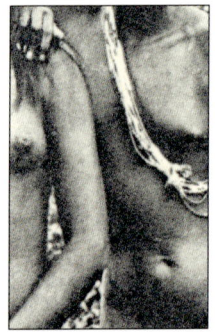

The Ethnographical Alibi

After several decades, a change became necessary. Once all the possibilities offered by the academic alibi were used up, it became a question of how to circulate erotic images in the large numbers that the general public were calling for, without clashing with the guarantor of moral standards, the authorities.

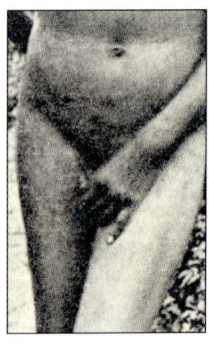

Indias do Sul do Brazil

c. 1903
Anonymous
Postcard, 14 x 9 cm

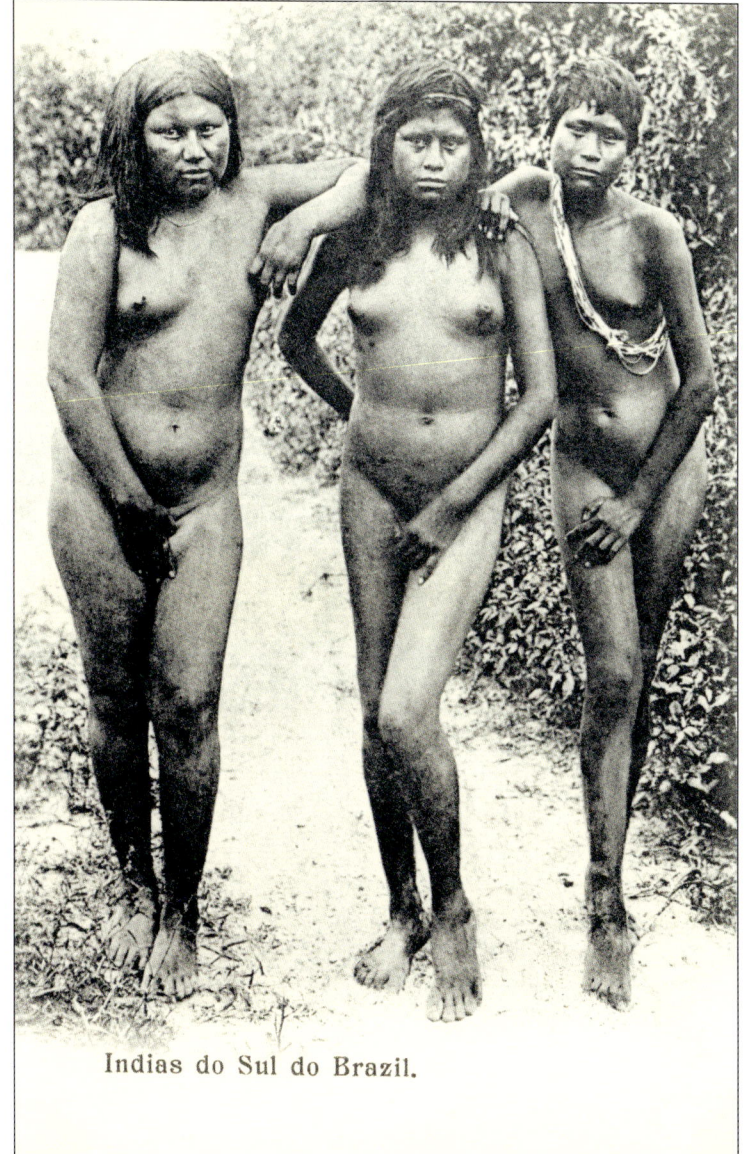

Indias do Sul do Brazil.

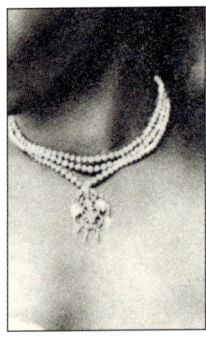

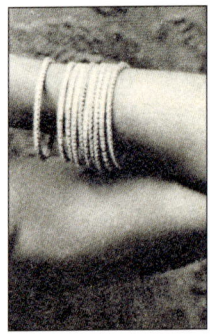

The colonisation of virgin territories fascinated the crowded Western world. These worlds were largely revealed thanks to photography, which brought the exotic into people's living rooms. The vastness of wild landscapes suffered little from distortion, but became impoverished, reduced to a monochromatic two dimensions. It is not the same with reproductions of an ethnographic nature. The natives of the four corners of the world were treated as primitive scoundrels.

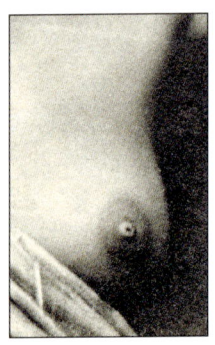

Rodiya Girl, Ceylan
_____

c. 1908
Plâté & Co.
Postcard, 9 x 14 cm

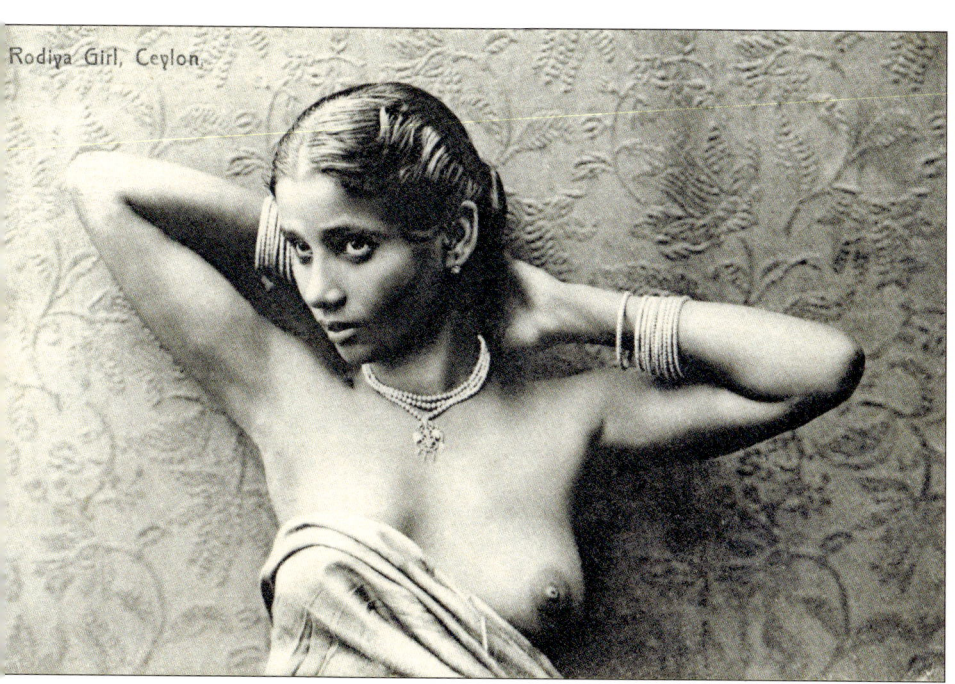

Rodiya Girl, Ceylon.

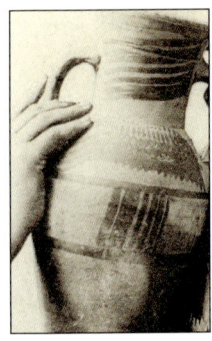

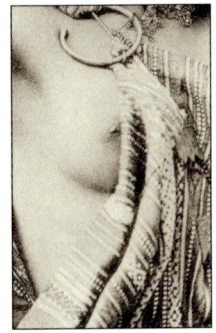

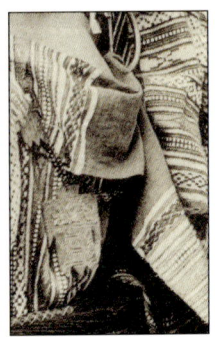

They were usually depicted naked under a blazing sun, or in studio reconstructions under the pretext of dubious morphological studies, and were used as examples for xenophobic and racist analyses. This justification for voyeurism in the form of the study of diverse populations of the world was in place at the end of the 19th century, when knowledge of feminine forms was generally restricted to wives and prostitutes.

Woman of Eastern Morocco

c. 1908
J. Geiser, Alger
Postcard, 9 x 14 cm

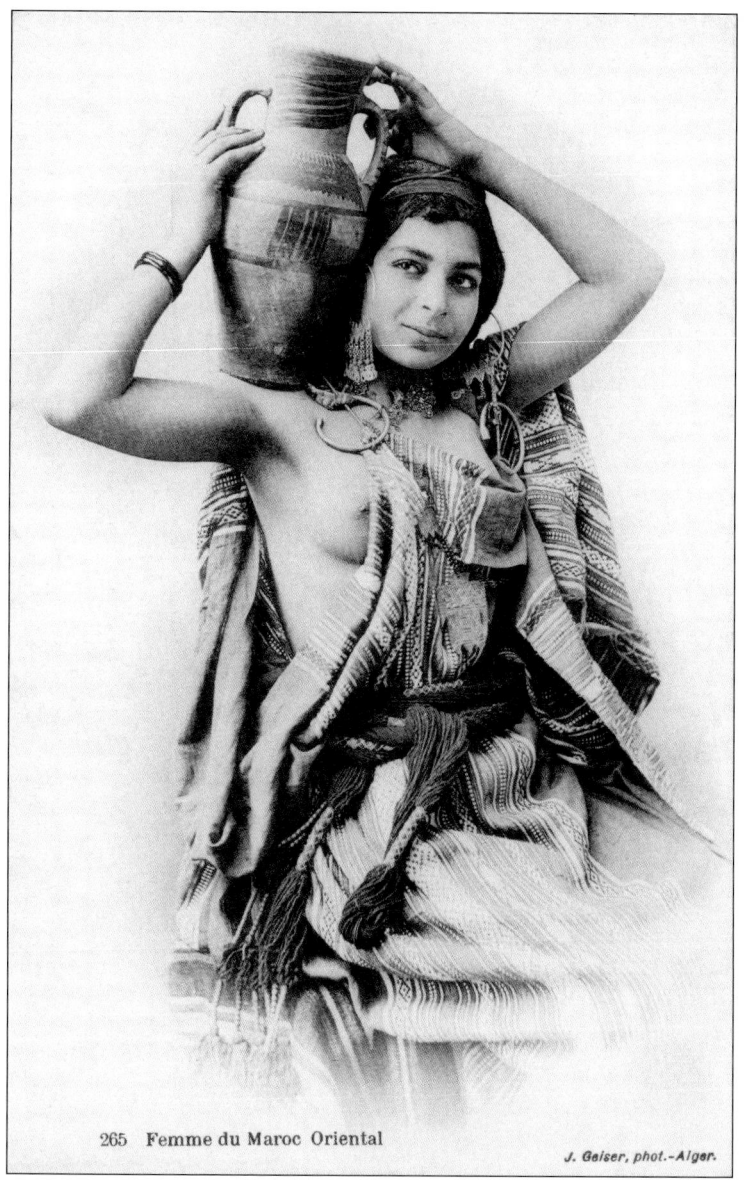

265 Femme du Maroc Oriental

J. Geiser, phot.-Alger.

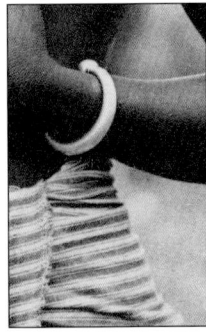

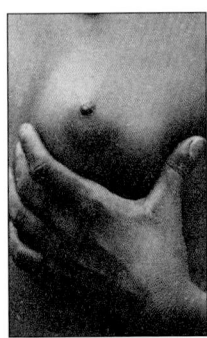

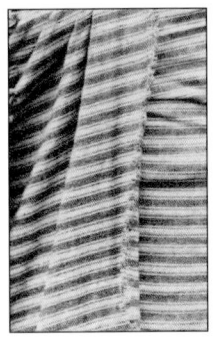

For the first time, new prospects opened up to little educated western woman via the discovery of nude photographs of men and the anatomy of the native women.

Christian morality was offended, more indignant at the presumed dissolute morals of these naked natives than by the shameless distribution of their images. The ethnological network expanded.

Woman of Timbo
_____

c. 1910
Fortier, Dakar
Postcard, 14 x 9 cm

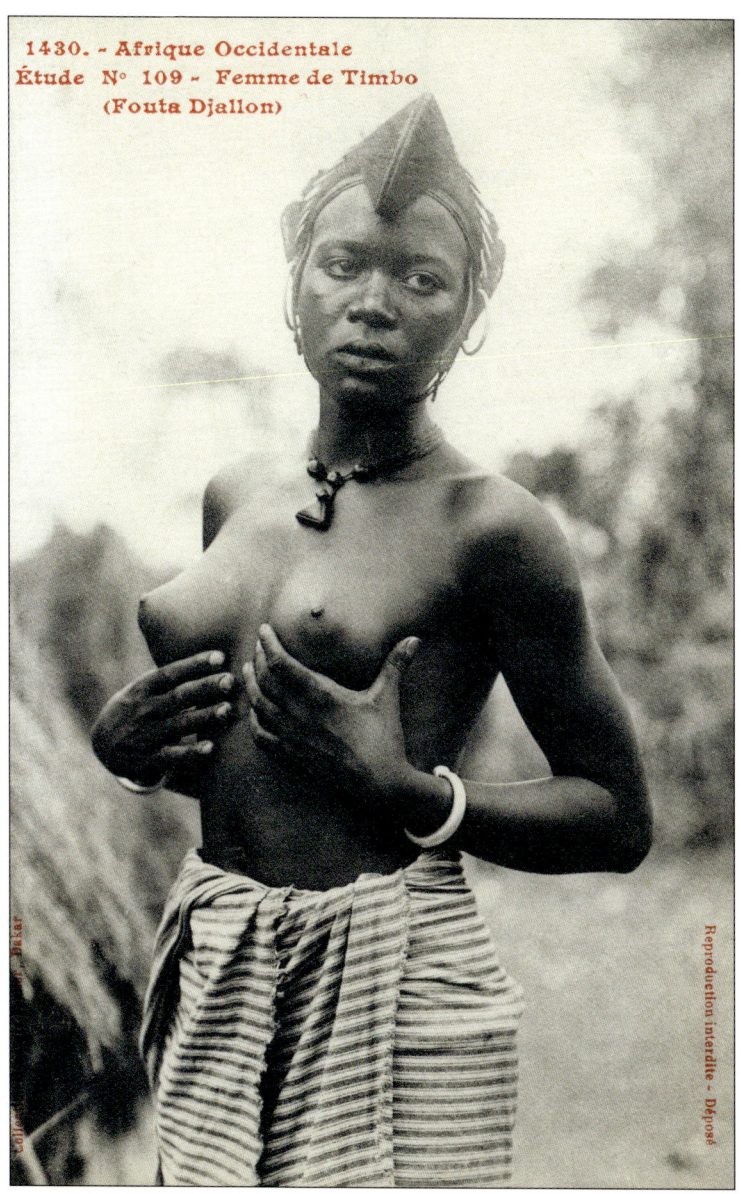

1430. – Afrique Occidentale
Étude Nº 109 – Femme de Timbo
(Fouta Djallon)

Reproduction interdite – Déposé

117

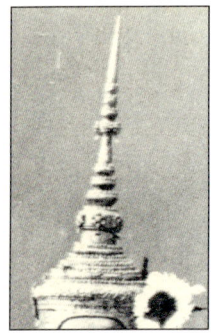

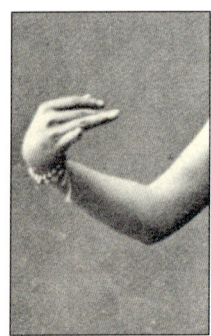

Suggestive scenes of harems were proposed for the delight of the middle classes; veritable production pieces guaranteed to transport people to another world, even if the "tableaux" were sometimes taken in Marseille.

For soldiers and the man in the street, postcards represented an inexpensive fantasy. It was easy to send a postcard to a friend in order to joke about the physique of a young Oriental woman and more vulgar than

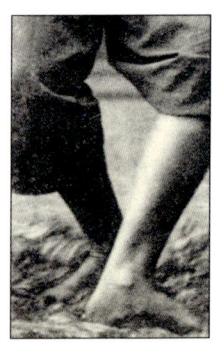

The Most Graceful of Laotian Ballerinas

c. 1910
Raquez A. F. Decoly Editions, Saigon
Postcard, 9 x 14 cm

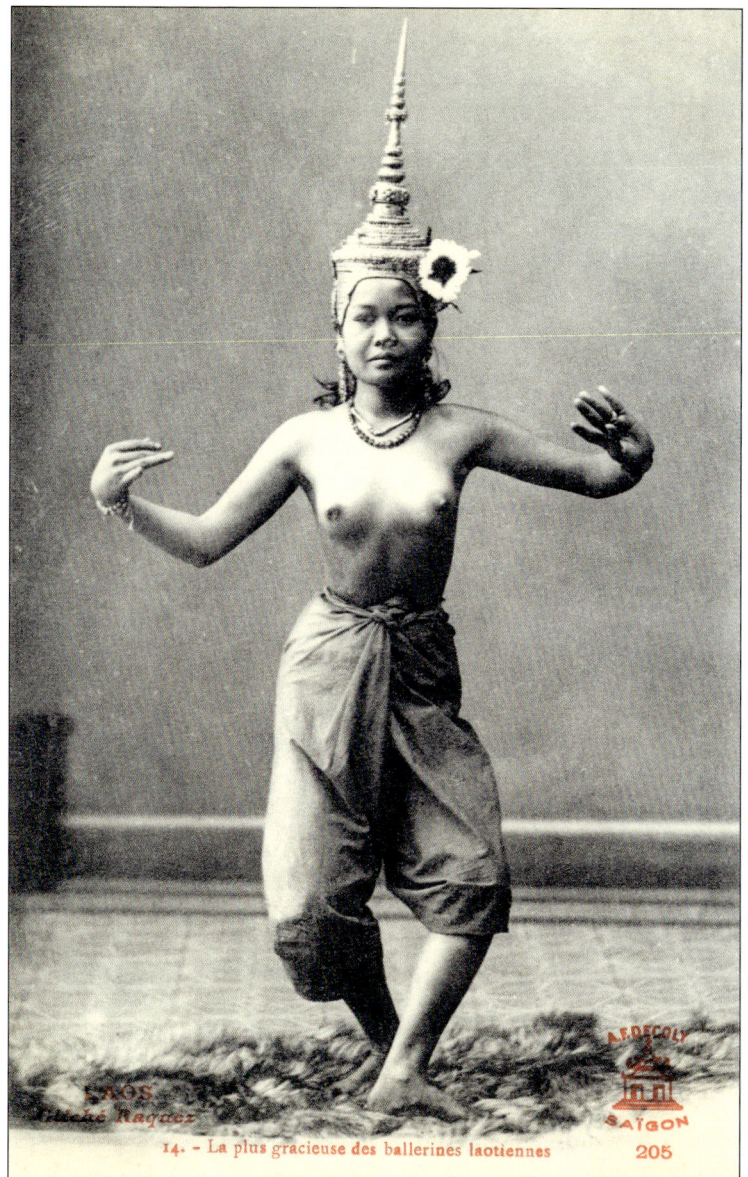

LAOS
Cliché Raquez

14. - La plus gracieuse des ballerines laotiennes

205

119

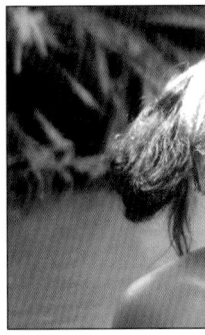

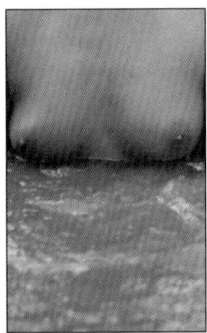

talking about one's fiancée, but so much more accessible as the body could be discovered for only a few centimes. The photographer-colonist cheated and deceived his clientele. The young girl who obligingly posed naked, or dressed in rags to appeal to the fetishist, was not the sort of girl that one would meet in the streets of Algiers, but a prostitute, a hireling, playing the part of an honest woman in a composition role.

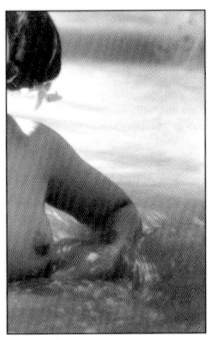

Young Asiatic Girls by the River

c. 1920
Anonymous
Gelatin silver print on postcard-sized print, 9 x 14 cm

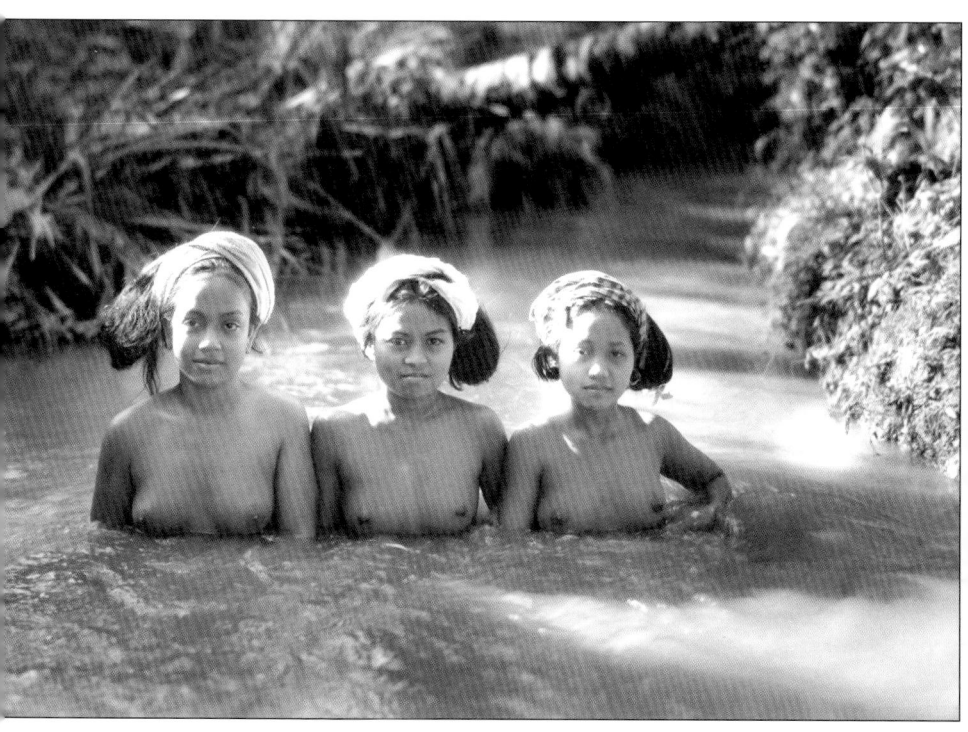

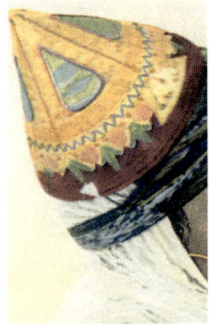

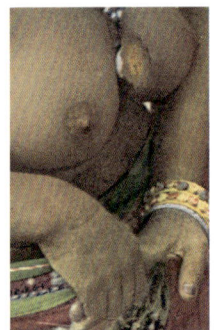

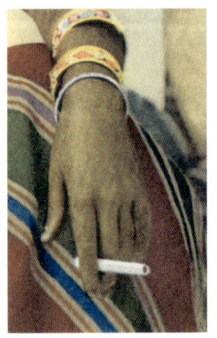

Women from Maghreb did not strip, especially in front of strangers. Those that agreed to do so were mercenary accomplices, bought by the eye behind the lens for the pleasure of voyeurs deceived as to the reality of the images.

Elsewhere, German aristocrats looking for the exotic and in a false concern for authenticity, wanted people to believe that Arcadia did exist.

Women of the South in their Interior, N° 8112

c. 1920
Anonymous
Photo A.D.I.A., 16.5 x 23 cm

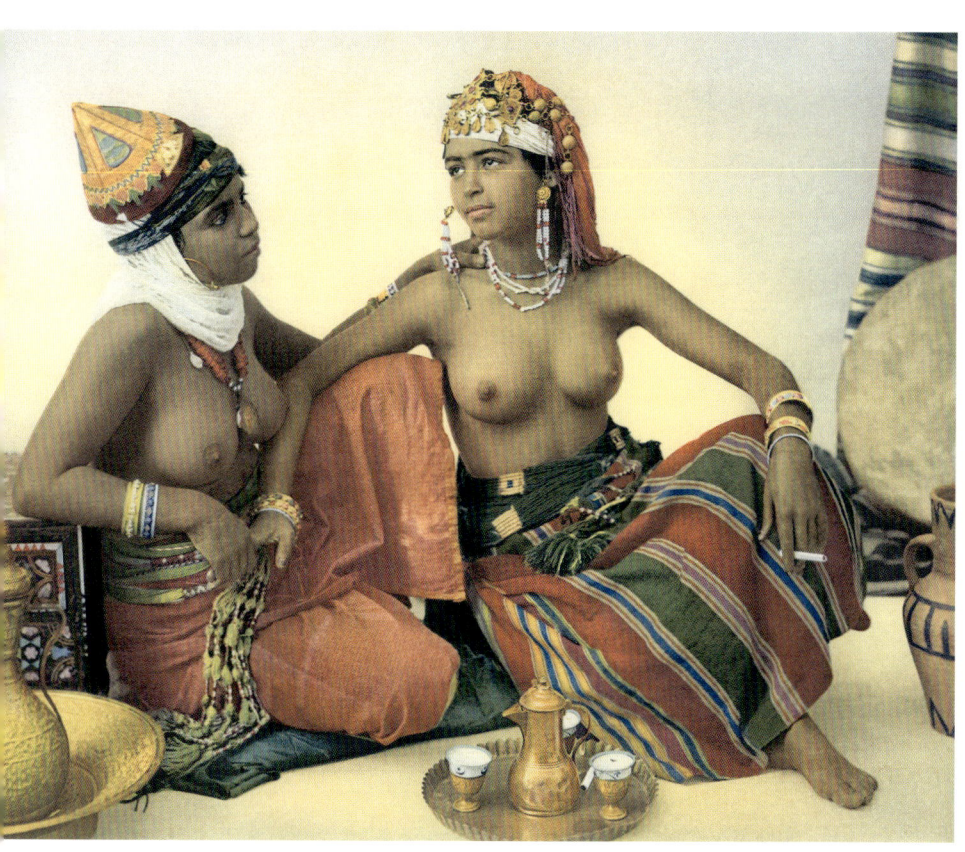

123

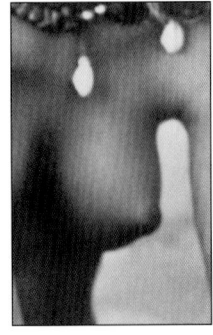

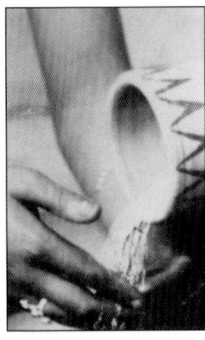

However, they, too, were obsessed by the attraction of the body, and took little care in their choice of accessories that comprised the decor. Such was the case with Wilhelm Plüschow (1852-1930) a descendant of an illegitimate branch of the Grand Duke Frédéric-François I of Mecklembourg-Schwerin. He was a wine merchant in Rome, who then settled in Naples where he took up photography and changed his name from Wilhelm to Guglielmo.

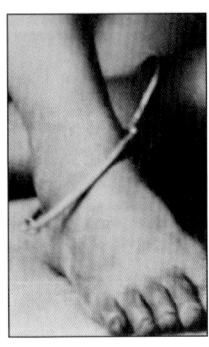

Study N° 1151

c. 1920
Anonymous, Photo-Albert, Alger
Postcard, 14 x 9 cm

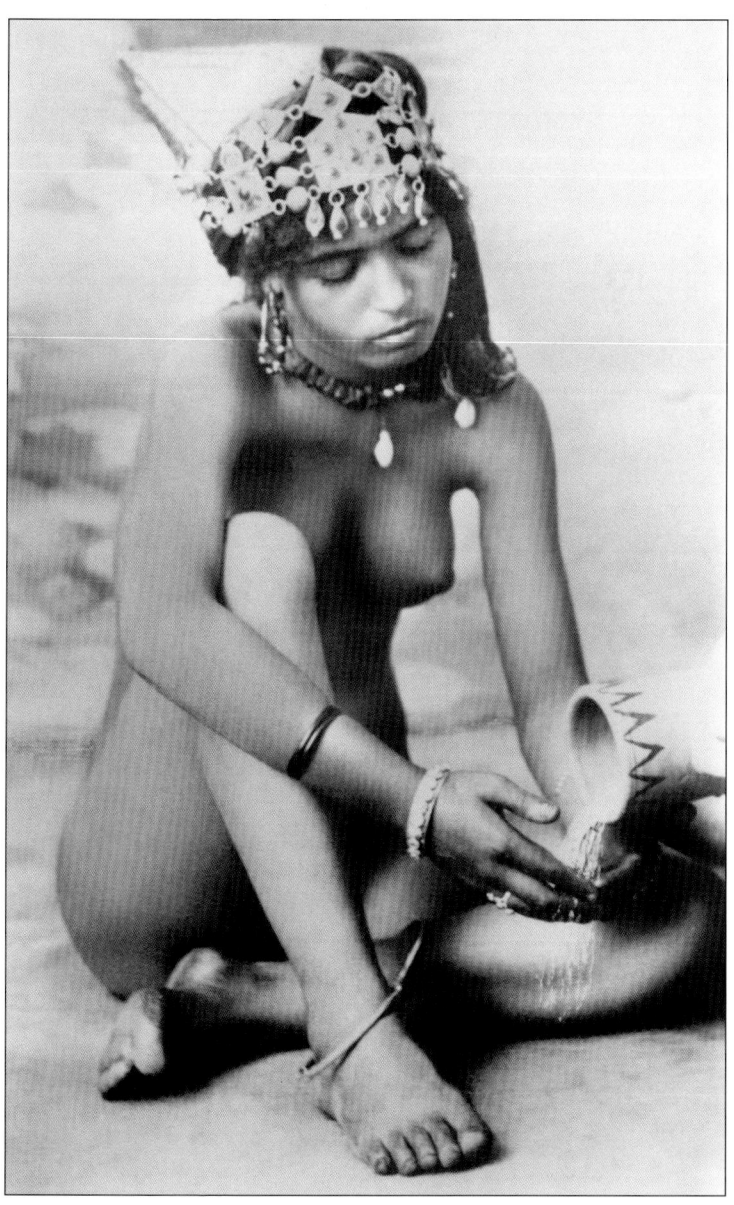

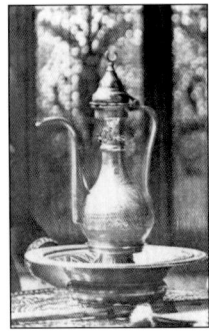

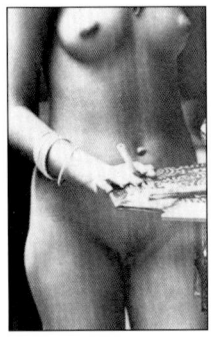

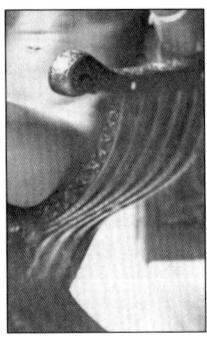

He initiated his cousin Wilhelm Von Gloeden (1856-1931) to the art of photography between 1876 and 1878. Baron von Gloeden took some seven thousand pictures, mostly of naked adolescents. In 1897, Plüschow went on a long trip to Tunisia, Egypt and Greece, during which he took several photographs. In 1902, the Italian authorities started proceedings against him for the procuring and corruption of minors.

N° 1512

c. 1920
Anonymous, Combier Editions, Mâcon
Postcard, 14 x 9 cm

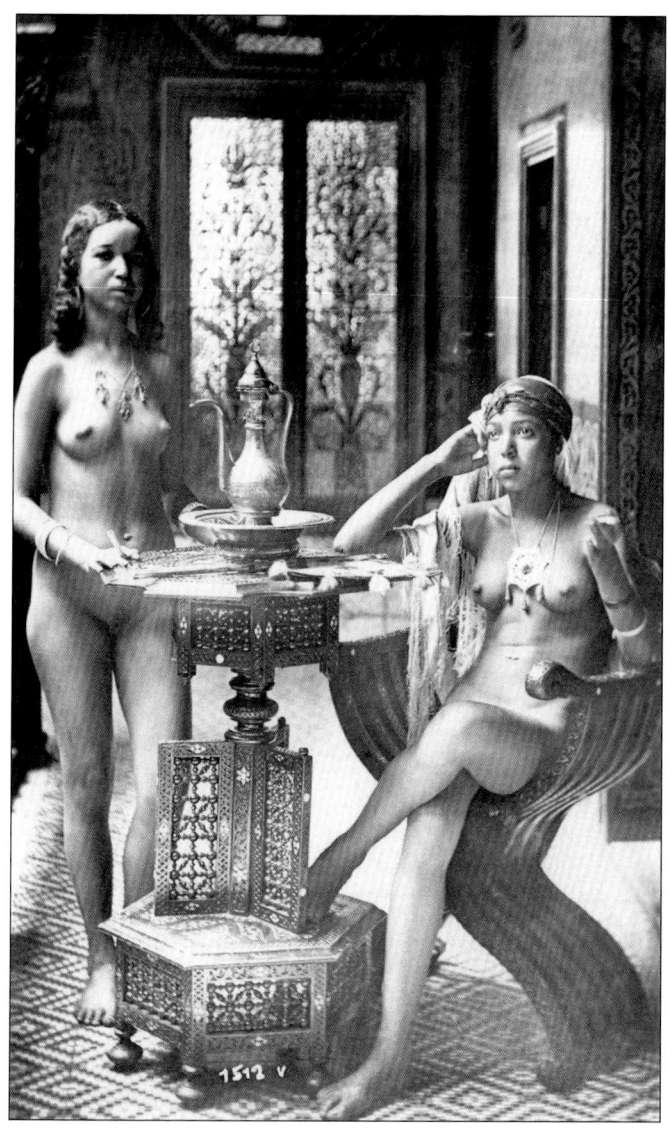

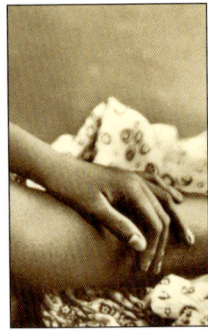

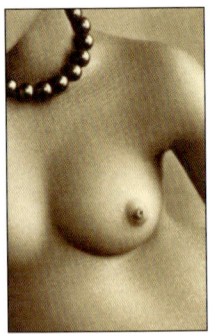

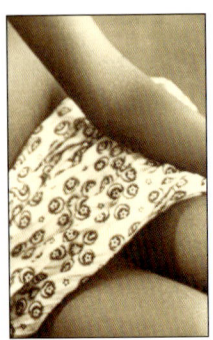

He returned to Berlin in 1910, where he died in 1930. The male nudes of Von Gloeden and Plüschow have been the subjects of numerous publications. The female nudes published here bear the stamp of a third accomplice, Vincenzo Galdi, who worked in Rome with Plüschow. Their pictures were sold together, making attribution somewhat difficult.

Untitled

c. 1920
Anonymous
Postcard of Italian origin, 9 x 14 cm

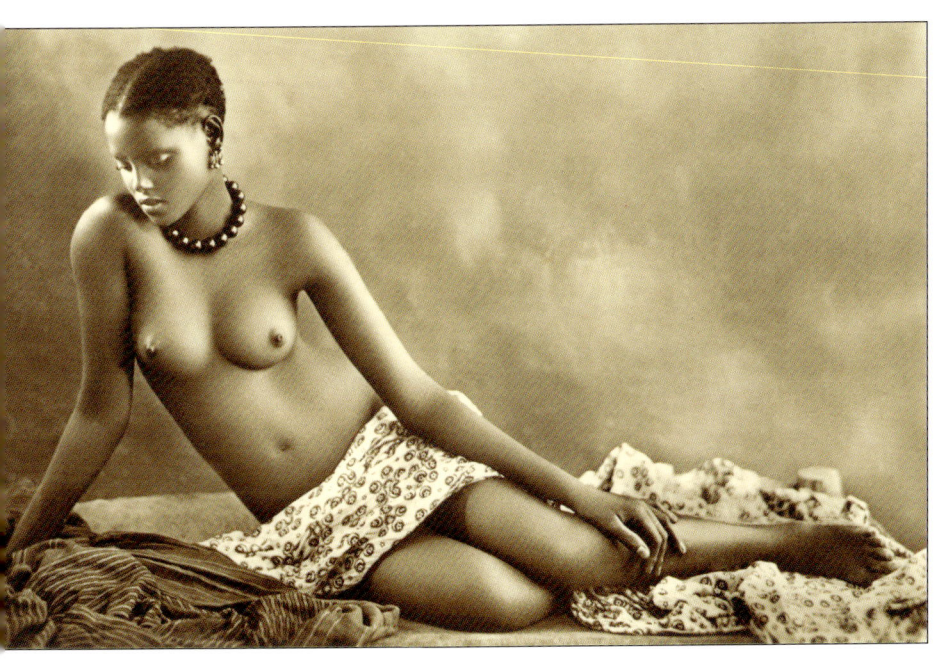

129

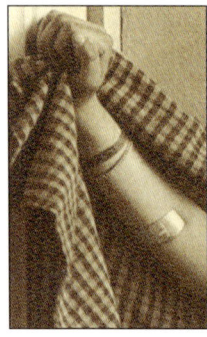

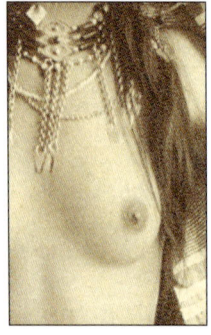

In 1949, Roger Peyrefitte, in *Les Amours Singuliers,* which is a sort of romanticised biography of Von Gloeden, states that Von Gloeden and Plüschow came to an agreement. The male nudes would be attributed to Von Gloeden and the female nudes to Plüschow. However, recent studies have highlighted the inaccuracy of this statement.

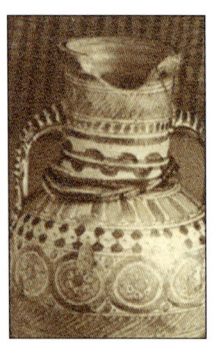

N° 3117

———

c. 1925
Lehnert & Landrock
Heliograve, 23 x 16.5 cm

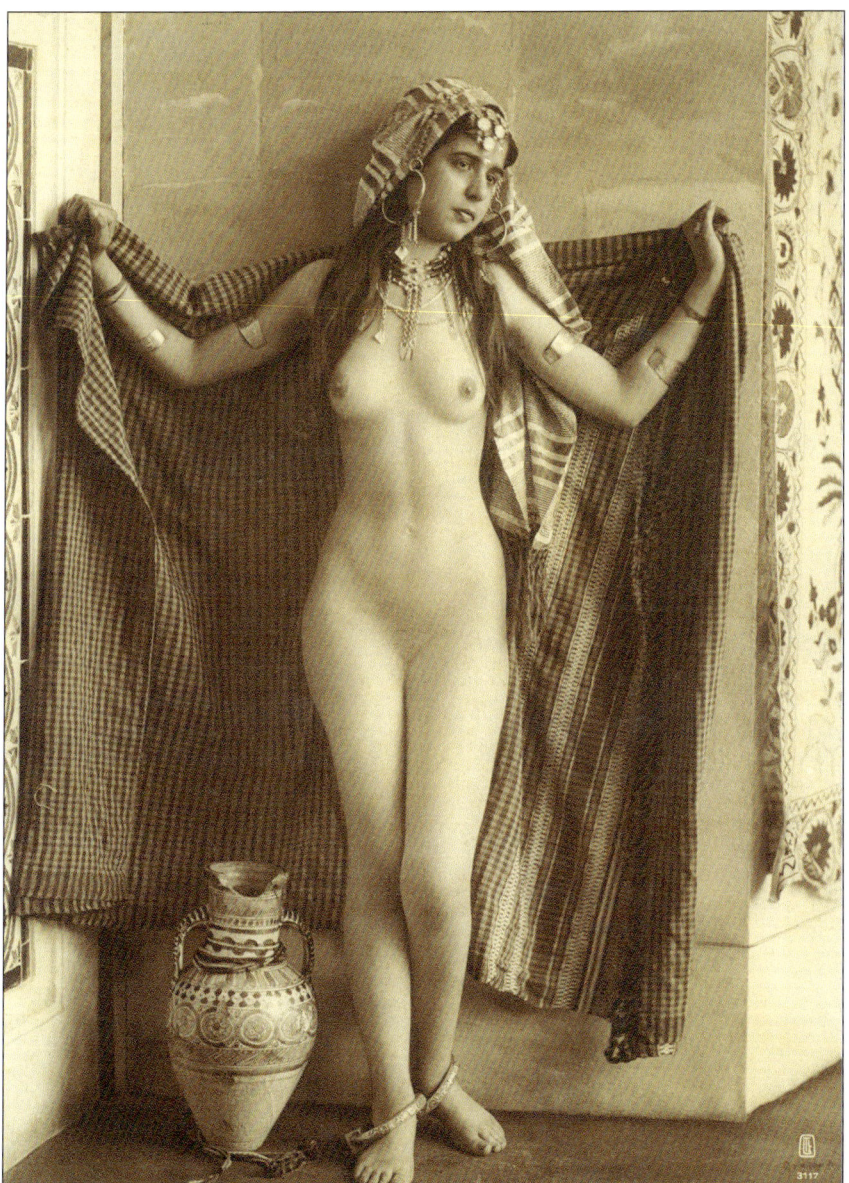

131

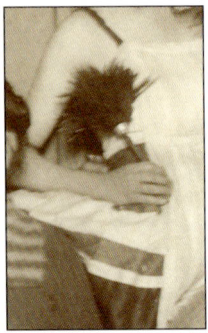

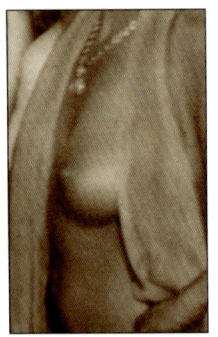

Habituation and Development

Among the different factors which marked the turn of the century, infatuation with the postcard was one of the more notable. At this time it was used in a way which is completely different from that of today, where it is only used while on a holiday.

At the beginning of the 20th century, the postcard was used for several different purposes. It was inexpensive and arrived quickly. It was the forerunner of the telephone and the televised news.

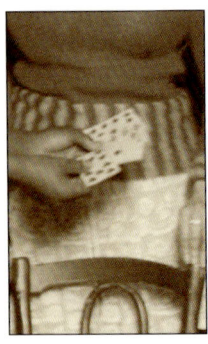

Through the Wings, Paris on Stage, N° 1011

c. 1920
Anonymous
Printed-back postcard, 14 x 9 cm

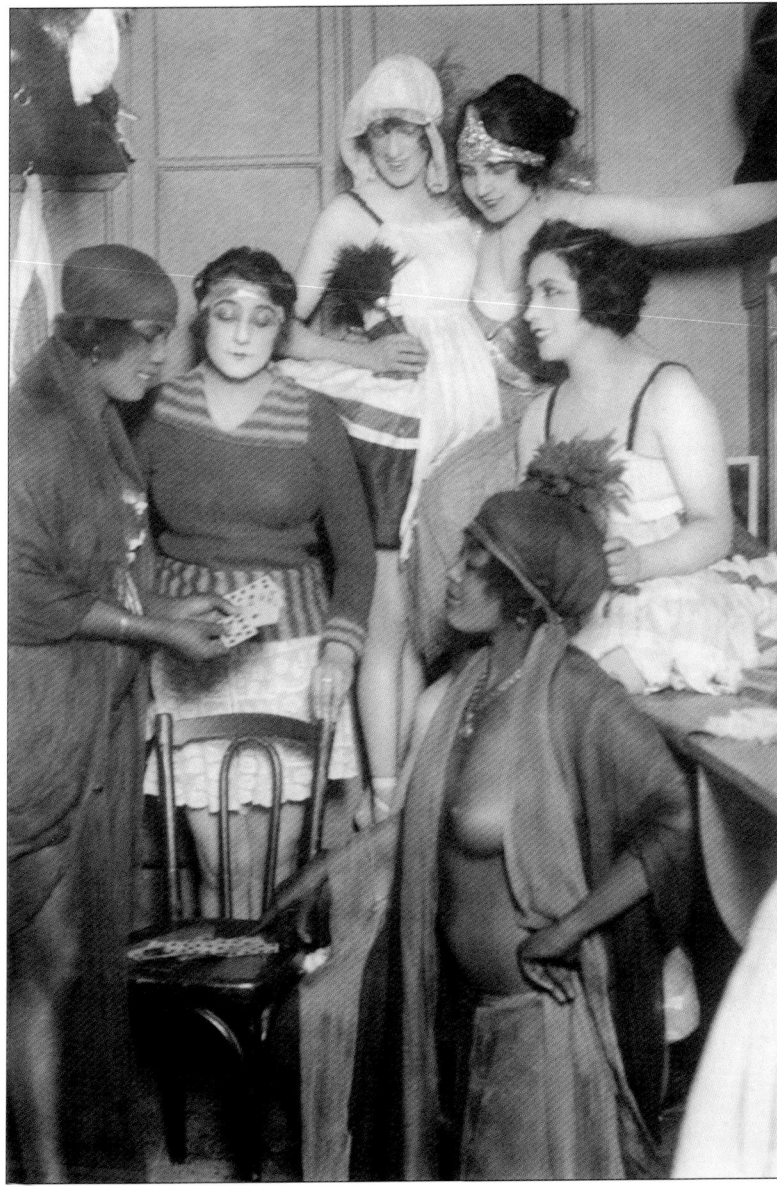

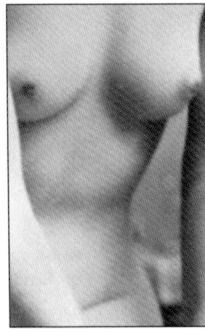

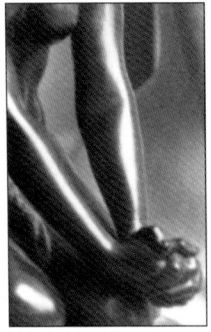

As soon as something happened anywhere in France - a catastrophe, social unrest, a discovery or an invention - postcards would be published and sent to the four corners of France. Postcards were also used to announce the arrival of longer correspondence, and it is not rare to see just a few words such as "I'll write tomorrow" on the back of postcards of this period. In short, they had a number of different uses which is difficult to imagine nowadays and millions were sold every year.

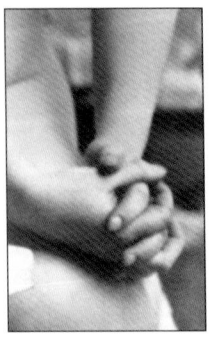

N° 4781
_____

c. 1920
V. d.S. A.-K. Editions, 173
Printed-back postcard, 14 x 9 cm

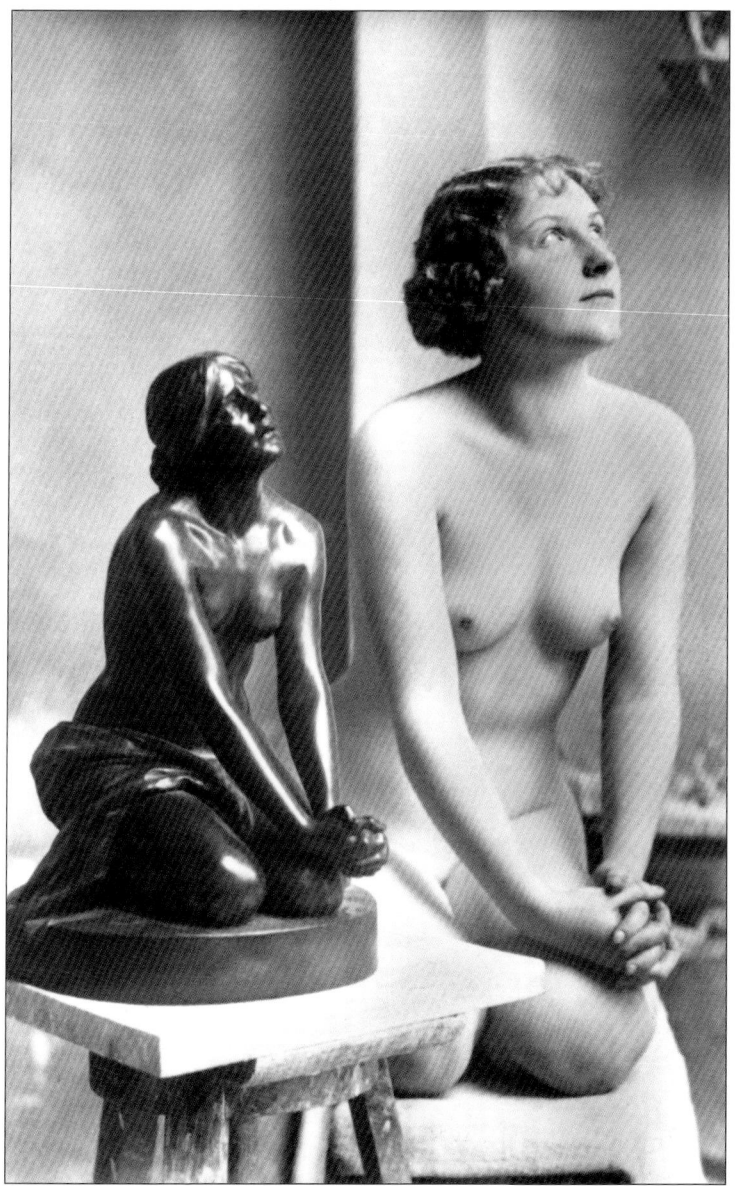

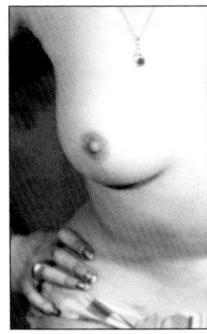

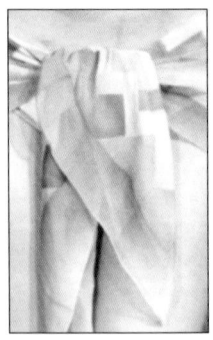

Although they existed from the end of the 19th century, the real explosion in the use of the postcard dates from 1904, the year in which the Postal Union between the most important countries was signed.

Photographic paper, which necessitated a great deal of care in the printing process, became popular in the shape of pictures the size of postcards. There were most often printed in collotype, a new procedure which allowed for screen printing without recourse to wood engraving.

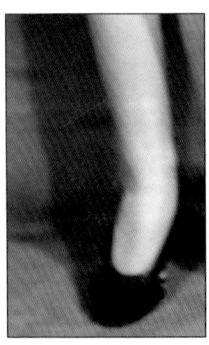

Untitled

c. 1925
Arès Editions
Gelatin silver print, 18 x 13 cm

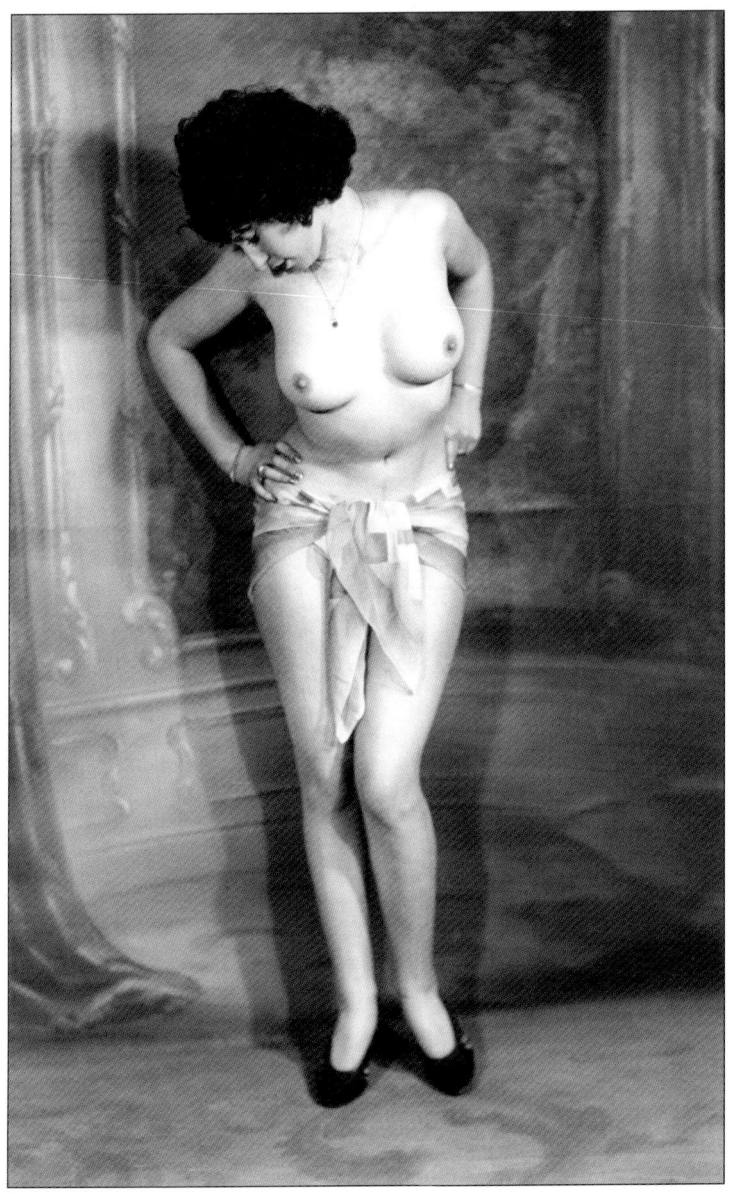

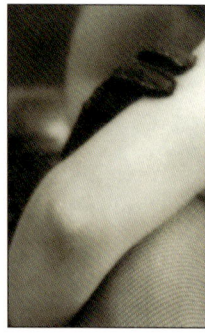

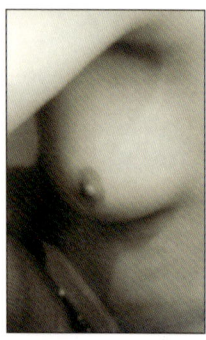

Following the discreet, cottage industry production of the 19th century, erotic images blossomed into an industrial production, printed in large numbers at the beginning of the 20th century.

As demand increased, photographers began to offer their work for sale through the medium of the written press in station kiosks at the very heart of the burgeoning industrial civilisation, to the great displeasure of the censors. In 1902, M. Emile Bayard founded *Le Nu esthétique* with the support of painters

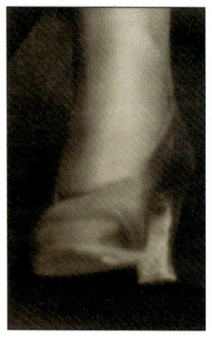

Untitled

c. 1925
Waléry
Gelatin silver print, 18 x 13 cm

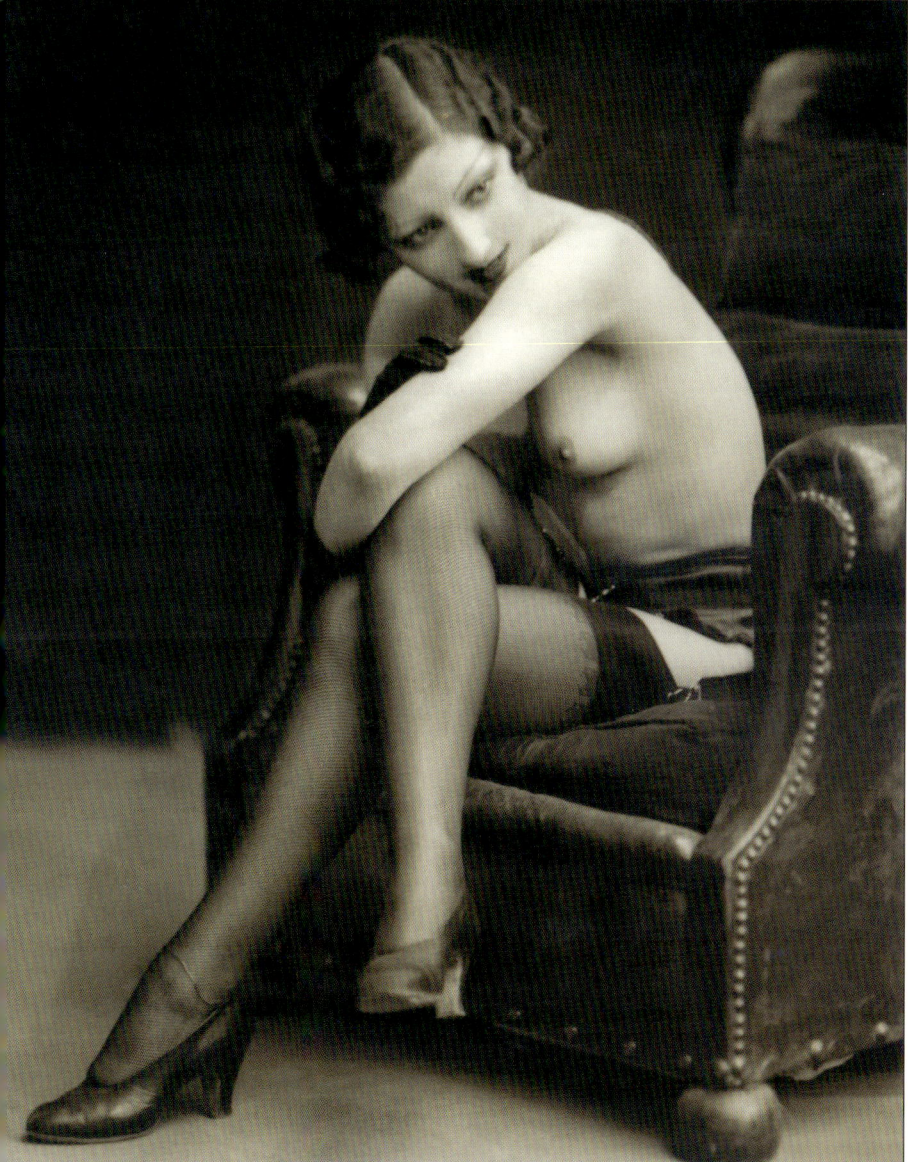

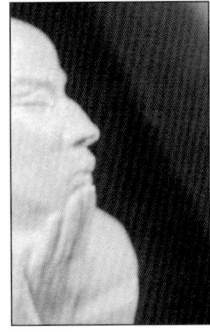

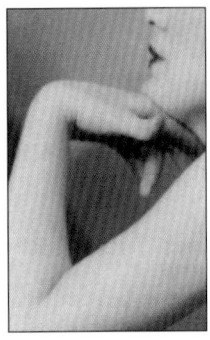

such as William Bougereau and Jean-Léon Gérôme. Gérôme referred to mythology in his preface: "It is impossible to imagine Venus with clothes on, any more than Hercules or Mercury", whilst confirming the importance of the contribution of photography to art at the same time.

"Photography has made remarkable progress in recent times, and has obliged Artists to divest themselves of the old routine and forget the old formulas. It has opened our eyes and forced us to see what we

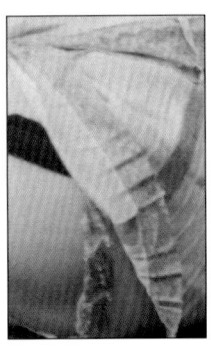

Untitled
———

c. 1925
Arès Editions
Gelatin silver print, 18 x 13 cm

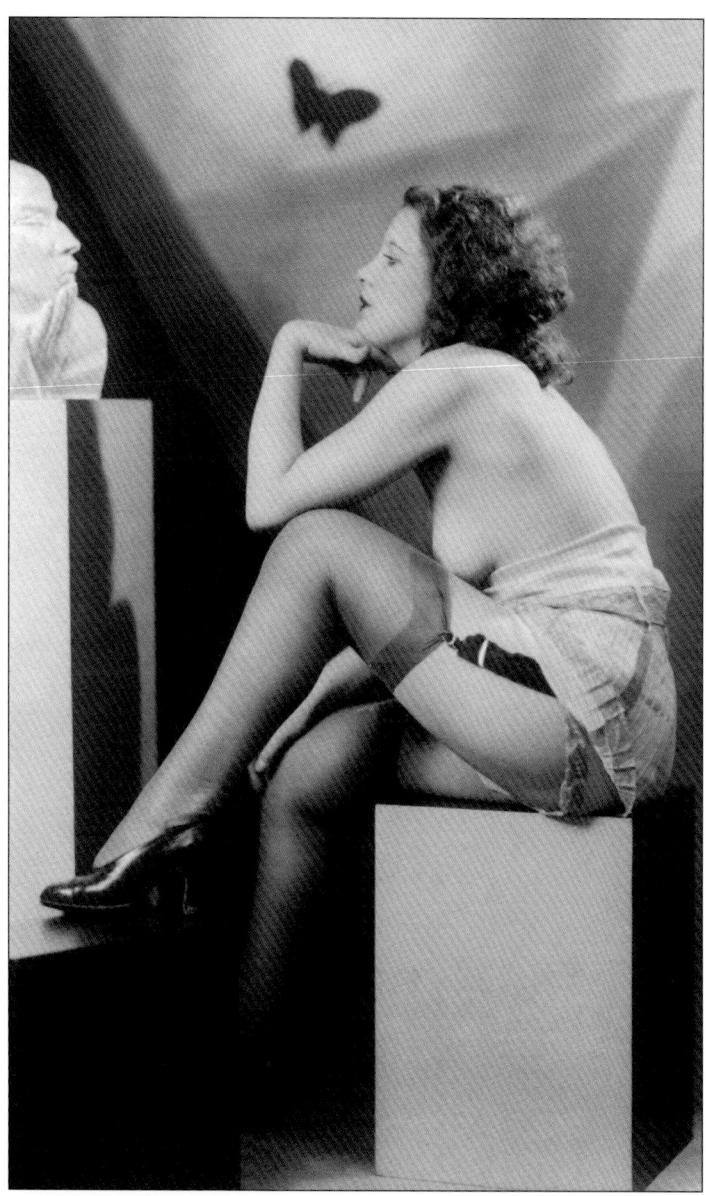

141

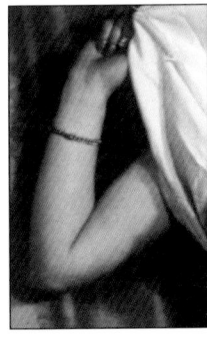

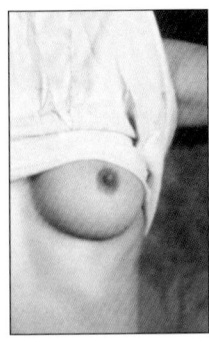

had never seen before, which constitutes a considerable and invaluable service to Art. Thanks to photography, the truth has finally come to light."

Pompous statements maybe, but hardly surprising coming from one of the leading Pompeïstic painters. Two years later, Amédée Vignola, an unknown artist, entered into competition with Bayard. He founded the journal *Etude Académique* – technical

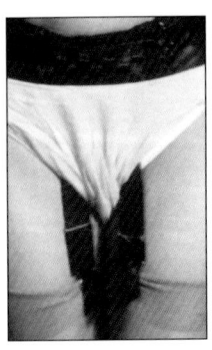

Untitled
———

c. 1925
Arès Editions
Gelatin silver print, 18 x 13 cm

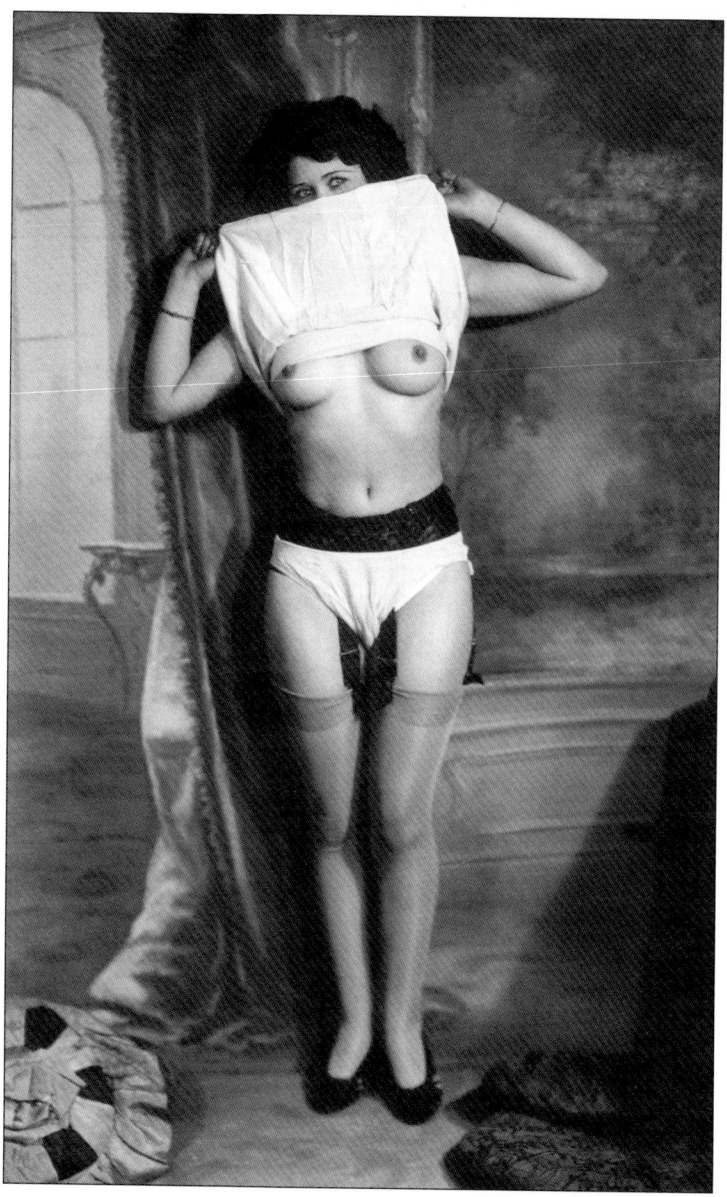

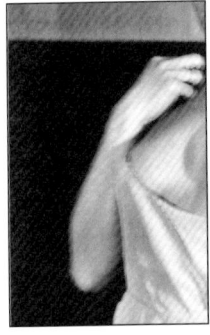

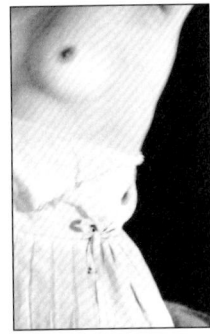

documentation strictly reserved for the use of painters, sculptors, and workers in the field of art. The alibi remained the same. Tens of fortnightly or monthly journals, and similar almanacs appeared at this time. Publishers also worked hard, stretching their imaginations to come up with catchy titles. Thus we find such titles as *Open Air Academy*, the *Beauty of the Woman*, the *Young Girl*, as well as anecdotal nude, Christian, taken from the fable or the Bible,

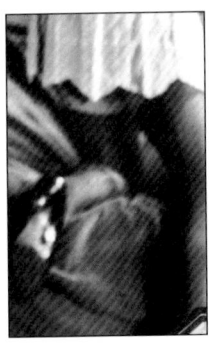

Untitled

c. 1925
Arès Editions
Gelatin silver print, 18 x 13 cm

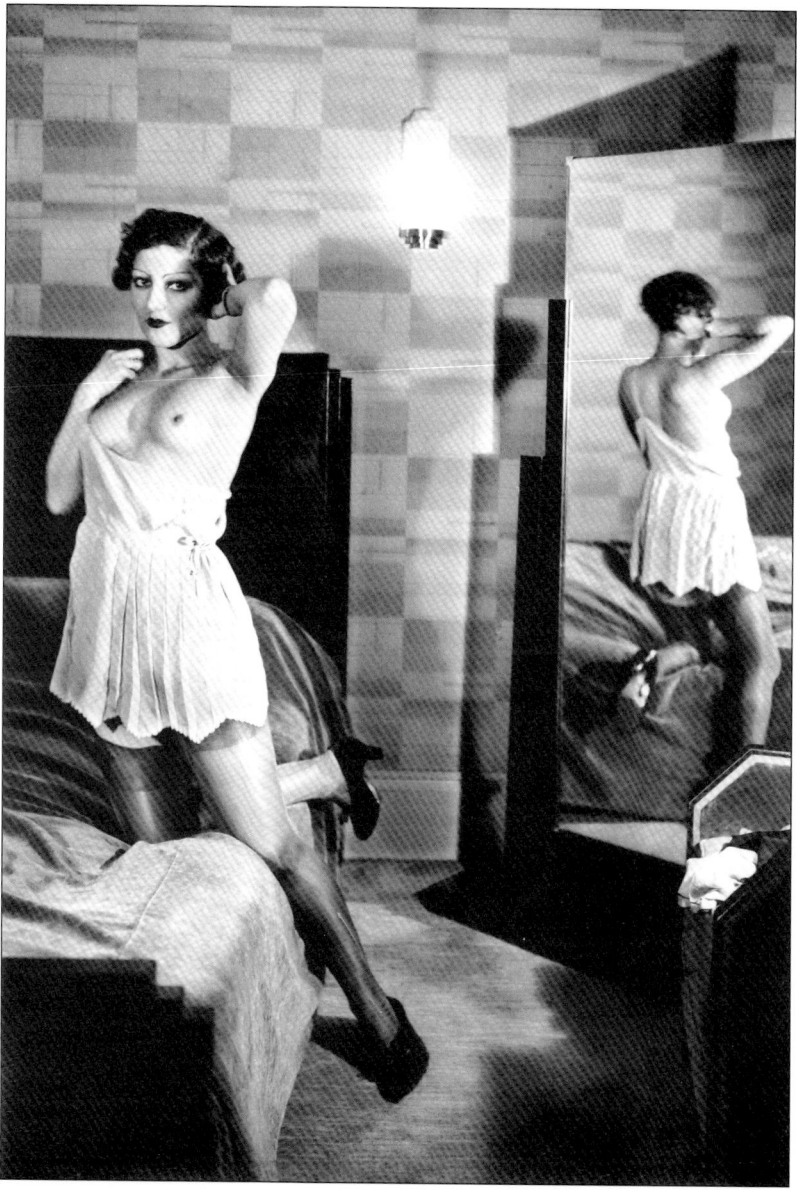

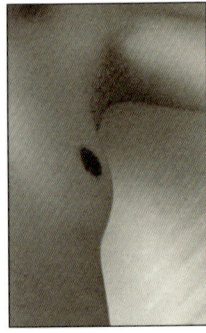

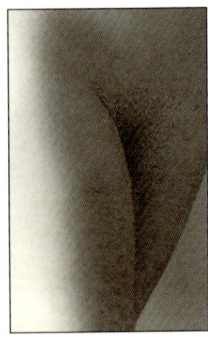

legendary, literary, pagan, profane, sacred or symbolic titles. Each volume is no more than a series of pretexts and camouflage that become less and less convincing, to exhibit the female body in a multitude of decors far from any requirement of art. In 1908, conscientious censors managed to prohibit the sale of journals from station kiosks, where it would be likely to find only a small proportion of "workers in the field of art". However, they were unable to put a stop to the surge in erotic images.

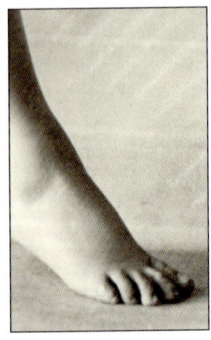

Untitled

c. 1925
François Bertin
Gelatin silver print, 23.5 x 17.5 cm

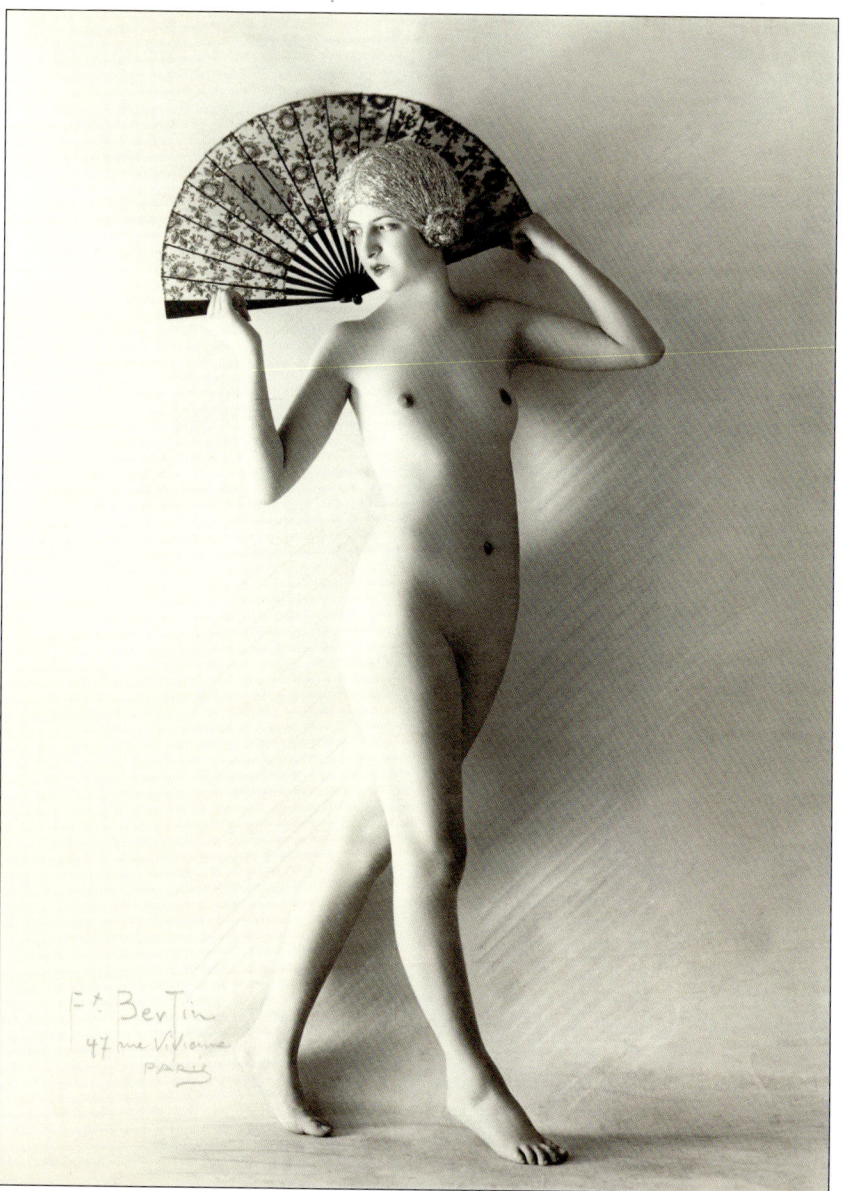

147

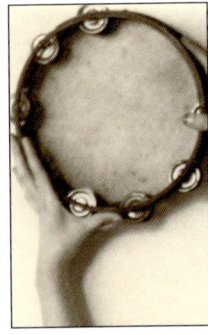

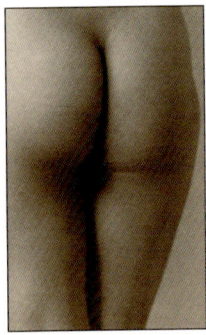

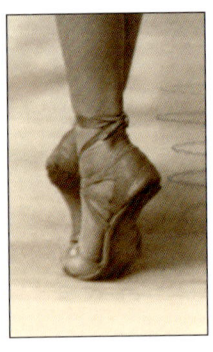

Manufacturers became involved. The stereoscope manufacturer Jules Richard put stereoscopic images onto the market.

Among these, his biographer Jacques Perrin made an inventory of 7500 erotic pictures of which 6350 were taken by Richard himself. His models came from different walks of life; professional and casual models, music hall dancers, especially from Le Tabarin where Jules Richard was a regular, and sometimes his own workers who were noted for their grace by the boss.

Untitled
———

c. 1925
François Bertin
Gelatin silver print, 23.5 x 17.5 cm

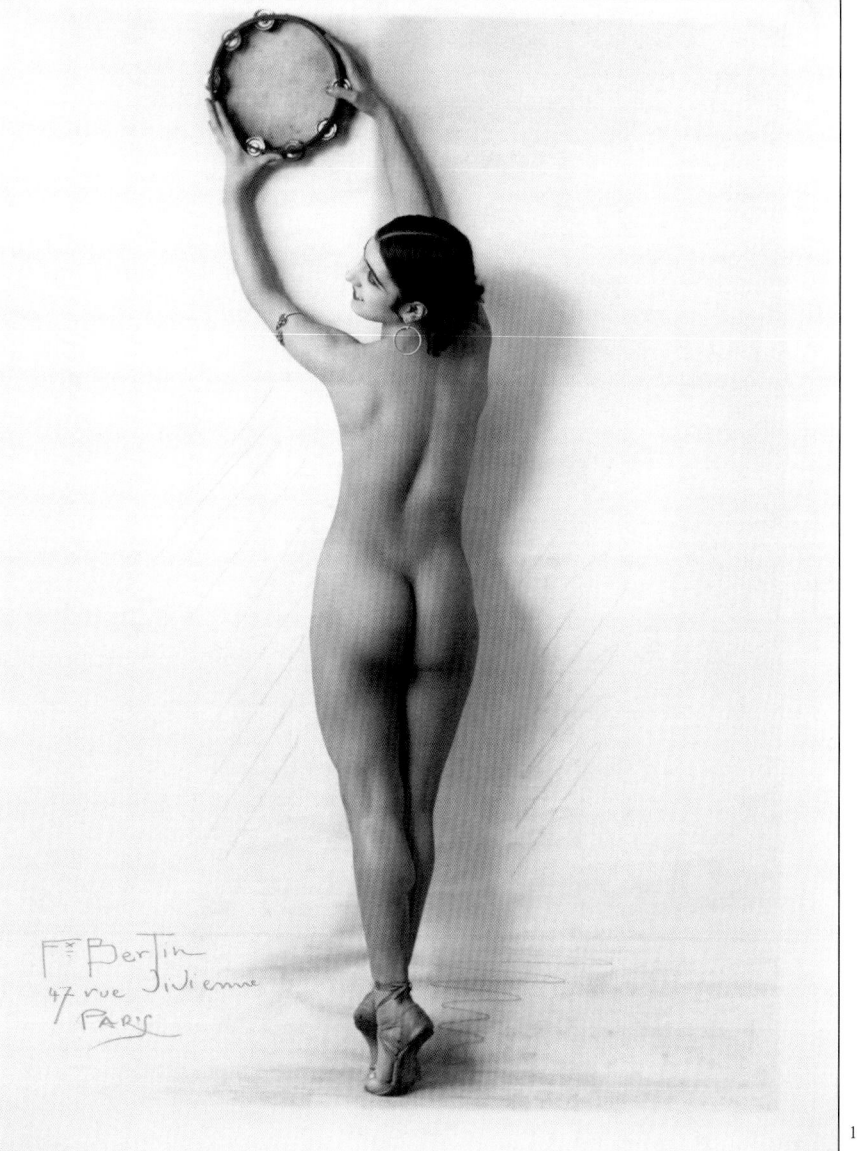

F:Berlin
47 rue Vivienne
PARIS

149

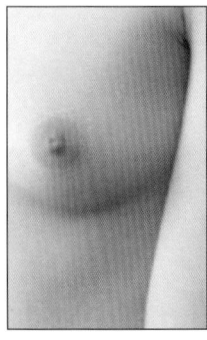

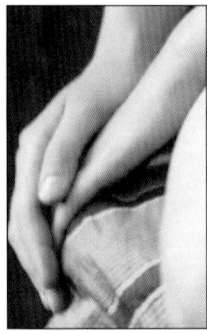

All the images were carefully listed. Among them we can find the names of Marthe, Renée, Hélène and Valentine who came from La Cigale, Le Moulin Rouge and Les Folies Bergères. The real spread of nude photography came during the course of the First World War. With the tacit approval of the authorities, wartime "pen-friends" sent millions of postcards to their dear, young soldiers, bringing to the sordid trenches the comforting image of a free and desirable woman – a relief which killed forever the academic alibi.

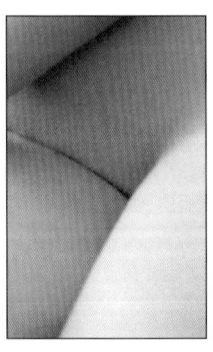

N° C 150

———————

c. 1925
Corona Editions (?)
Gelatin silver print, 24 x 18 cm

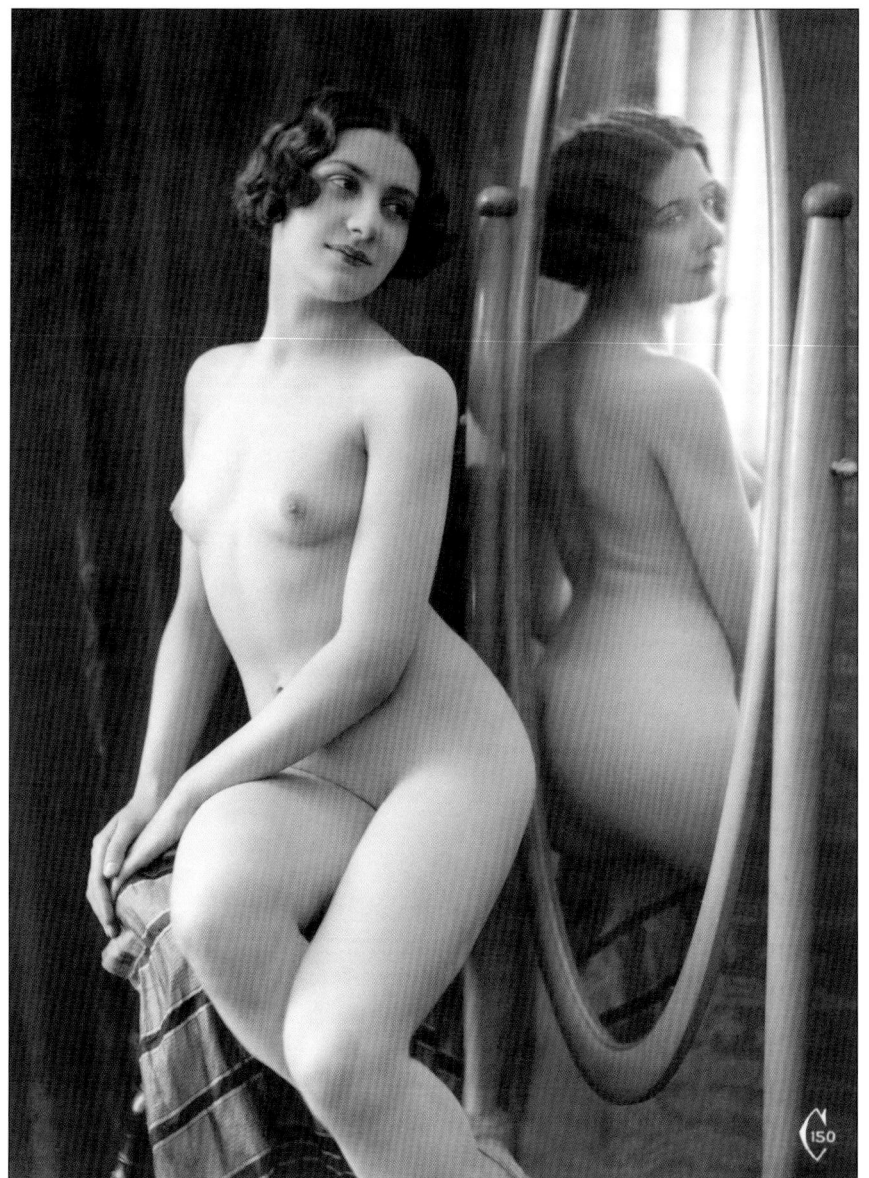

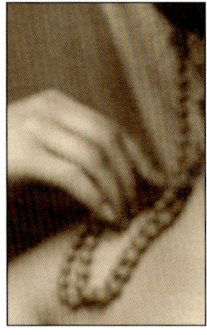

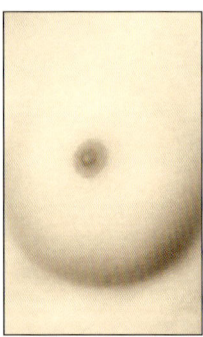

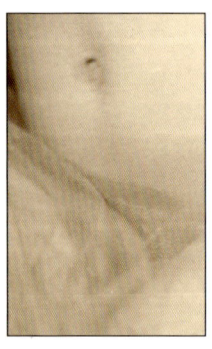

Once again, Paris acted as a beacon for erotic images. This "free and desirable" woman could only be Parisian, at a time when France was at the centre of a conflict involving protagonists from many different nations and origins. Photography even entered the brothels, allowing for the making of catalogues, including the rates and specialities of the girls. When these young ladies were busy, the client could serenely make his choice whilst waiting.

N° 61

———

c. 1925
P. C.
Gelatin silver print, 24 x 18 cm

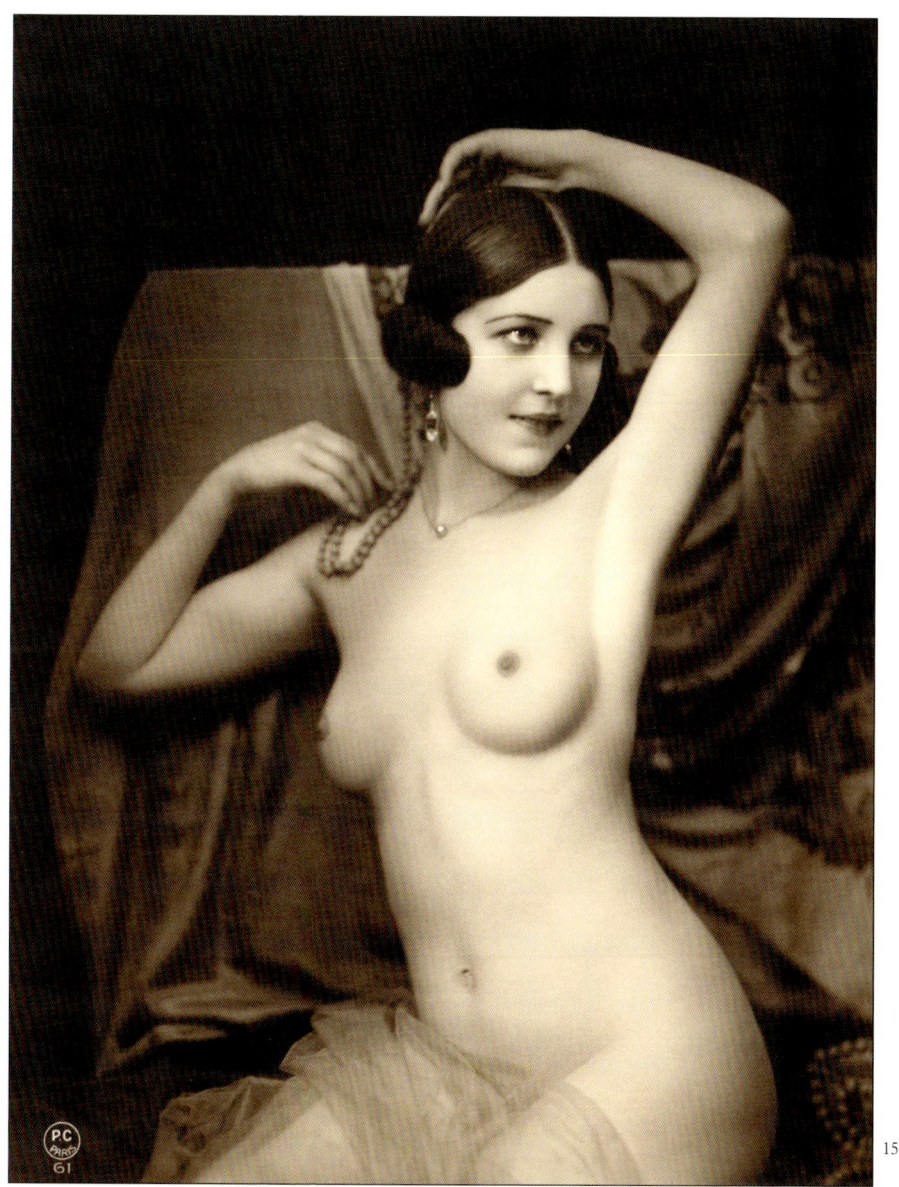

153

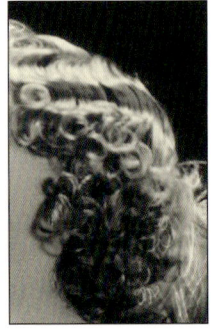

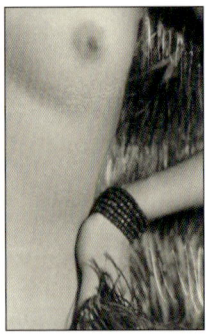

The Euphoric Ecstasy of the Crazy Years

After making parodies in the army theatres of the femininity of the café concert actresses who were far from the front lines, the returned soldiers were able at last to find once more the idealised woman that they had dreamed about in the trenches. Meanwhile, stage artists would get round the question of nudity by being smothered in thick body stockings.

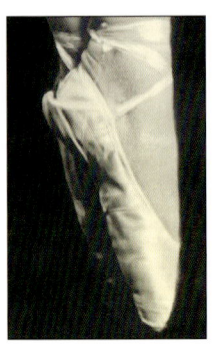

Untitled
———

c. 1925
Anonymous
Gelatin silver print, 24 x 18 cm

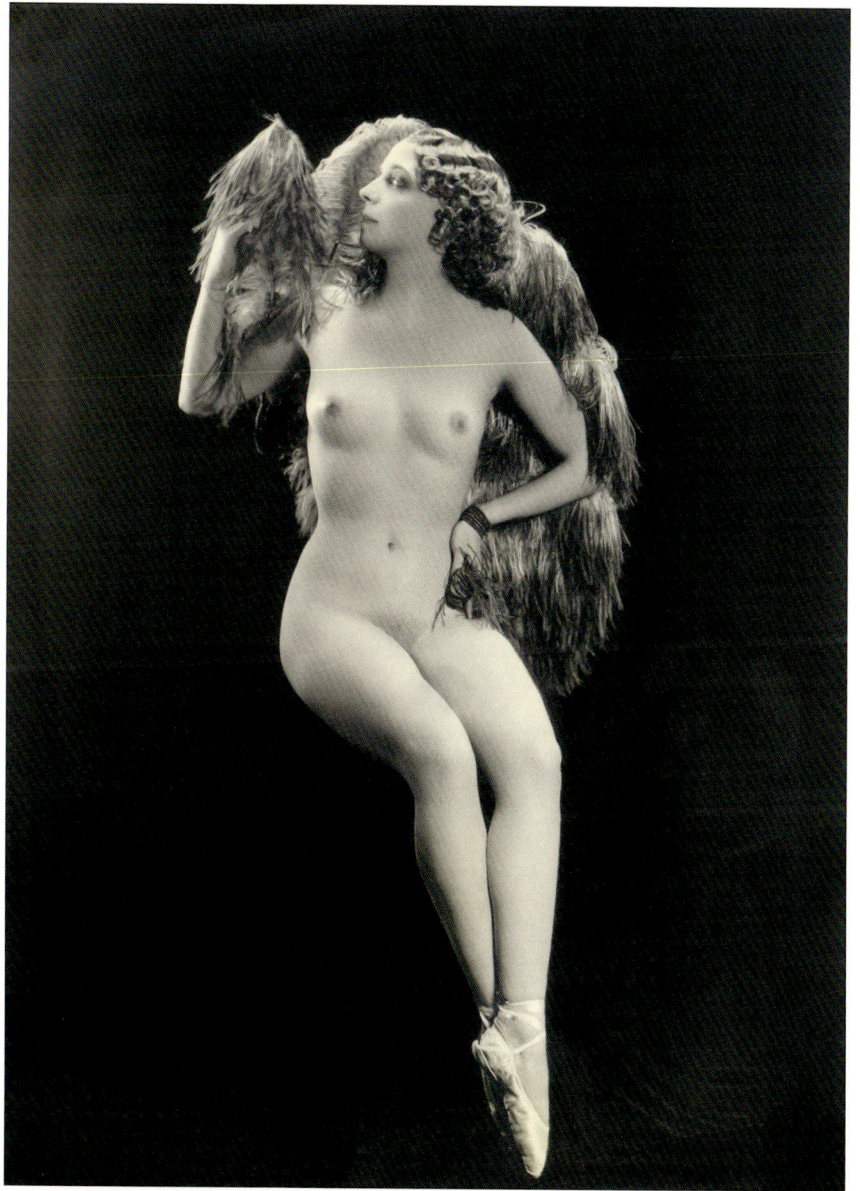

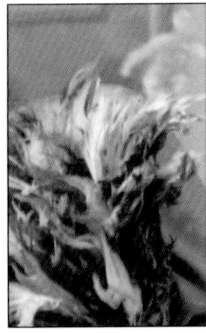

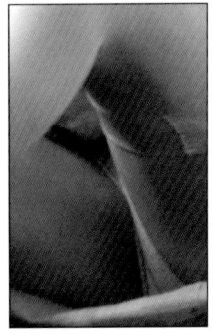

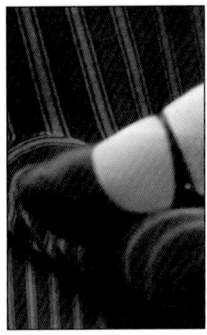

Some would reveal themselves timidly, showing that the progressive conquest of nudity also took place in the theatre and more particularly in the music-hall; at first in 1910 in an operetta at the Concert Mayol, and then two years later at Les Folies Bergère, where a woman portraying Eve sitting imposingly on a flower-decked float entered the stage, personifying Love.

Taking advantage of the euphoric ecstasy that reigned at the end of hostilities, the Casino de Paris decided that all of its

N° C 83
————

c. 1925
Corona Editions (?)
Gelatin silver print, 24 x 18 cm

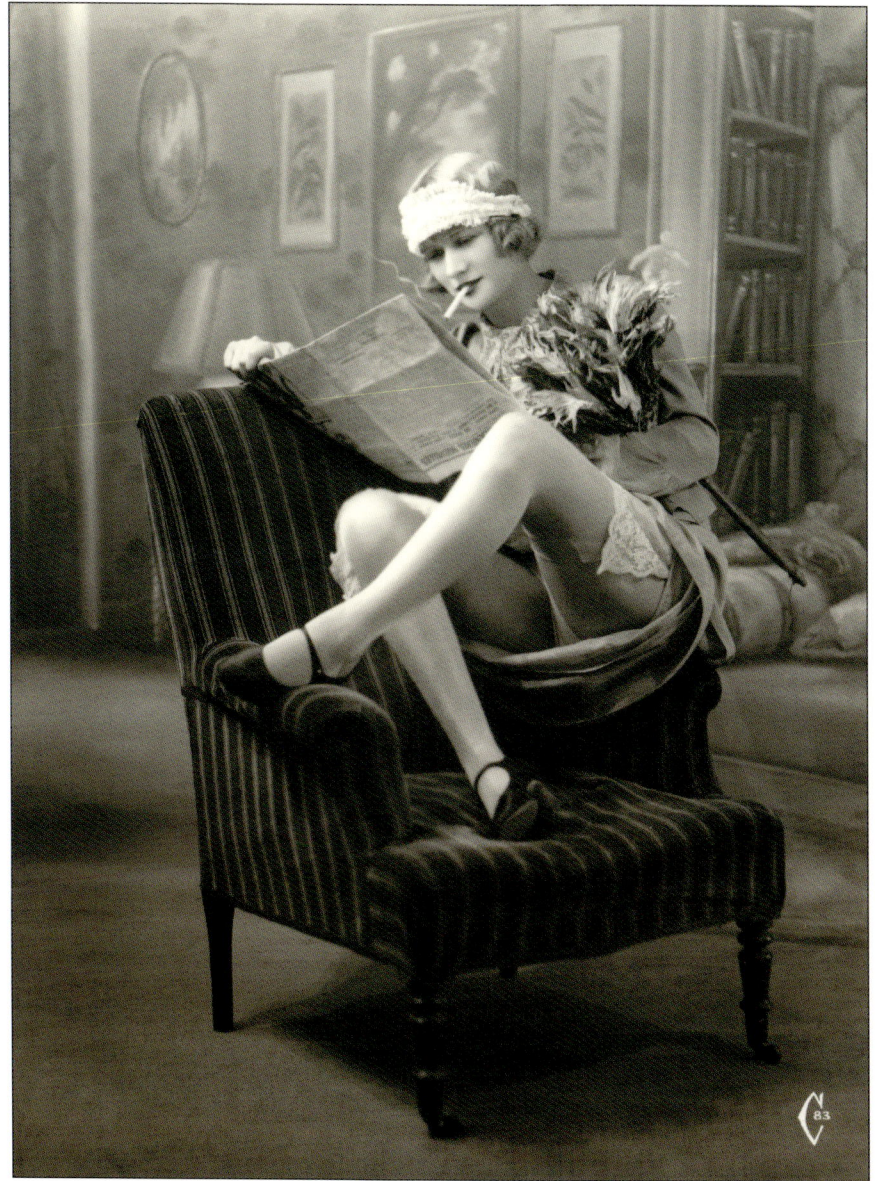

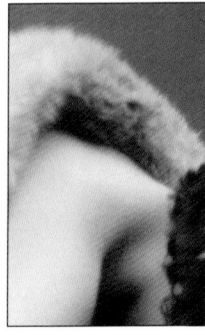

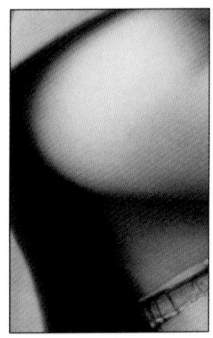

dancers would appear nude for its show *Paris Dances*. People were fascinated by naked women whose images were easily affordable, and the prudish denouncers of vice were scandalised. However, the movement had reached the point of no return. The effect of shock at the end of the Great War brought about a liberating explosion of artistic movements on both sides of the Rhine, resulting in Dada, Bauhaus, The Paris School, Surrealism and Cubism, amongst others. It was the coming of a new world.

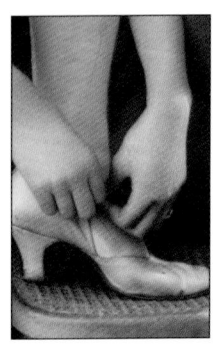

N° 751

———

c. 1925
Anonymous
Blank-backed postcard, 14 x 9 cm

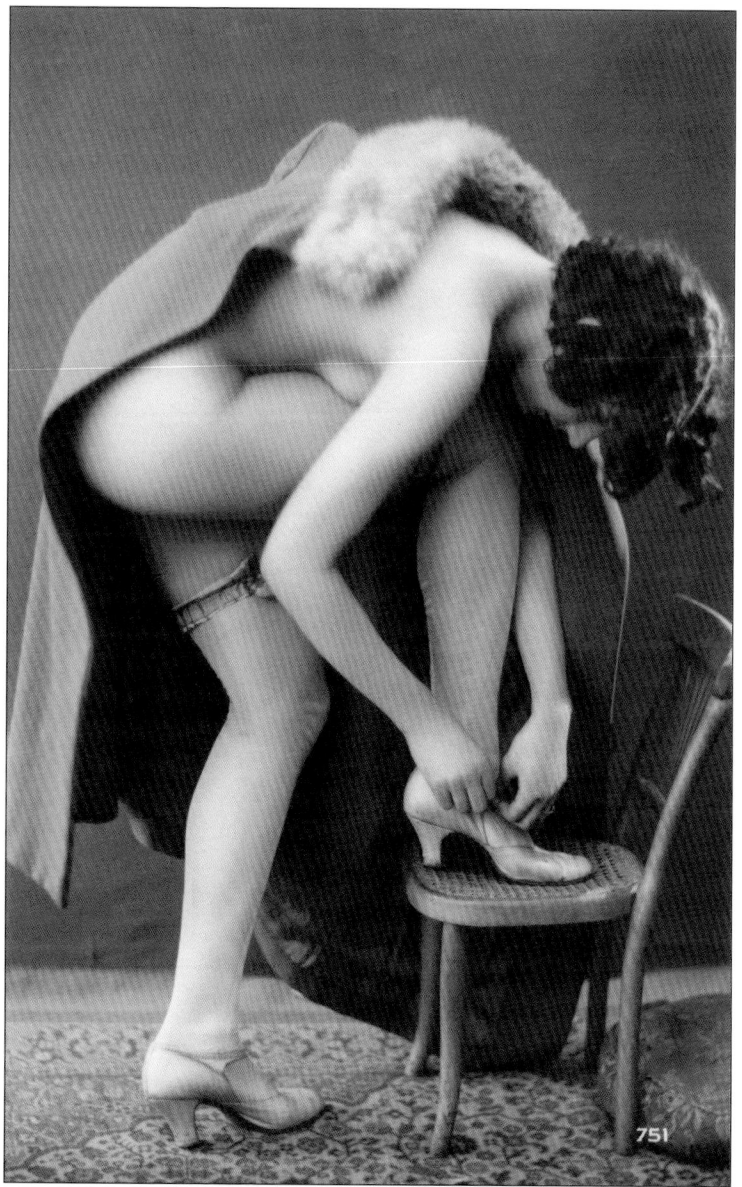

751

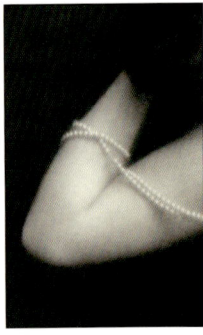

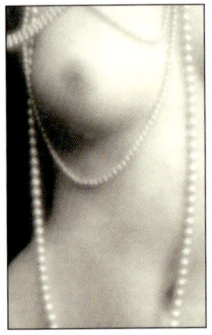

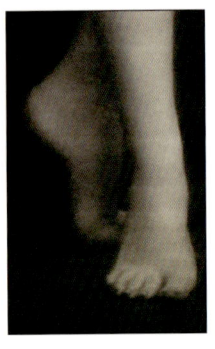

In just a few years, the dynamism and the joy of life generated by the music-hall shows rejuvenated the atmosphere on stage - which became the centre for the exhibition of nudity. The Crazy Years were at their peak. After the bloody years of the war, survivors thought only of sampling all pleasures. Le Tabarin, Le Moulin Rouge and Les Folies Bergère reflected this prevailing spirit of pleasure, and were an excellent alibi for proposing nude women to spectators. This was far from the time when Monsieur Courtelat du Roché,

N° 103

---

c. 1925
Yrélaw (anagram of Waléry)
Gelatin silver print, 24 x 18 cm

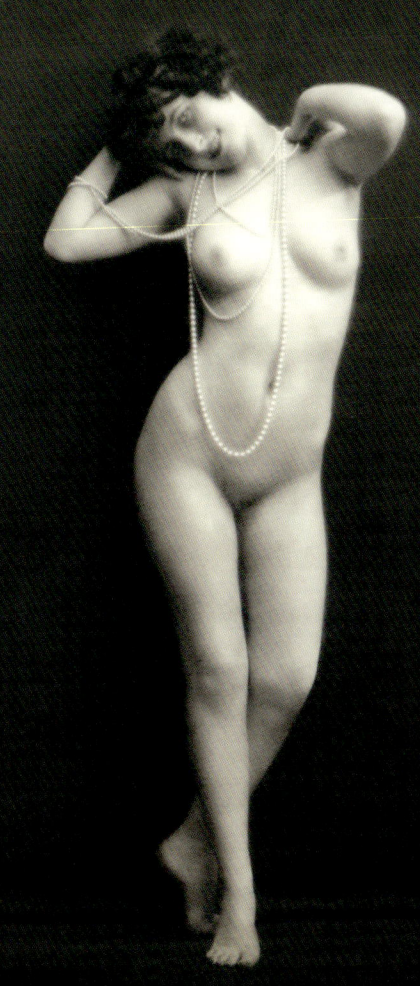

Yrelaw

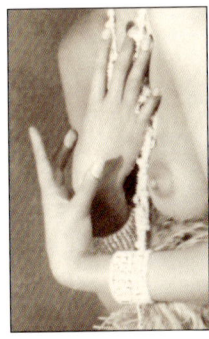

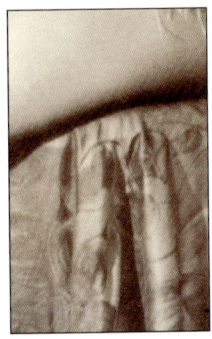

nicknamed Father Modesty, would check the undergarments of La Goulue and her friends for the presence of suitable attire.

Josephine Baker, the undisputed queen of the Folies Bergère shows (*La Folie du Jour* in 1926 and *Un Vent de Folie* in 1927), now leapt out on stage with nothing but a row of bananas for a costume. She was photographed from every angle and the pictures sold by the thousands. The image of drunken revelry conveyed by the music-halls would be repeated elsewhere.

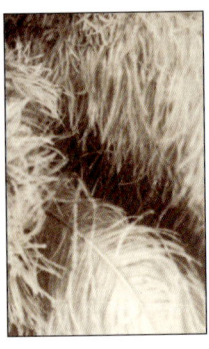

Josephine Baker, N° 130

c. 1925
Waléry
Printed-back postcard, 14 x 9 cm

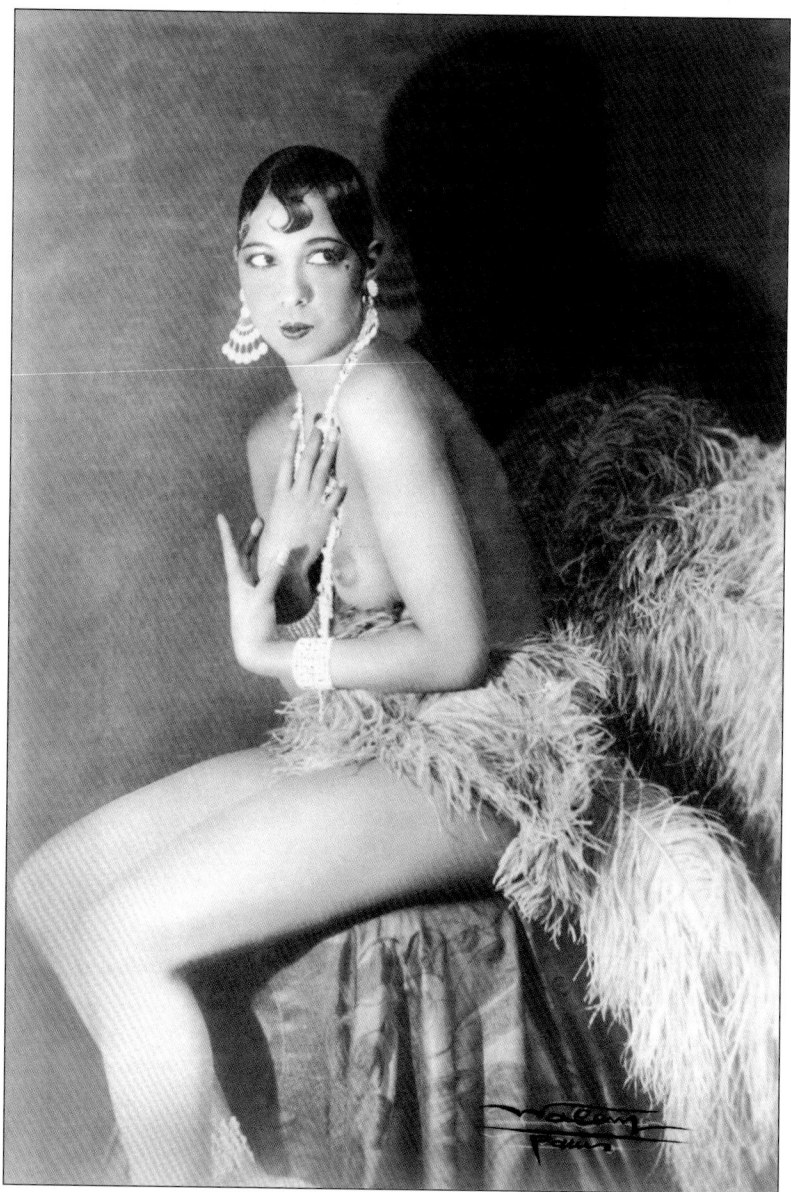

163

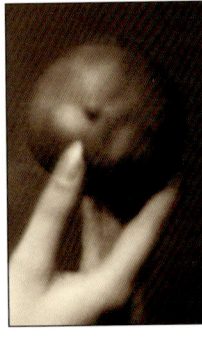

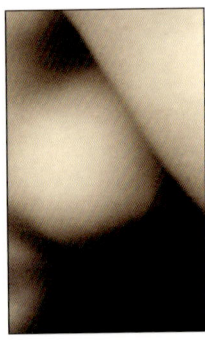

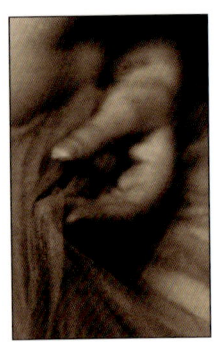

Josephine Baker, Mistinguett and their fellow entertainers had the same celebrity status at this time as the super models do now.

The phenomenon continued. Women became freer and their naked and insolent image became unavoidable. Emancipation was not far away.

The struggle between the sexes reached its height in 1922 when Victor Margueritte was involved in a scandal. Margueritte, the Zola of the Crazy Years, who was a well-known novelist and Commander of the Légion d'honneur, published his thirty-seventh novel

N° 84

―――

c. 1925
P. C.
Gelatin silver print, 24 x 18 cm

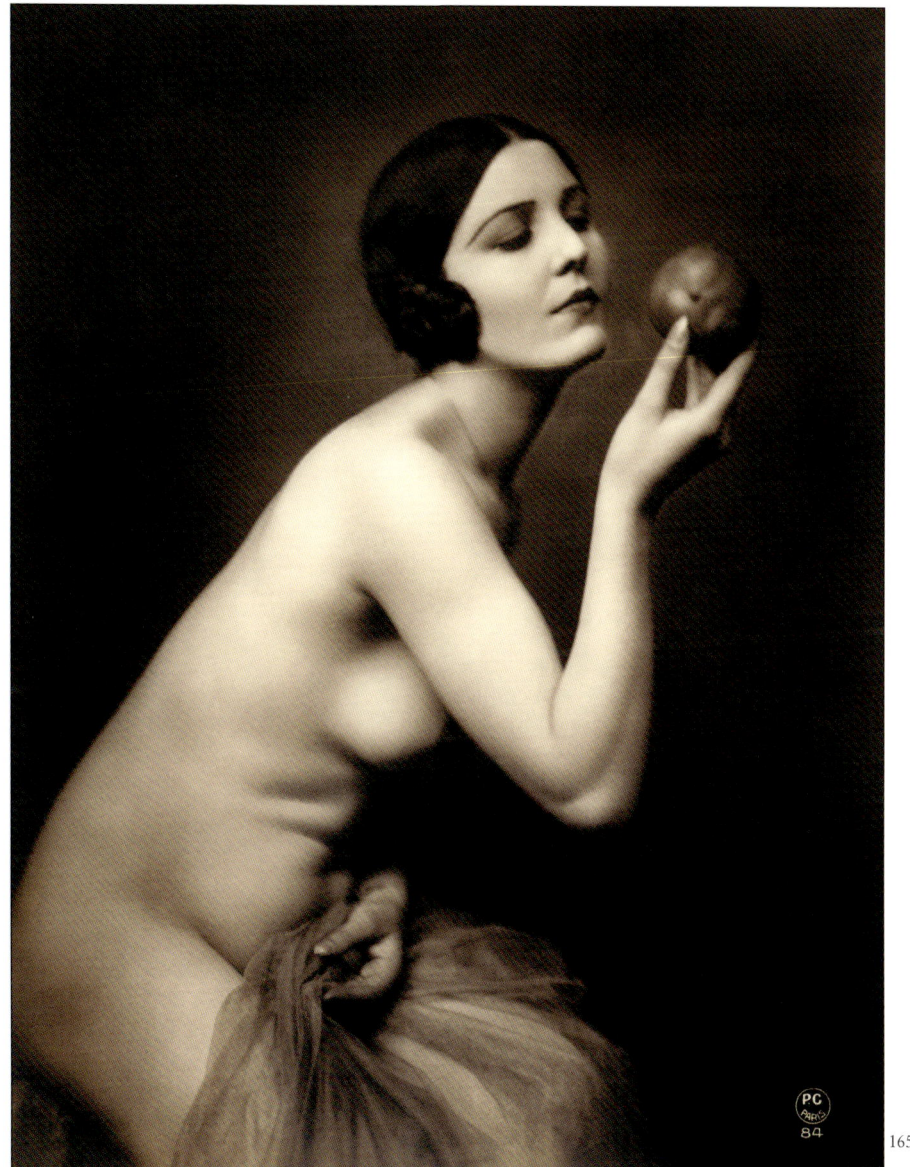

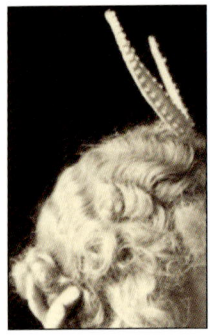

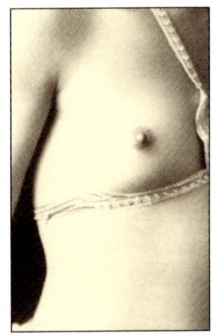

entitled *La Garçonne*. In the novel, Monique Lerbier, on finding out the day before her wedding that her husband-to-be had been unfaithful, looked for solace in the arms of her mother, a self-interested middle-class woman. Her mother minimised the facts in order to secure a social match contrary to the wishes of her daughter. Being a woman of her time, Monique decided not to accept the prevailing middle class hypocrisy, which was summed up by a statement made by her mother: "In this world, and consequently in life, what is

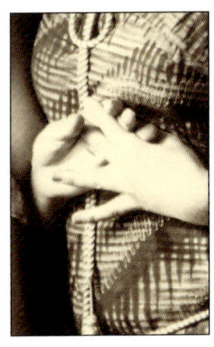

Untitled

c. 1925
François Bertin
Gelatin silver print, 23.5 x 17.5 cm

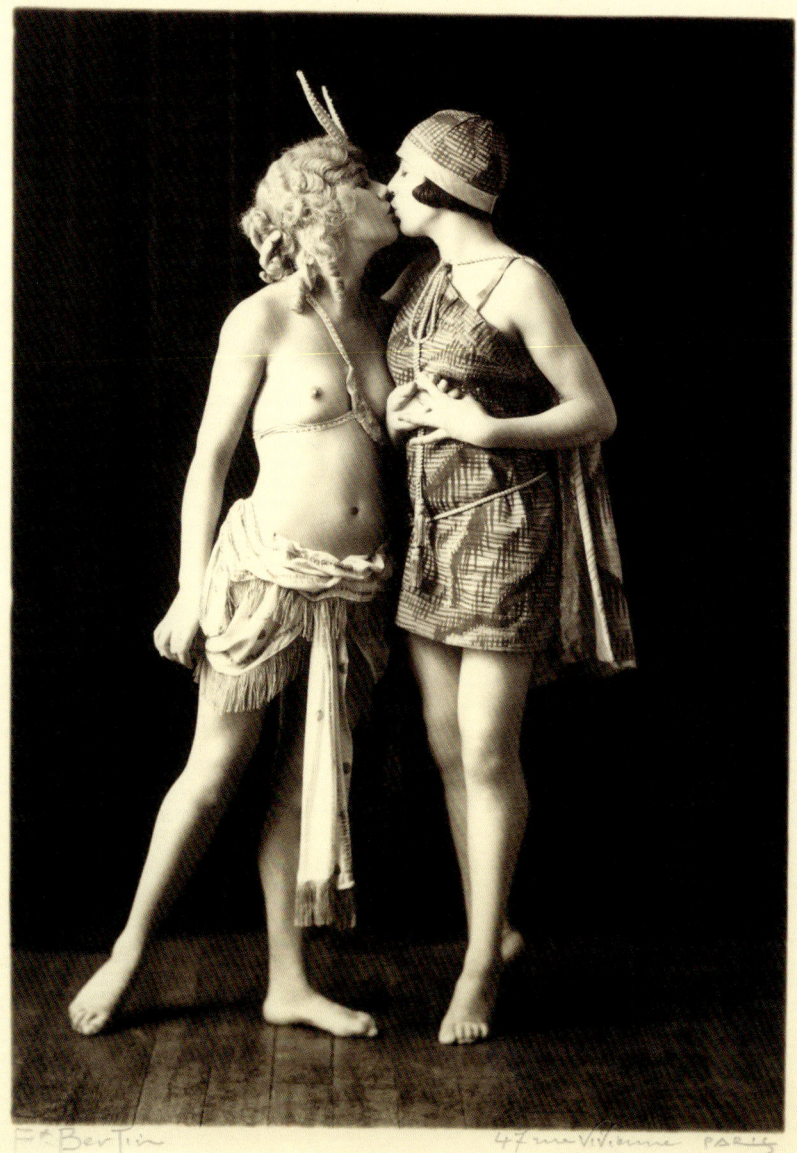

Ft Bertin   47 rue Vivienne PARIS

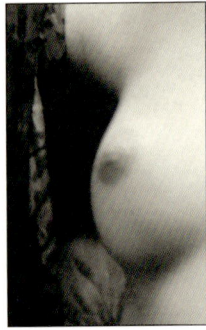

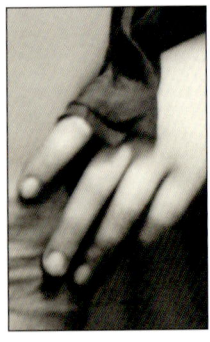

important is not what we do but what we say and especially what is said of what we say." Incensed by these family values, Monique challenged institutional laws, the laws of marriage, the patriarchal moral laws dating from the preceding century, those macho laws which ignored the rights of women and were rooted firmly in the interests of men. Victor Margueritte underlined the pitfalls of this difficult period. "Women have been prisoners for centuries. They have been slaves, used to

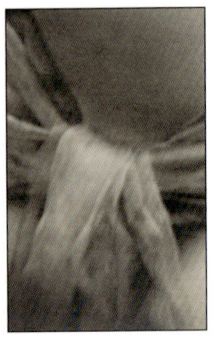

Nº 51

———

c. 1925
A. Noyer Editions
Gelatin silver print, 24 x 18 cm

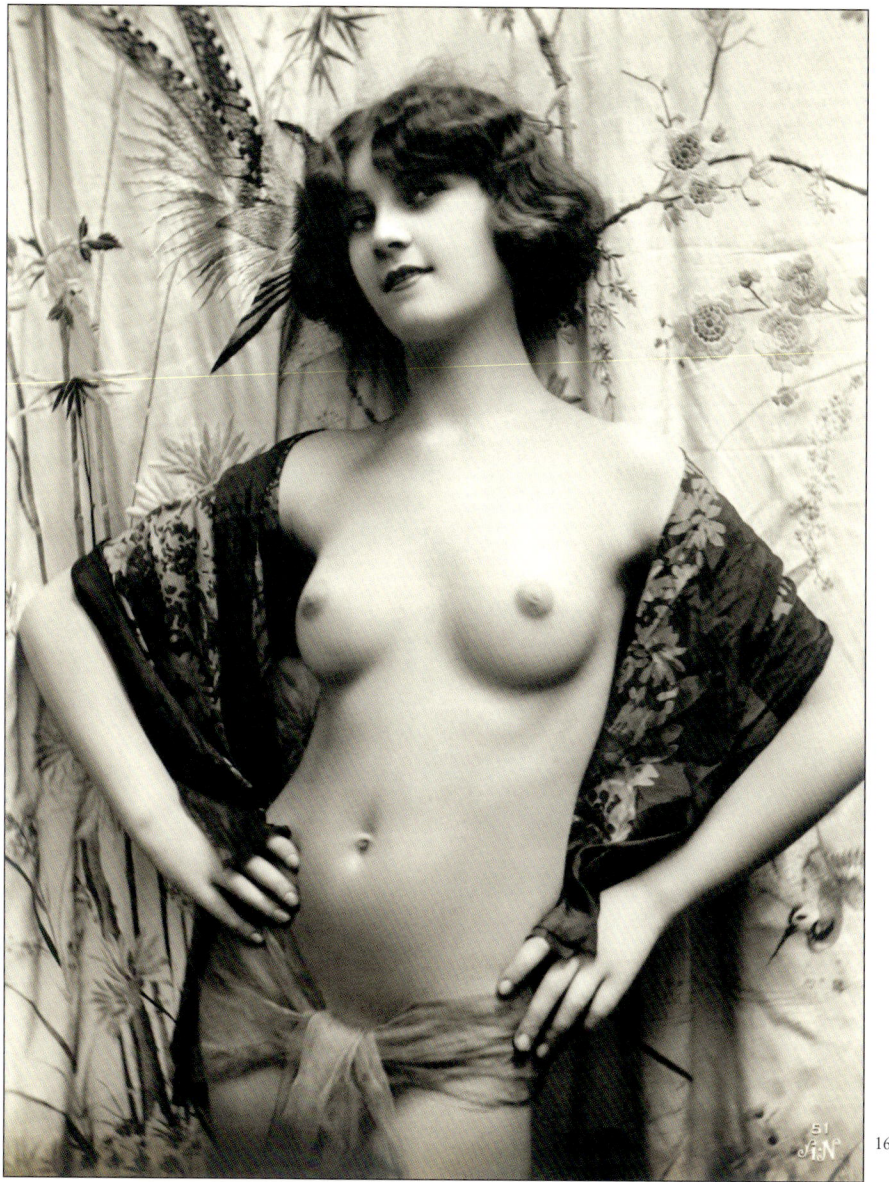

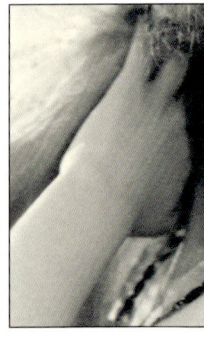

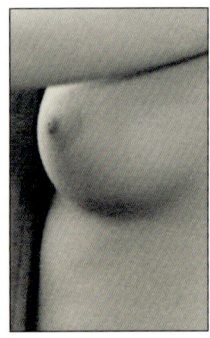

resignation and being overshadowed by men. They now stumble at the sudden opening of the doorway of light and freedom." Struggling against the instinct of masculine sovereignty, the emancipated heroine turns towards women, conveying the image of these "worldly women", half-heterosexual, half-lesbian, typical of the Crazy Years, who were known as "les garçonnes".

Victor Margueritte would be stripped of his *Légion d'honneur* as a result, and became the victim of a virulent press campaign.

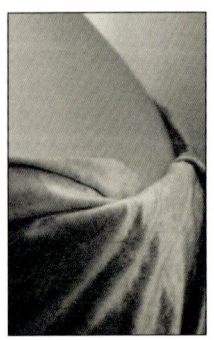

N° 1

———

c. 1925
Biederer Studio
Gelatin silver print, 24 x 18 cm

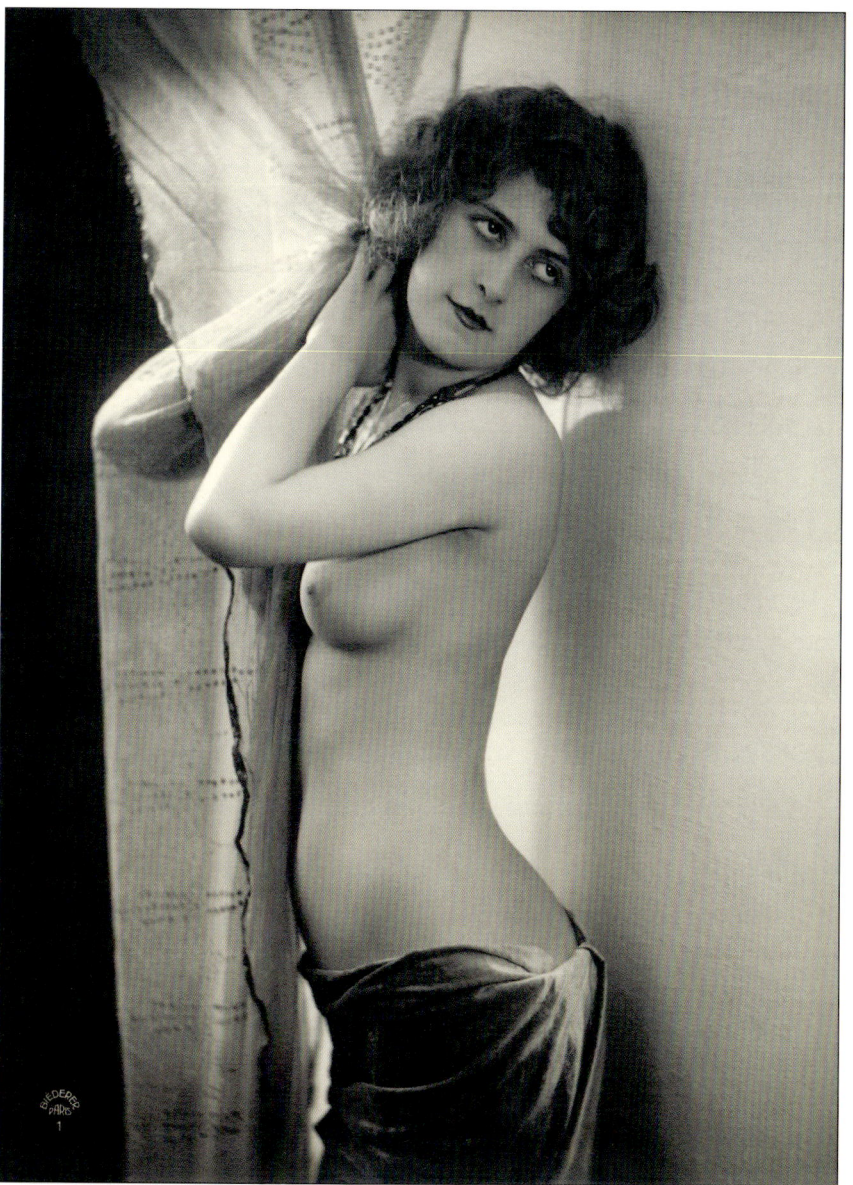

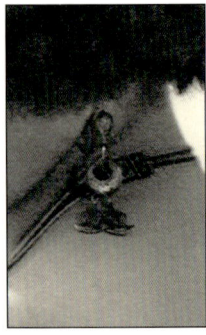

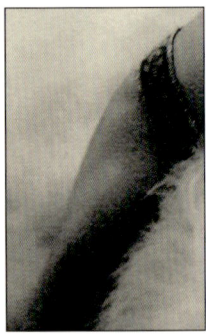

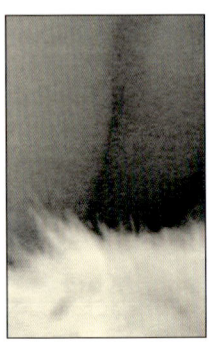

The novel was blacklisted by the Vatican, and removed from the station kiosks by the publisher *Hachette*. However, the damage had already been done. Women's attitudes changed, even as far as photography was concerned. They no longer posed for the photographer in an academic manner as models for hypothetical artists, but in order to seduce. This also heralded the period of "dark room" professionals who specialised in eroticism, where the pictures were available in shop windows or at the back of sex shops.

N° 7

c. 1925
Biederer Studio
Gelatin silver print, 24 x 18 cm

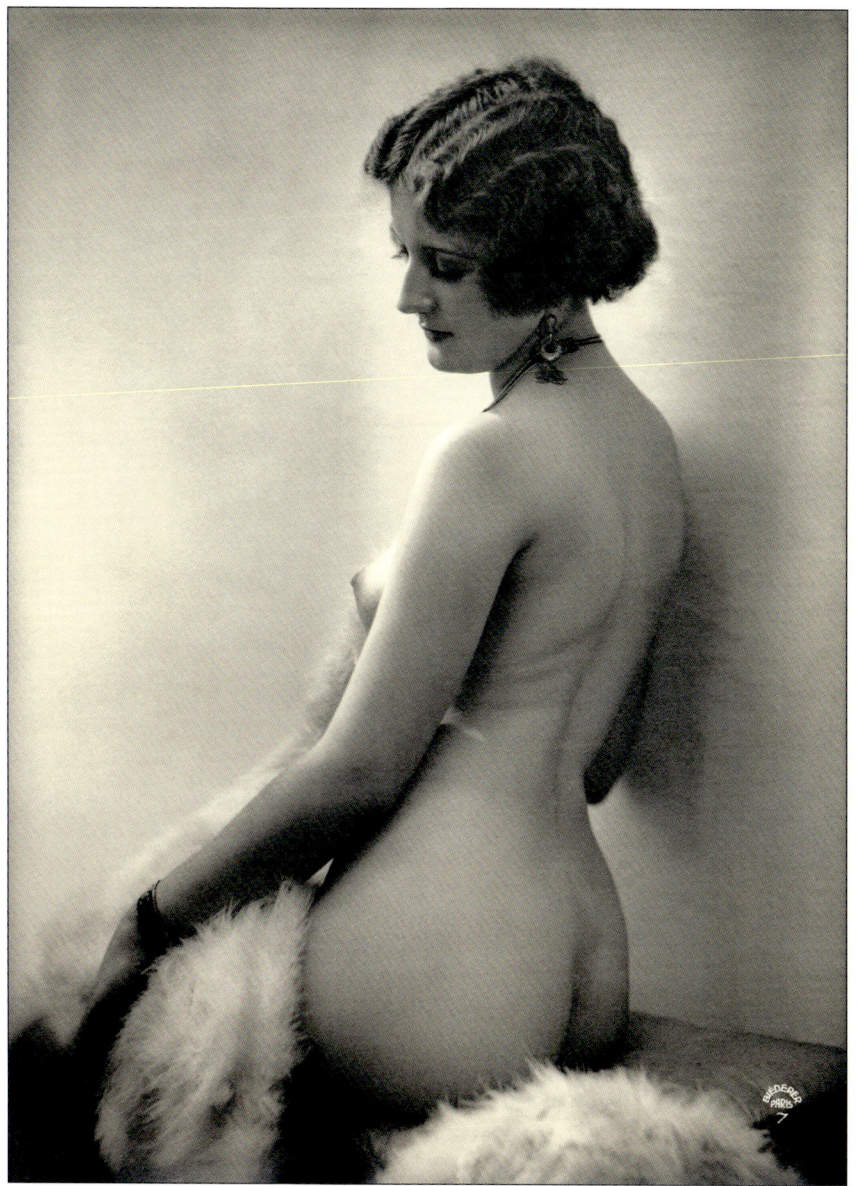

173

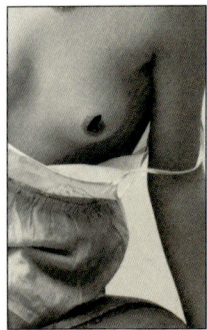

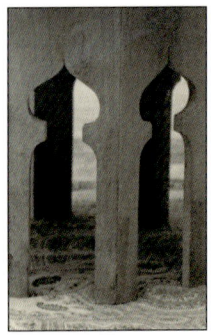

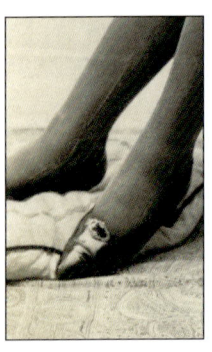

Erotic Bookshops: Between Anonymity and Audacity

In the *Didot-Bottin* professional directory of the twenties, Henri Manuel appears in the list at no. 27 rue du Faubourg Montmartre, as the President's official photographer. He moved easily from the presidency to the music-hall, where he took a number of nude photographs for clients such as *Yva Richard*, a lingerie company, which also sold "soft" photographs as a side line to its principal activity.

Untitled

c. 1925
J.B. Editions
Blank-backed postcard, 14 x 9 cm
Note from the sender: "*It's been one year, during the month of Ju
I saw her in Creuner, dressed even better.*"

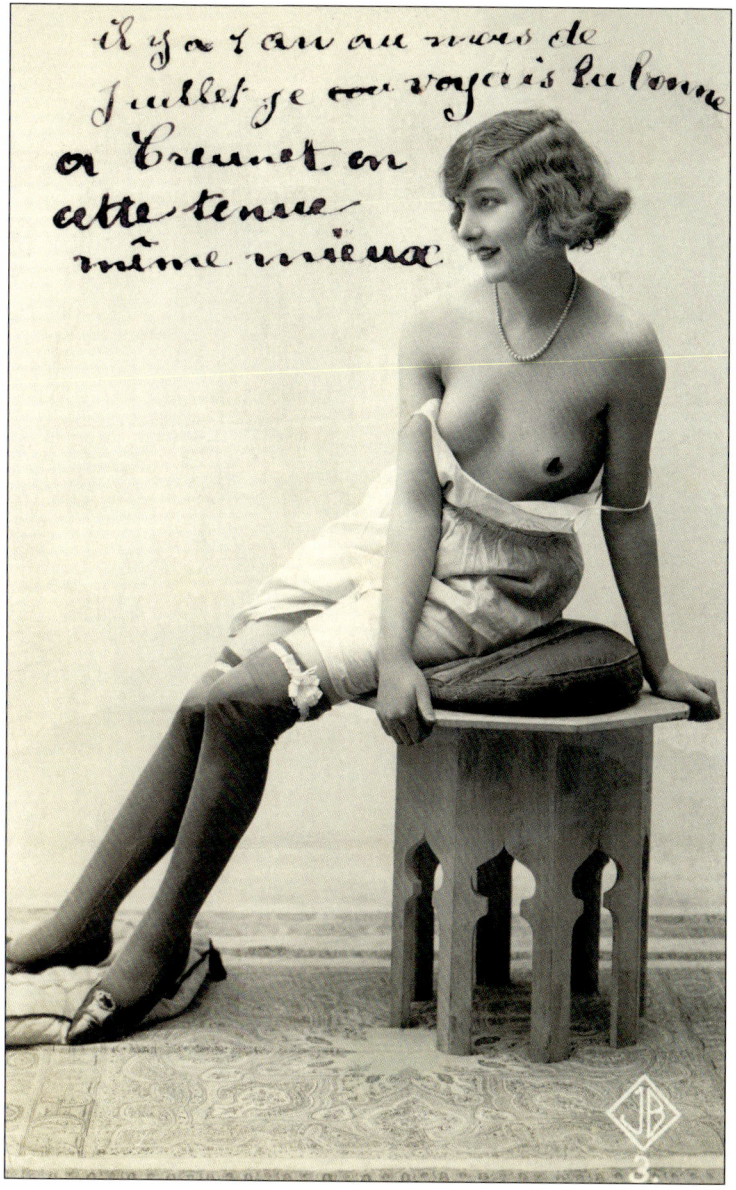

il y a 4 an au mois de
Juillet je vou voyais La bonne
a Treunet en
cette tenue
même mieux.

175

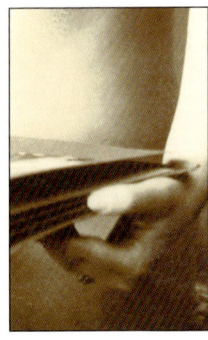

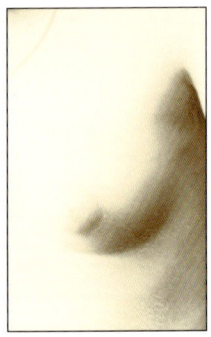

Yva Richard also bought photographs from Bertin, one of the most famous music-hall photographers. The proprietors of *Yva Richard* were several fashion designers, who took advantage of the infatuation for photographs of an erotic and fetishist nature. At first, they bought photographs from several photographers, and then they began to take the pictures themselves, with the husband behind the camera and the wife in front, dressed in a basque or in a fishnet swimming costume.

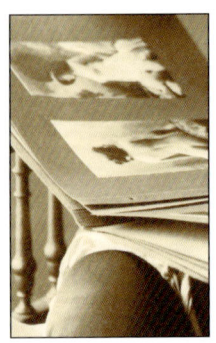

N° 204

———

c. 1925
A. Noyer Editions
Blank-backed postcard, 14 x 9 cm

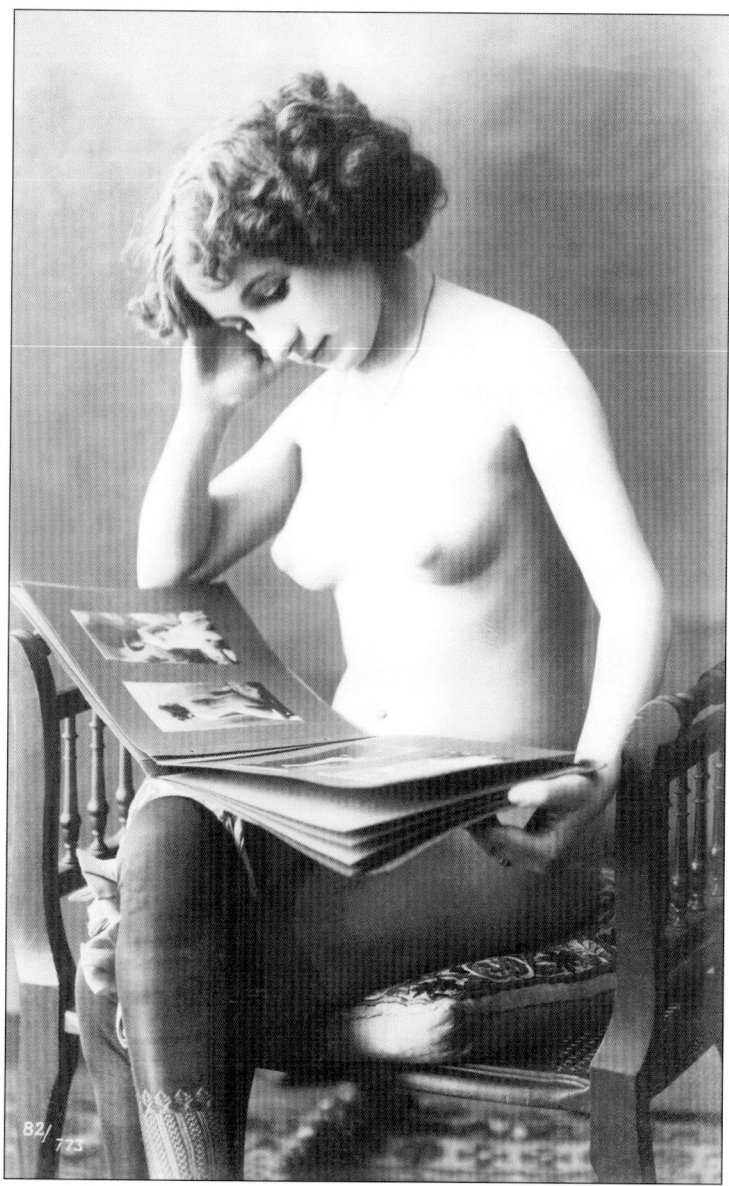

82/
773

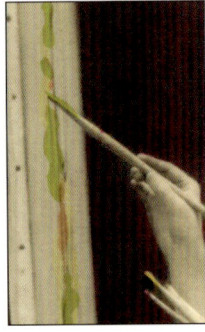

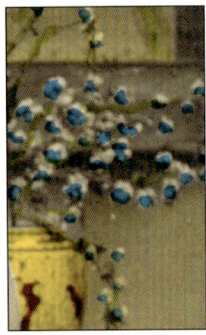

For the pictures of a fetishist nature, involving "kidskin and patent leather", the demand became so high that they were helped by another photographer called Biederer who was located at an address on the boulevard du Temple. At first, Biederer signed his photographs, but when he began to specialise in domination scenes, he signed the pictures only with a B and then, stopped signing at all. However, the discovery of a souvenir album of a model from this period revealed his name, thus doing away with his anonymity.

N° 1045

c. 1925
P. N. Editions
Printed-back postcard, 14 x 9 cm

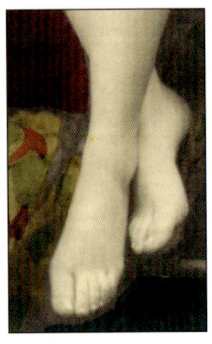

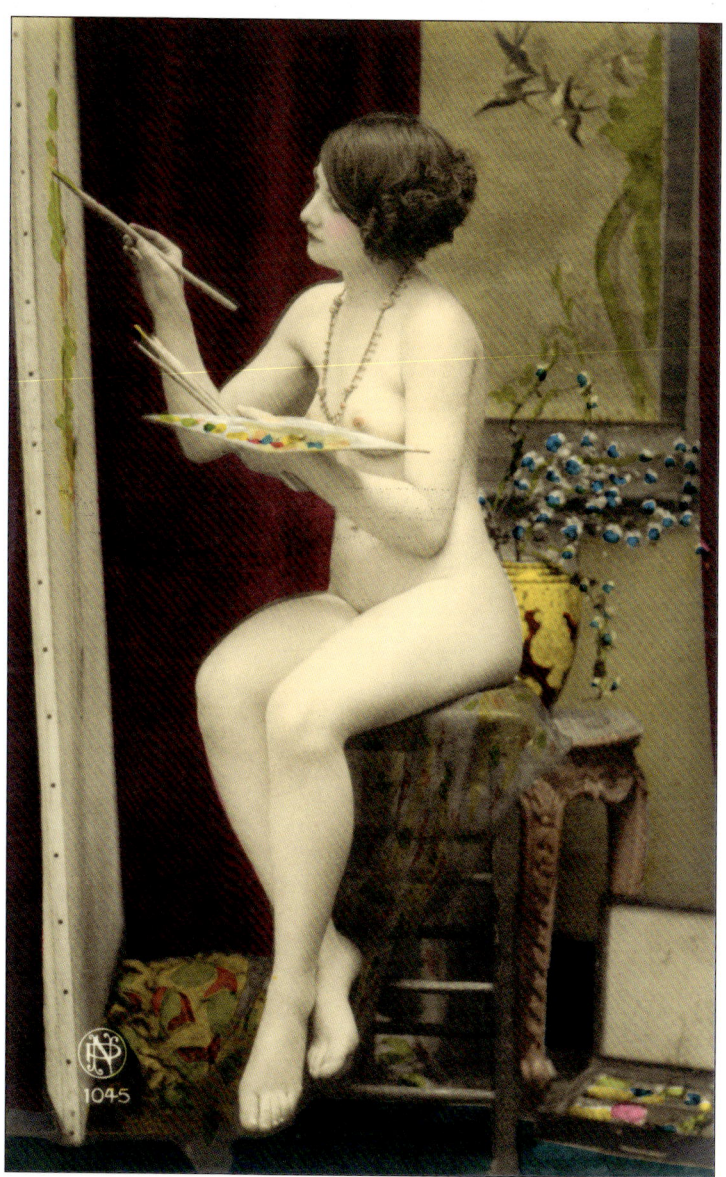

179

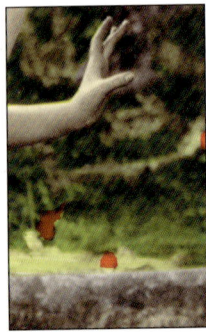

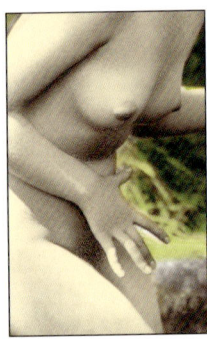

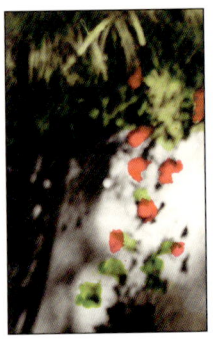

Another name is that of Albert Wyndham, located at no. 13 rue Auber. He worked, at the beginning of the Thirties, for minor magazines with enchanting names such as *Petit choc*, *Jambes Savantes*, and *Honni Soit*, which regularly appeared under the publisher's name *Aux Deux Tourelles* registered in Paris and London. He was also responsible for several little catalogues, called *Poupées Parisiennes* or *Camera Prints*, which were published in English and aimed at an Anglo-Saxon clientele.

N° 3613

———

c. 1925
S. O. L. Editions
Hand-printed printed-back postcard, 14 x 9 cm

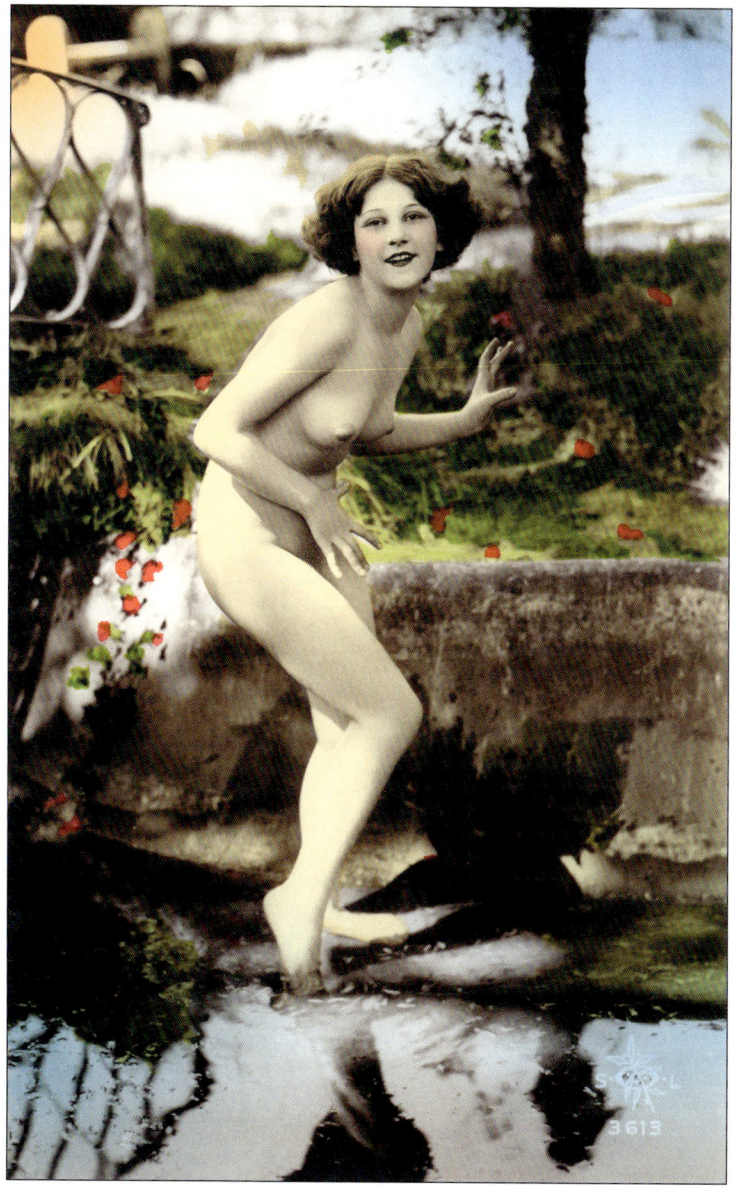

3613

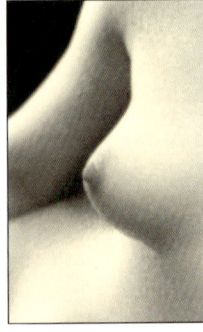

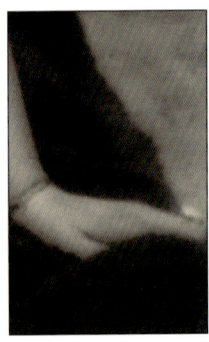

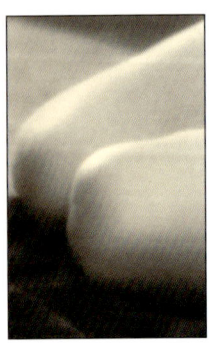

Those interested could order pictures postcard size or 18 x 24 that he would sign with either *Film Art* or in his own name. It was such a success that it is not rare to find his work nowadays by chance, in the boxes of old postcard dealers. His larger works are less common.

Even if a postcard or photograph is not signed, after studying photography and handling thousands of pictures, analysing lighting, accessories, models, emotional and erotic content, it becomes relatively easy to

Untitled

c. 1930
Albert Wyndham
Gelatin silver print, 24 x 18 cm

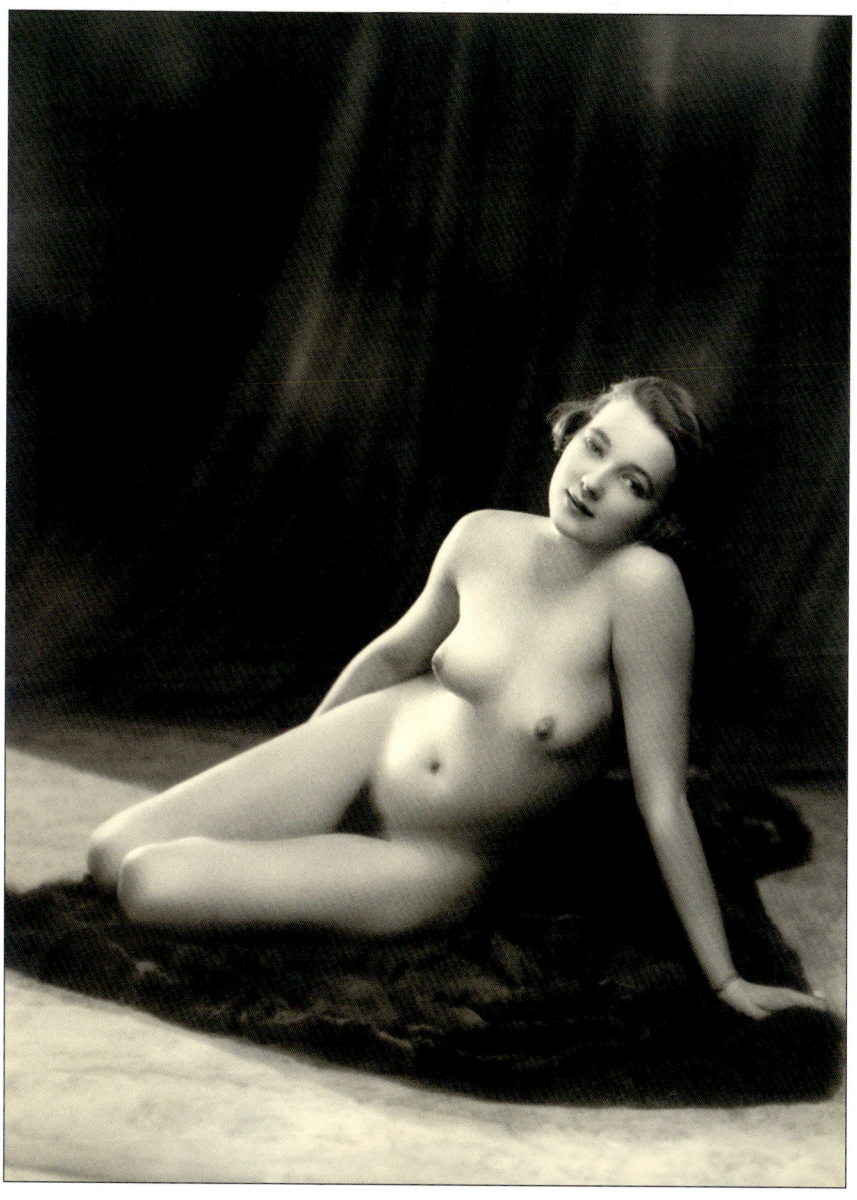

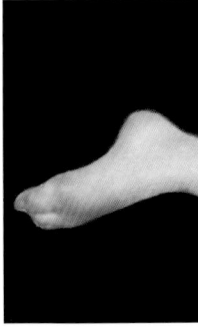

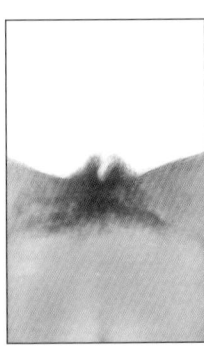

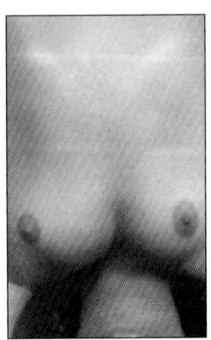

identify a disparate image in a homogenous collection, or to be in a position to confirm that such and such a photograph is or is not of the same photographer. Putting a collection back together is certainly possible; however, attributing it to someone remains impossible if none of the elements are signed. Some prints of a very high quality were made on the same paper as others signed by Albert Wyndham. However, the use of industrial paper proves nothing and moreover, the erudite researcher of the forerunners of 19th century eroticism,

Untitled
————

c. 1930
Anonymous
Gelatin silver print, 18 x 24 cm

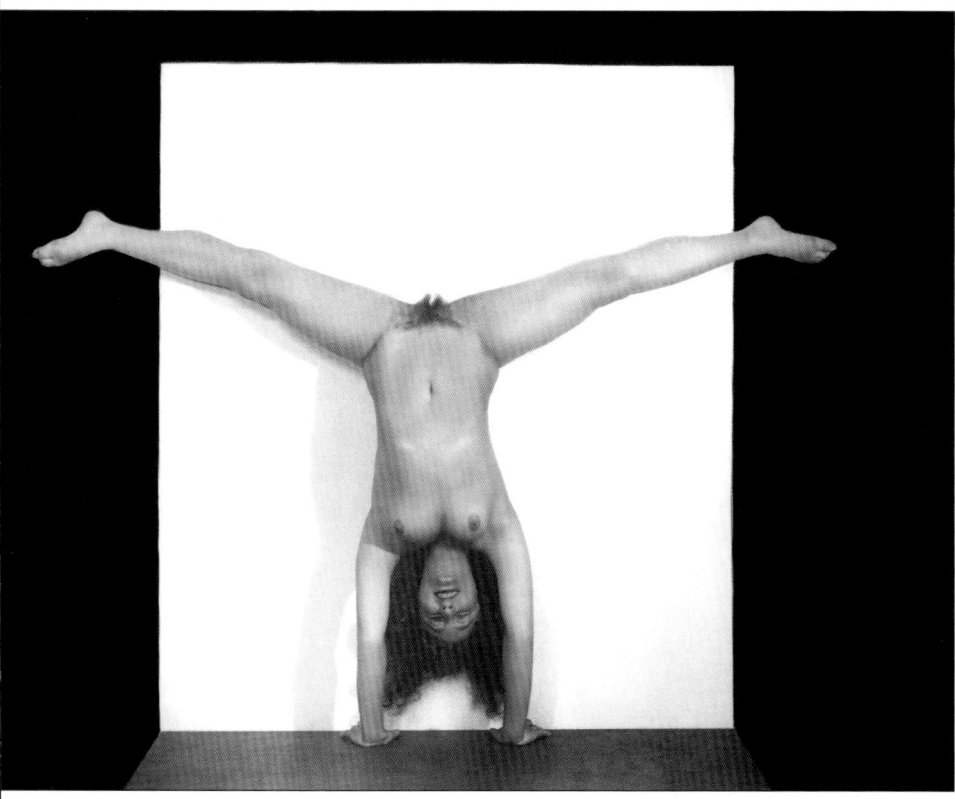

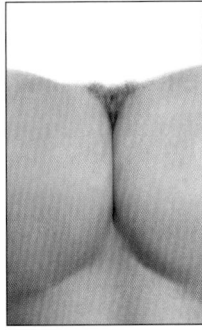

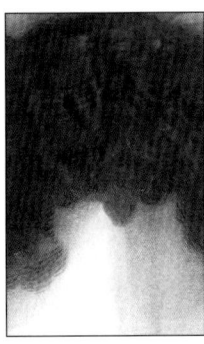

Serge Nazarieff, had handled the negative plates of this photographer under the name of *Grundworth*. Unfortunately, this name appears nowhere else.

Grundworth is almost an anagram of Wyndham, and it would be so simple if such a pseudonym was used. In this case, it could be that under the name of Wyndham, the photographer took almost academic pictures aimed at the surviving French soldiers of the First World War or their sons, used to images of a sentimental nature in order to dilute their erotic connotation.

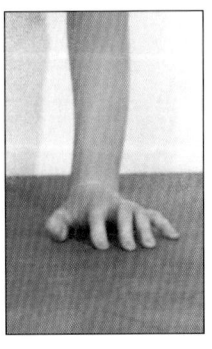

Untitled

c. 1930
Anonymous
Gelatin silver print, 18 x 24 cm

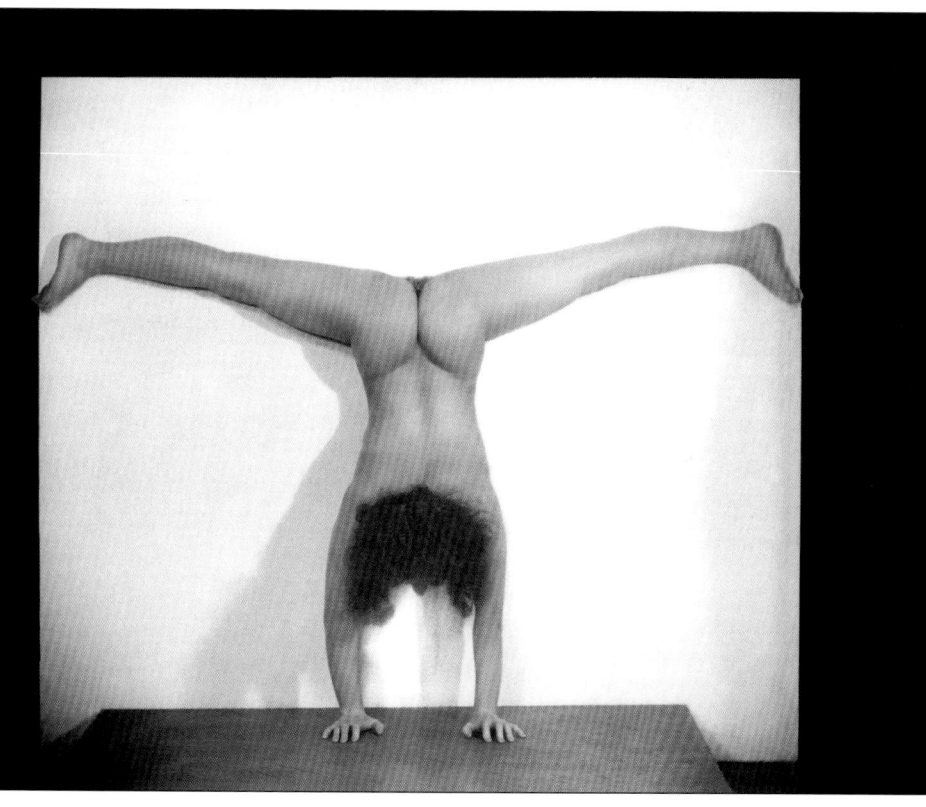

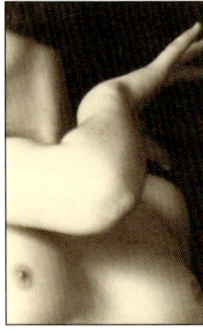

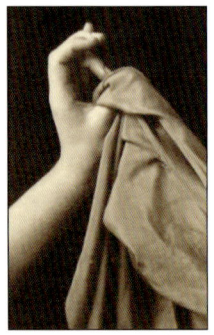

Then, under the other name, Grundworth, the cunning photographer proposed illicit images bordering on pornography. However, there is unfortunately no proof. If we compare the images of Grundworth with those of Wyndham, although the same paper is used and the compositions are similar, there is no sign of the same piece of furniture, the same models or even the same accessories. It is hard to believe that the photographer, if it was the same person, did not use either the same chair or candlestick holder that could be identified in both sets of

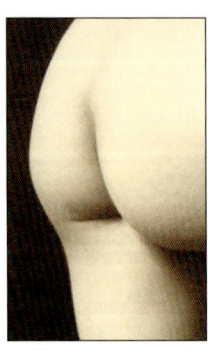

Untitled

c. 1930
François Bertin
Gelatin silver print, 23.5 x 17.5 cm

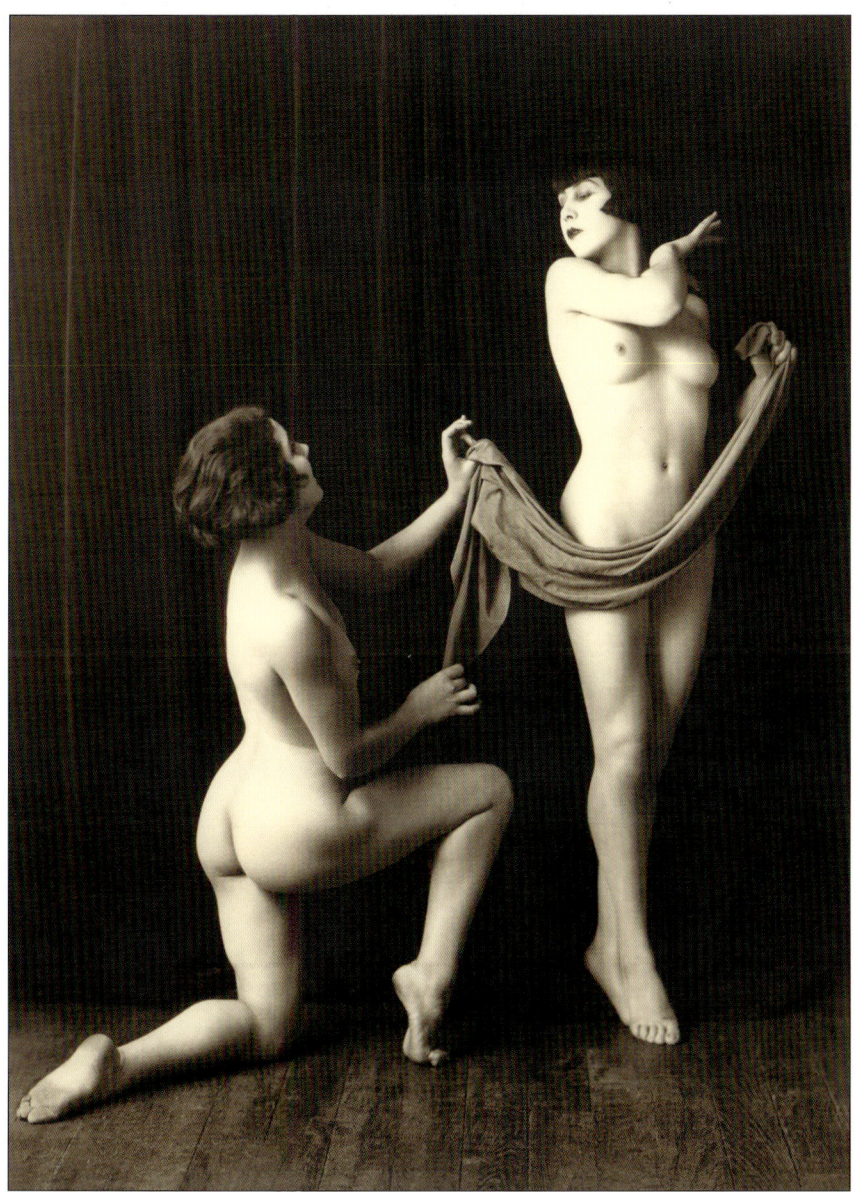

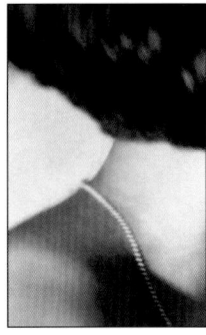

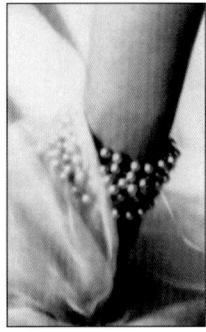

photographs, or, and even more importantly, that the photographer did not ask one of Wyndham's models, whom he found to his liking, to become a model for Grundworth or vice versa. Unlike what has been able to be proved in the case of Biederer, nothing proves that Grundworth was Wyndham. In spite of his anonymity, this underground photographer remains a reflection of this time, when women, from the middle classes to the prostitutes, rejected the shackles imposed on them by men for centuries.

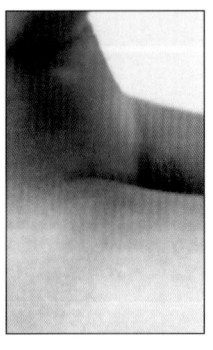

N° 75

———

c. 1930
Hide Mayer Kupfer, A. Noyer Editions
Gelatin silver print, 24 x 18 cm

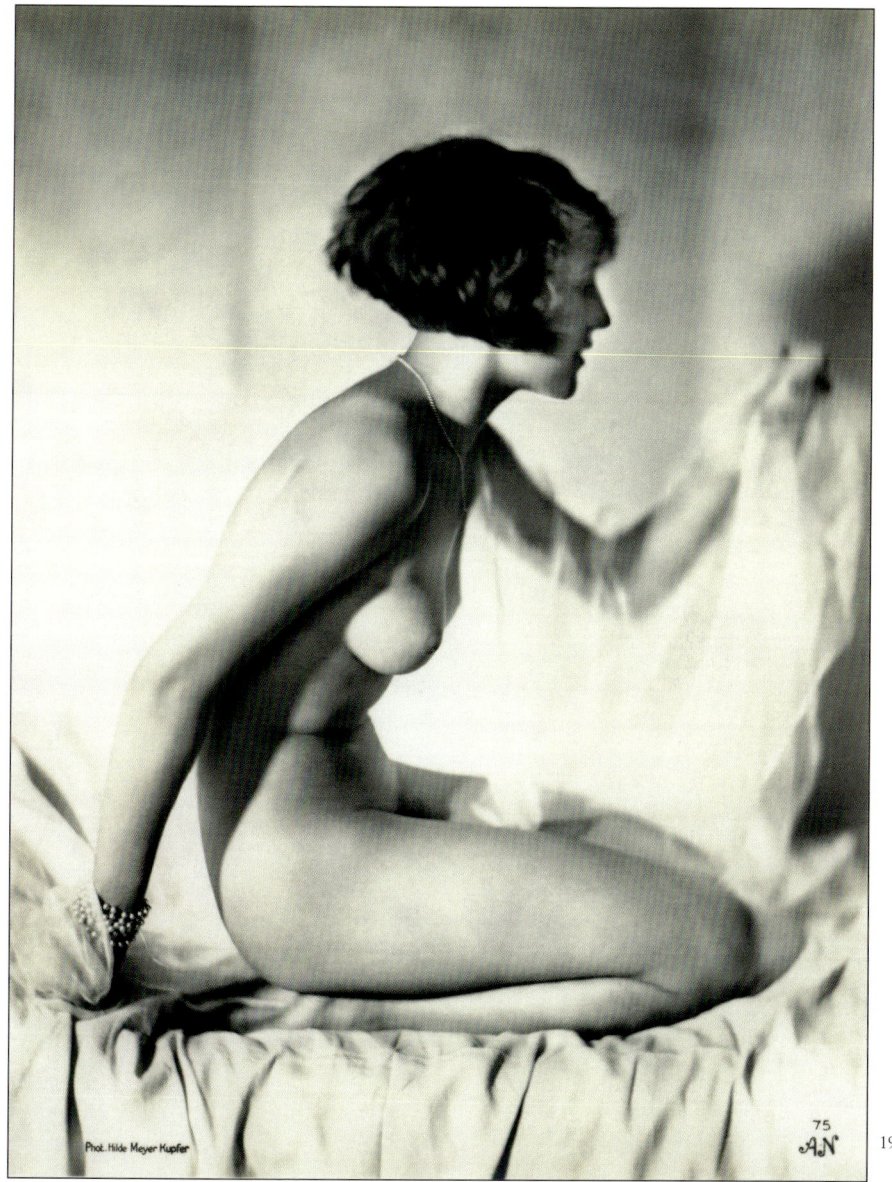

Phot. Hilde Meyer Kupfer

75
A.N.

191

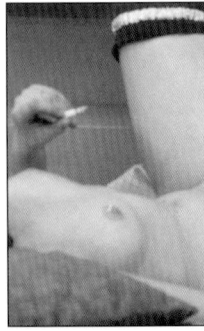

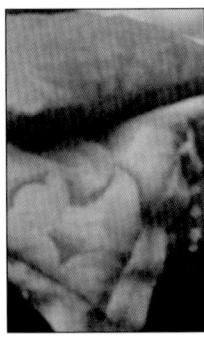

Better than any other photographer, he immortalises the modernity of his time without deceiving us. His models, often in groups, provoke the photographer by staring hard at him through the lens, violently revealing their differences to the gaze of men. It is however possible that this is not that case, that it is he who is the guilty one, who by taking advantage of the situation, uses these women to immortalise his most obscene fantasies on his photographic plates.

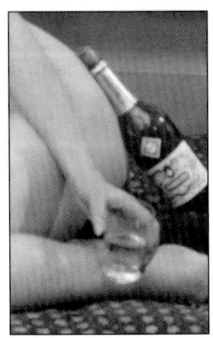

Untitled

c. 1930
Ostra Editions (?)
Blank-backed postcard, 9 x 14 cm

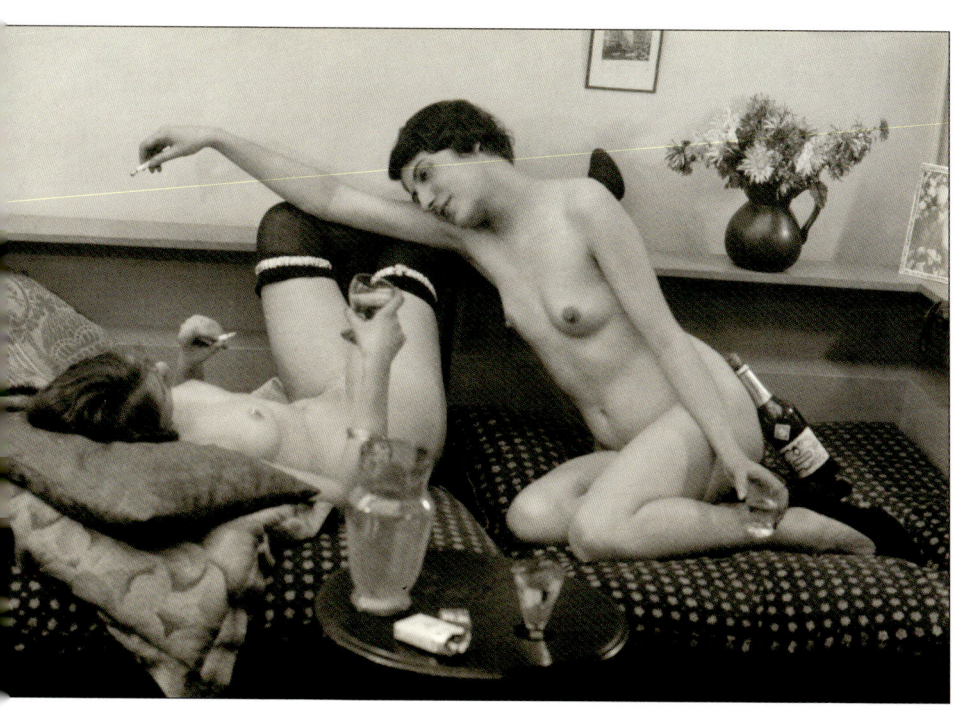

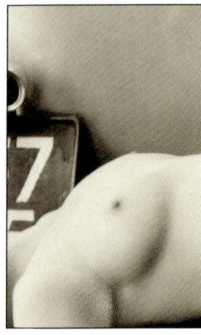

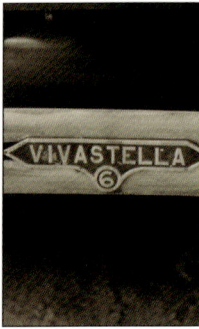

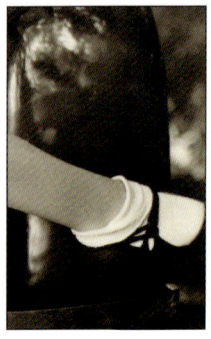

The 1930's. The beginning of the decade was full of events. Wall Street collapsed, turning the worldwide economy upside down. The market economy commenced its ascension to the dominant place that it occupies today. Aviators crossed the Atlantic. Theatres closed and were replaced by cinemas; Le Bataclan in 1927, La Cigale in 1928, L'Olympia and Le Moulin rouge in 1929 and L'Eldorado in 1930. Les Folies Bergère and the Casino de Paris were the only halls to remain open.

N° 915

———

c. 1930
Ostra Editions (?)
Blank-backed postcard, 9 x 14 cm

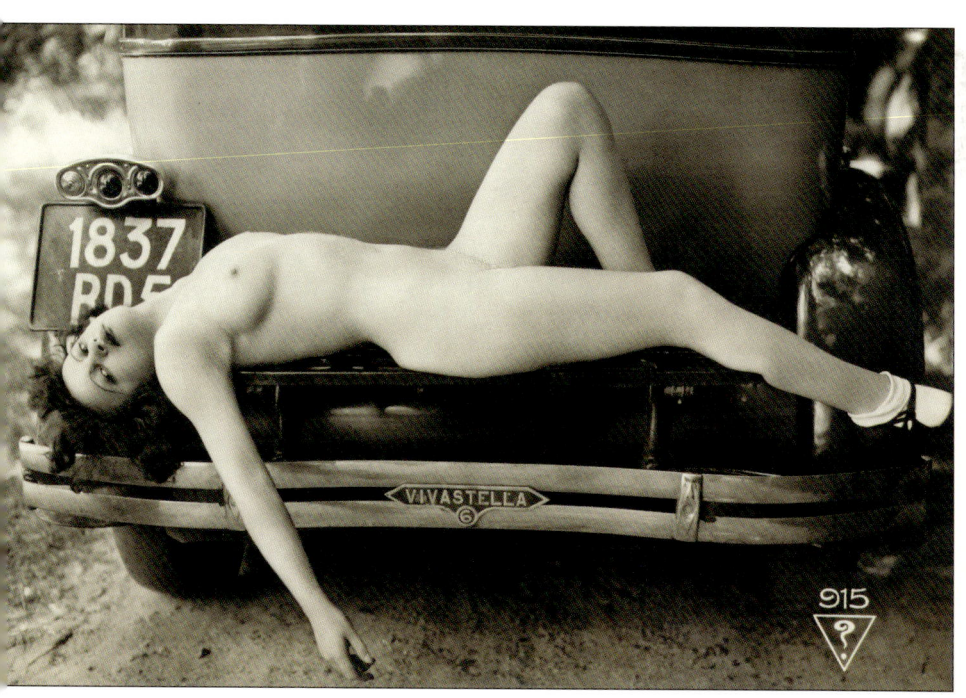

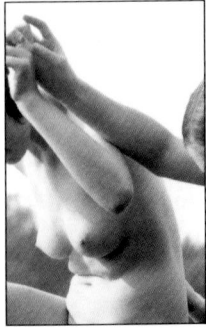

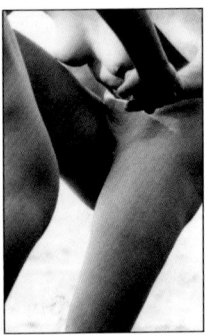

After having taken over the stage, the nude established itself on the streets of Paris, bringing about the beginnings of bookshops which were similar to the sex shops of today.

A further examination of the professional directories of the time shows that the entry *Vidal, Bookshop* appeared for the first time at no. 4 rue du Ponceau in the red-light district of the rue St. Denis, a hot spot of Parisian prostitution. Monsieur Vidal and his lady friend set up the *Editions Gauloises* company at the end of 1930, the head office

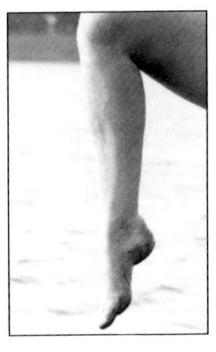

N° 6449

———

c. 1930
G. Riebicke
Gelatin silver print, 13 x 18 cm

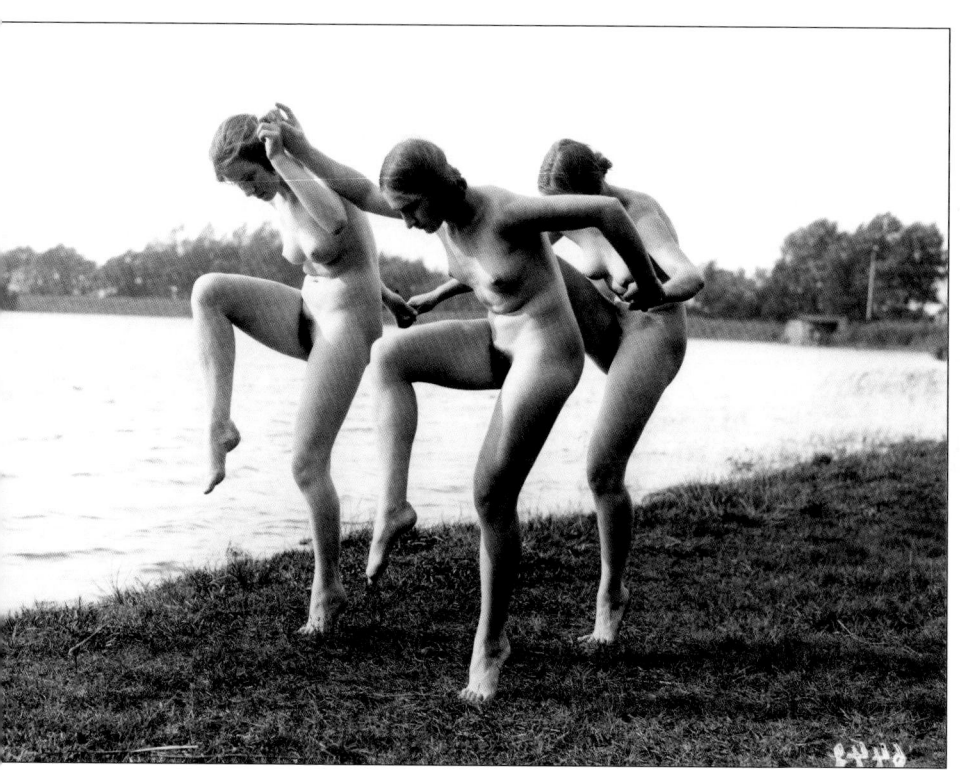

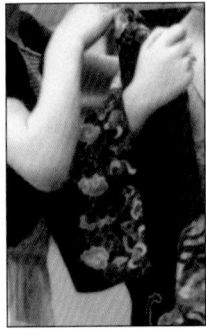

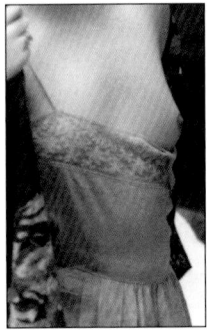

located at rue de Ponceau, and three branches located at four different addresses (39 rue Beauregard, 7 rue de la Lune, 1 rue Blondel and 227 rue St. Denis) although two of them were in fact in the same building in the rue St. Denis district. The reasoning behind two and sometimes three addresses very close to each other came from sound commercial logic. This bookshop wanted to offer its clients a maximum of variety in its sales outlets.

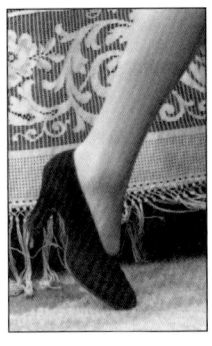

N° 2787

c. 1930
SAPI Editions
Blank-backed postcard, 14 x 9 cm

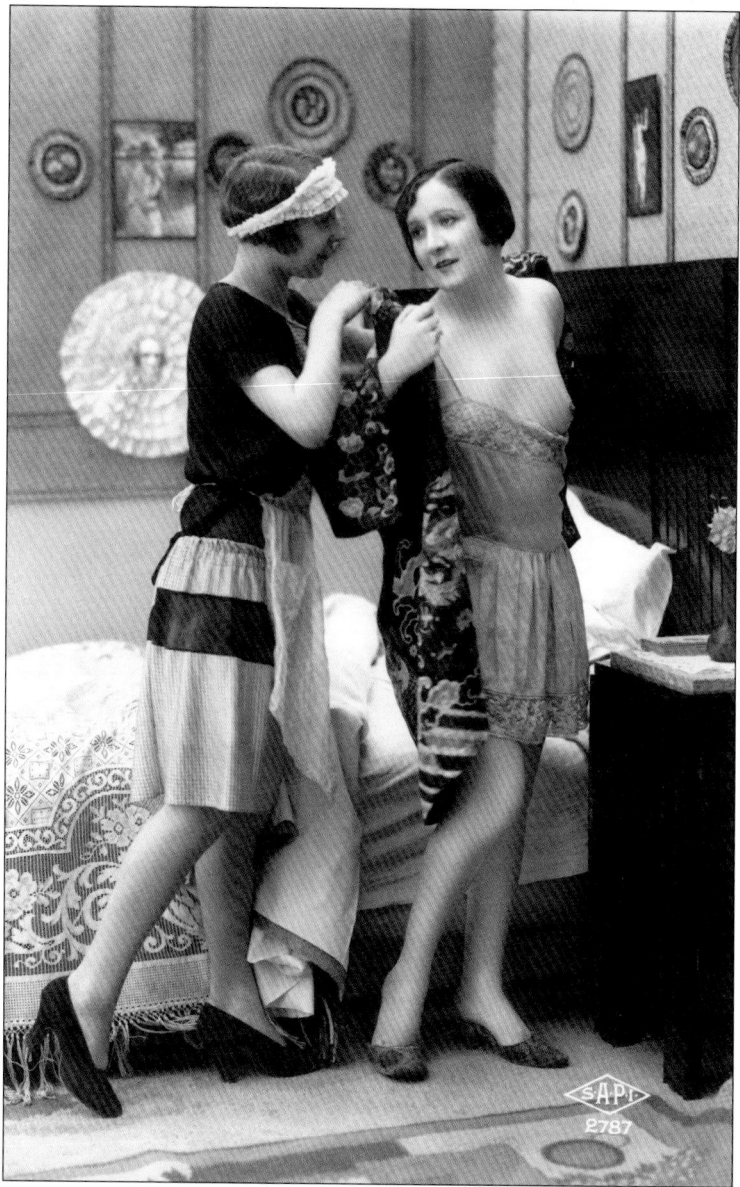

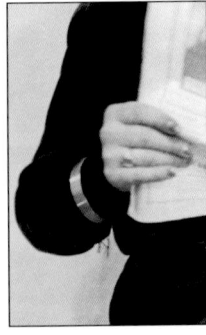

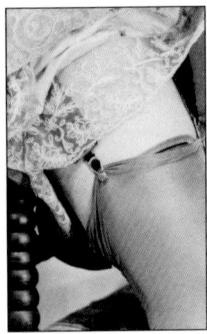

Its advertising in the lightweight journals of the time took the form of blocks of unequal size, covering entire pages of which it was the sole source. It quickly created its own journals, thus minimising drastically the cost of advertising space. In direct competition with Yva Richard, *The Lingerie Bookshop,* located at no. 9 rue Richepanse, would change its name firstly to *Richepanse Bookshop* and then finally to *Diana-slip.*

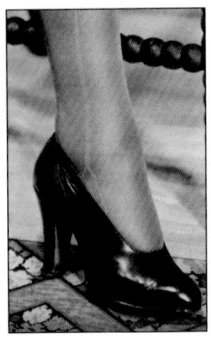

Untitled
———

c. 1930
Biederer Studio
Gelatin silver print, 18 x 13 cm

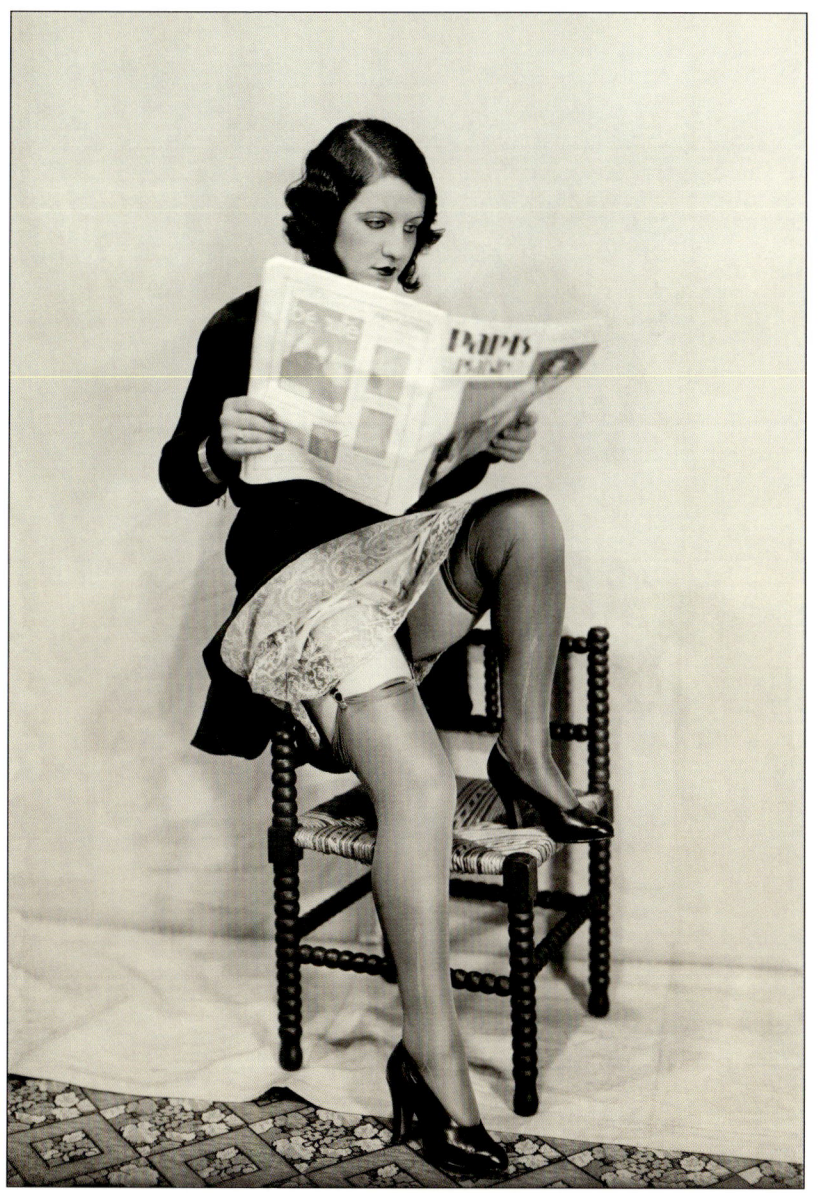

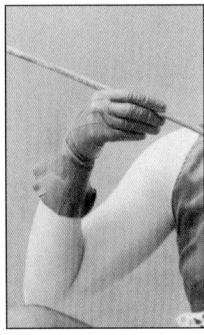

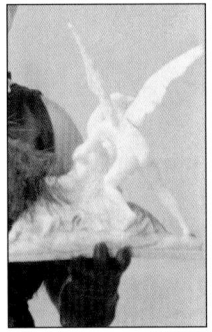

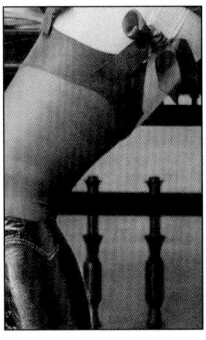

Yva Richard versus Diana-Slip

Just as the fashion designer *Yva Richard* became a photographer, the *Editions Gauloises* began to deal in lingerie, and copying the idea of their predecessor, invented the character of *Diana-Slip* who would present her creations herself. Paris became the centre stage of a terrible duel: *Diana-Slip* versus *Yva Richard*. Patent leather versus kidskin!

Untitled
_____

c. 1935
Yva Richard
Gelatin silver print format postcard, 14 x 9 cm

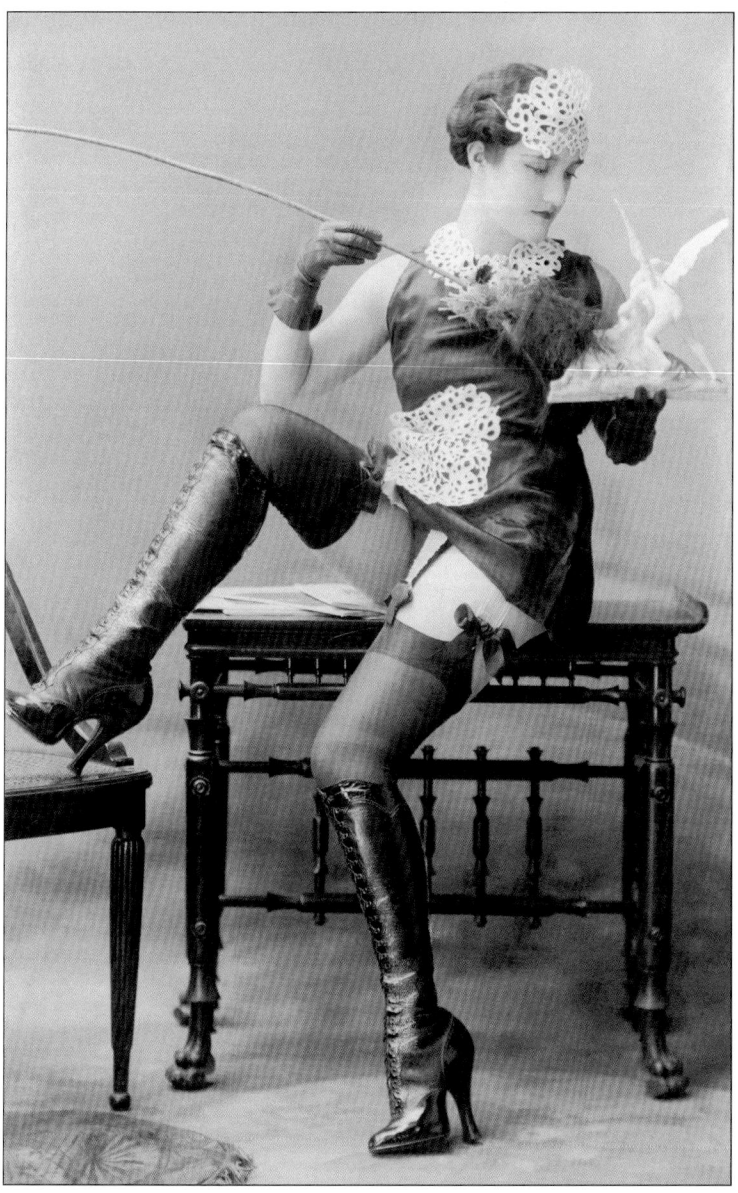

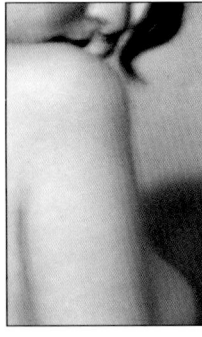

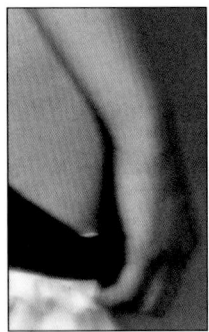

Of all the businesses in the *Editions Gauloises* group, the company located at rue Richepanse targeted the same clientele as that of the company located at rue Pillet-Will. With large financial backing, it was able to offer the clientele more lavish catalogues. Moreover, it was not difficult for *Diana-Slip* to find competent photographers; they could choose from those working for the group's magazines.

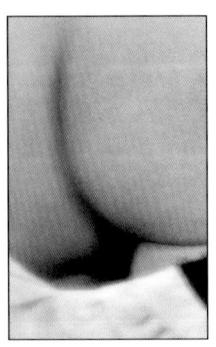

Untitled
———

c. 1935
Anonymous photograph for Diana-Slip
Gelatin silver print, 14 x 9 cm

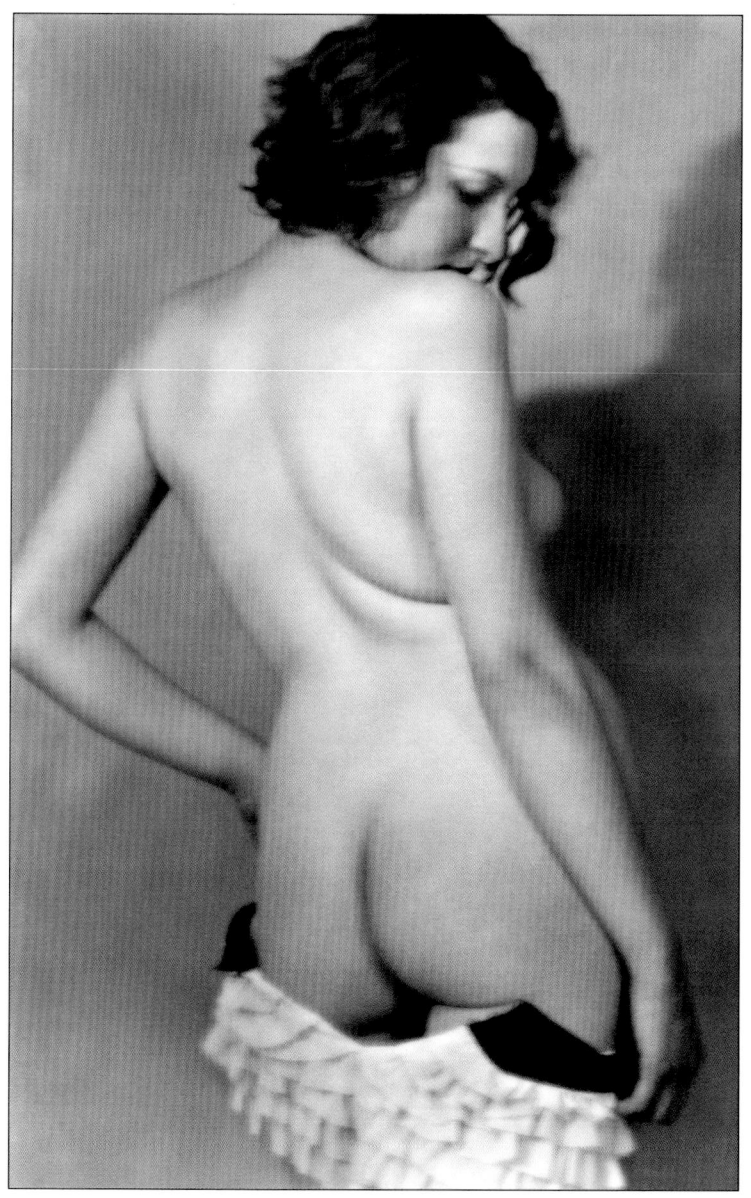

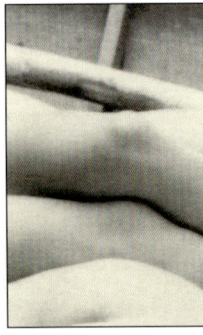

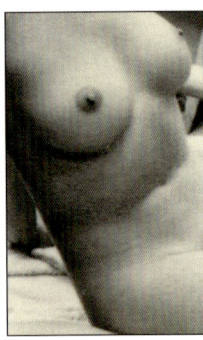

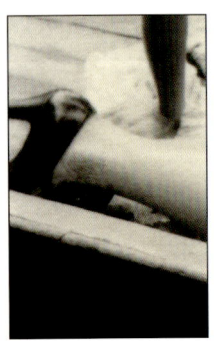

The names of famous photographers of the century such as Brassai, Kertesz and Krull feature discreetly amongst others that have since been forgotten.

The two companies were now proposing the same products, but the fight was unequal as the financial means were not the same. Pressure from its competitors upset the commercial strategies of *Yva Richard*, but nothing could halt the process that had been initiated.

Untitled
———

c. 1935
Anonymous
Gelatin silver print, 13 x 18 cm

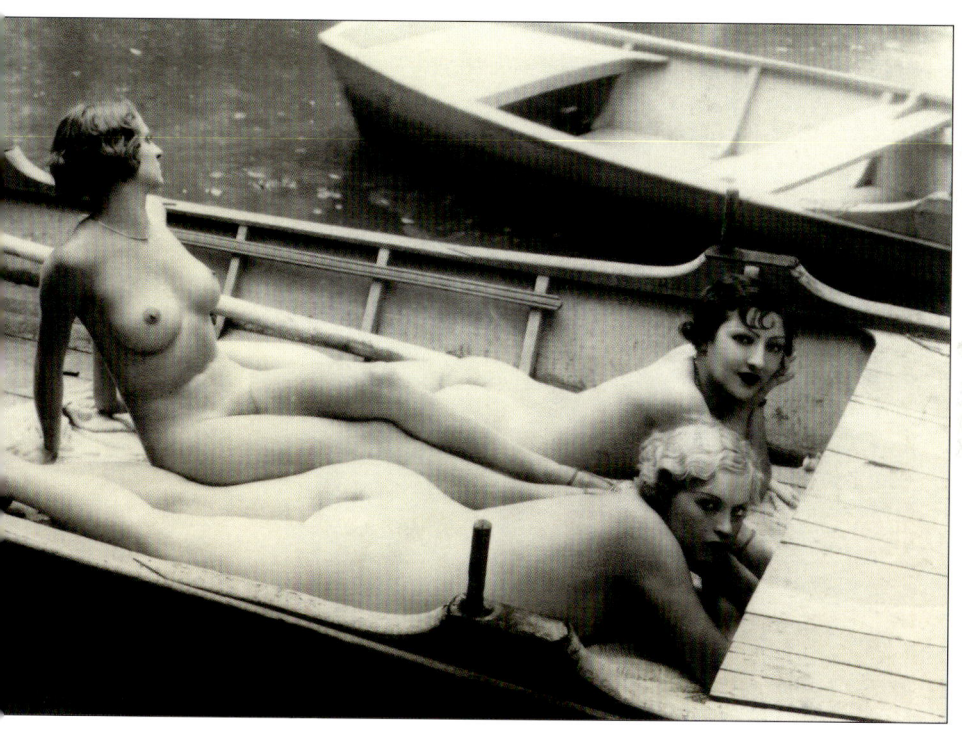

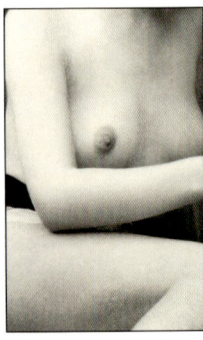

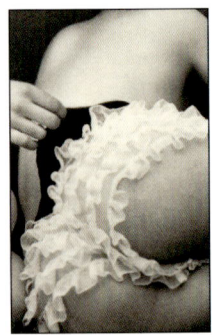

In 1936, *Editions Gauloises* changed its name to *The New Bookshops*. The different companies were given bewitching names such as *Miss Lulu*, *Luna Studio*, *Venus Administration*, *The Two Moons Bookshop*, *Luna Bookshop*, *The Sun Bookshop*, *Moon Editions*, *The Full Moon Bookshop*, *Collectors Club*, *Opéra d'Antin Bookshop*, *Erotik Studio* and *Miss Malou*. All these shops, publications, journals and studios were part of the same company.

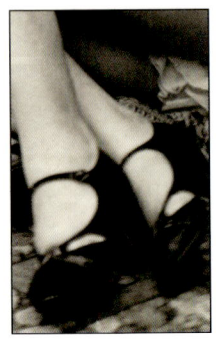

N° 508

———

c. 1935
Biederer Studio for Ostra Editions
Blank-backed postcard, 9 x 14 cm

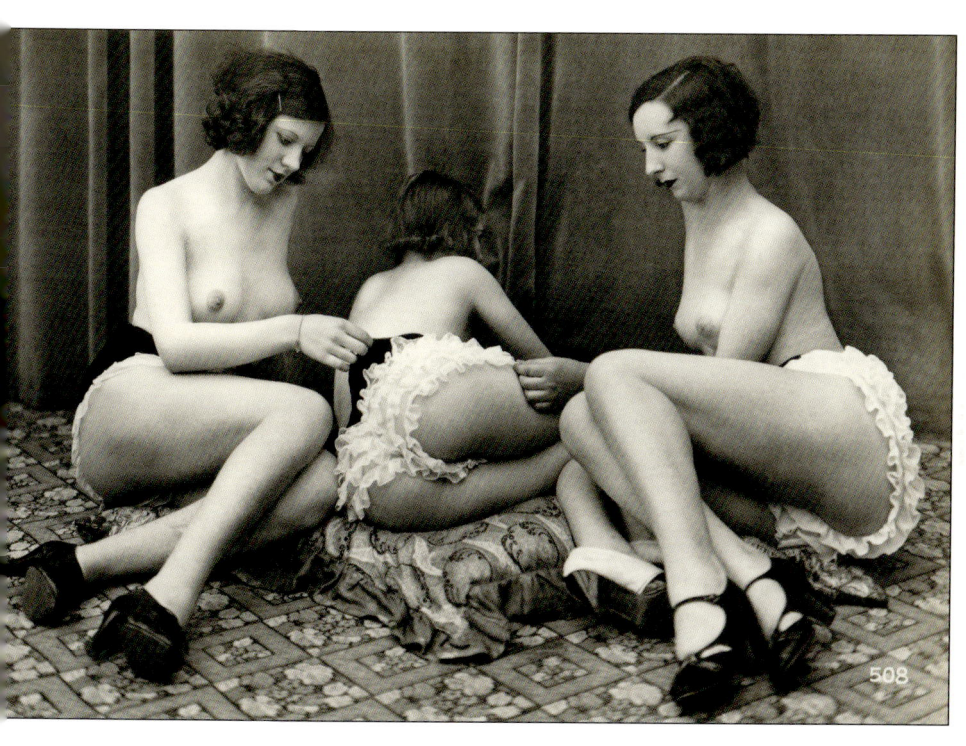

508

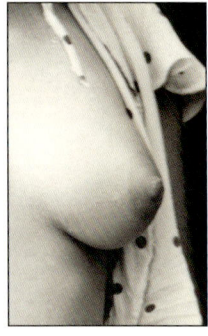

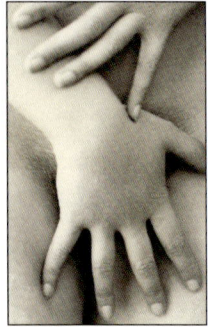

It became a veritable corporation, dealing a fatal blow to *Yva Richard,* at least as far as its presence in the press was concerned. As a direct competitor, advertising for *Yva Richard* was never to appear in the *New Bookshops* magazines. The numerous advertising inserts of the beginning of the decade were over, even in magazines such as *Parisian Life* or *Amusing Journal,* where they had appeared on a regular basis, their disappearance leaving a huge gap in the columns.

N° 59

c. 1935
Biederer Studio for Ostra Editions
Blank-backed postcard, 14 x 9 cm

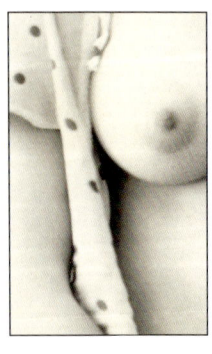

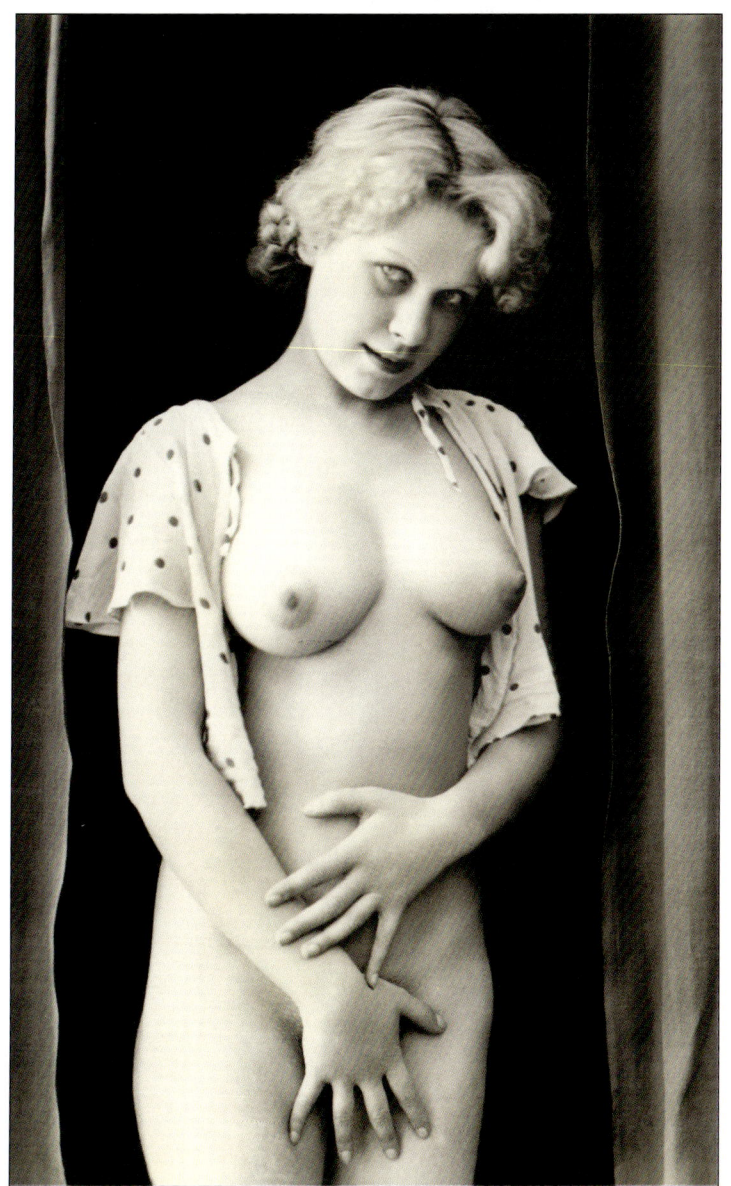

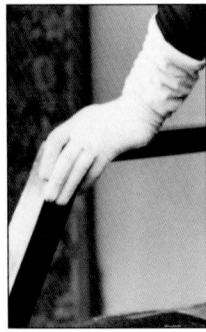

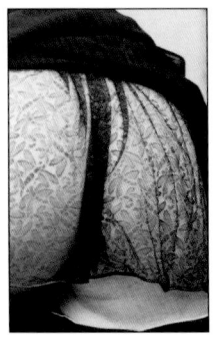

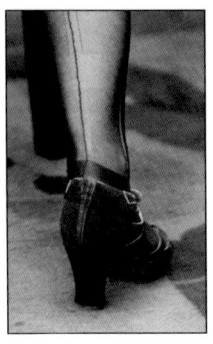

The *New Bookshops* continued to expand. It went through several administrative changes without changing the head office. On the 7th of January 1937, a new bookshop opened at no. 11 rue Tronchet, called the *Madeleine Bookshop*. This was the year in which Martoune, who was an important client of both *Diana-Slip* and *Yva Richard*, remarked on the size of the queue in front of her brothel The Sphinx, which employed one hundred and twenty girls with a turnover of one hundred and fifty thousand

N° 17

———

c. 1935
Biederer Studio for Ostra Editions
Blank-backed postcard, 14 x 9 cm

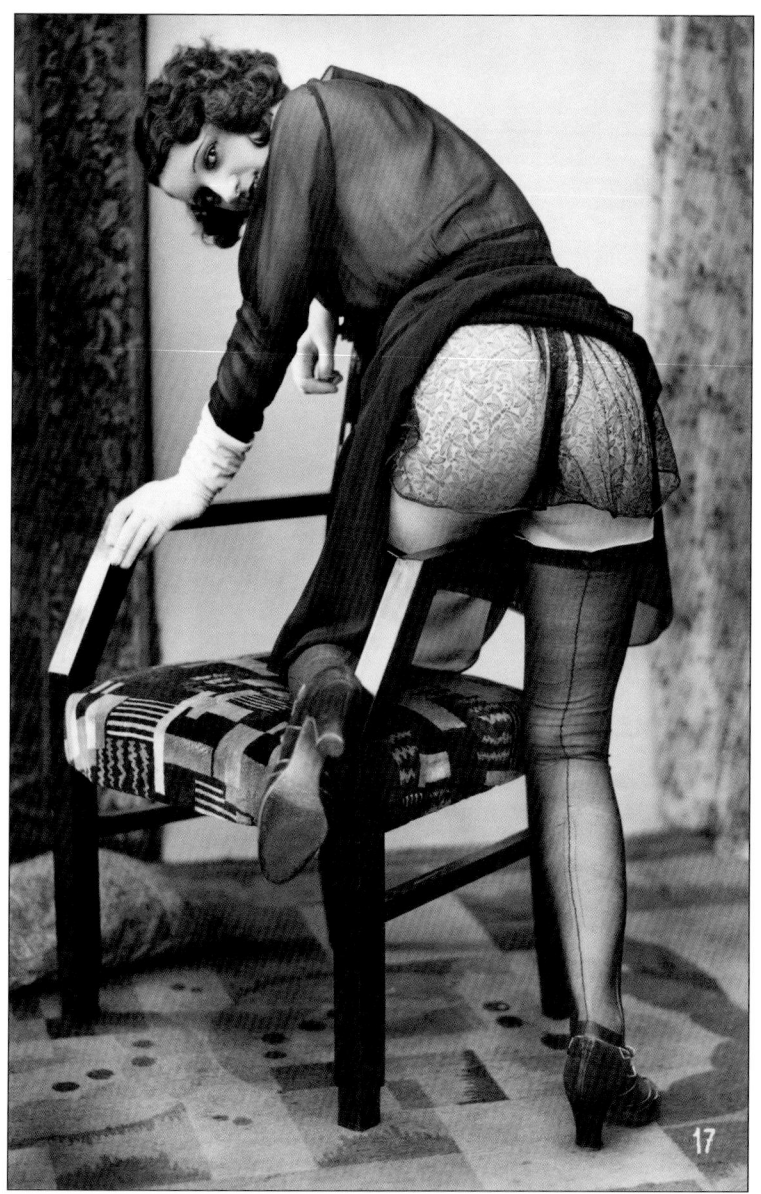

17

213

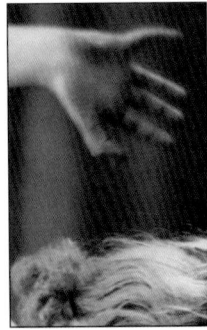

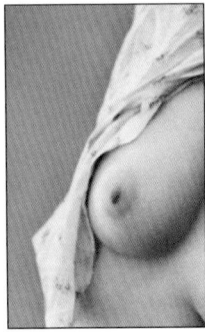

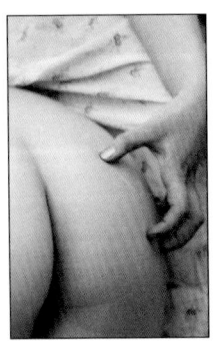

francs per day and catered to the important people of this world.

It was a lavish period of pleasure, yet the greatest of all cataclysms would soon take place. This carefree attitude of the time takes us to 1939, when on the 17th of April the Commerce Register records no less than 18 companies in the New Bookshop group. *Curio Publications, Ponceau Bookshop, Réaumur Sébastopol Bookshop,* the *Moon Bookshop, Moon Library,* the *Richepanse Bookshop, Diana Slip, Richepanse Publications, Libertine*

Untitled
————

c. 1935
Biederer Studio for Ostra Editions
Gelatin silver print, 16 x 11 cm

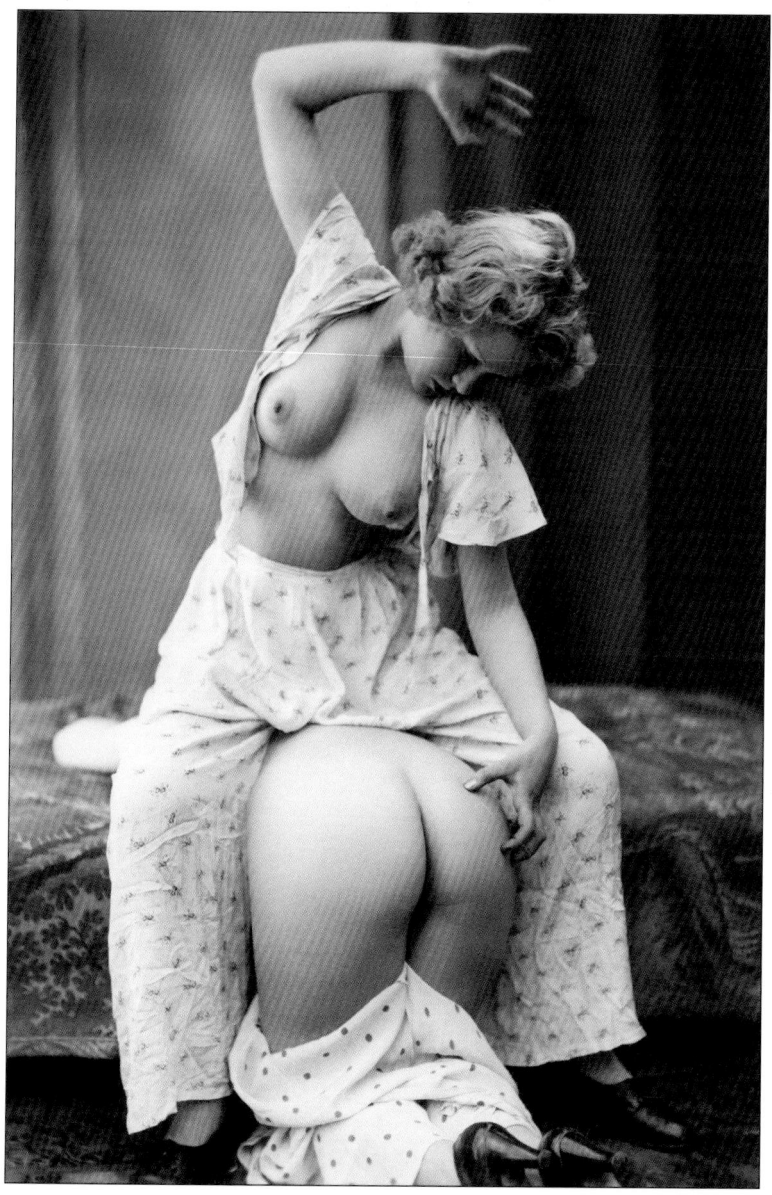

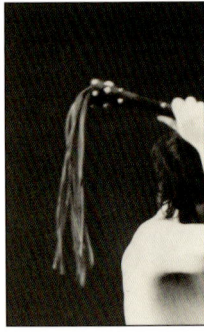

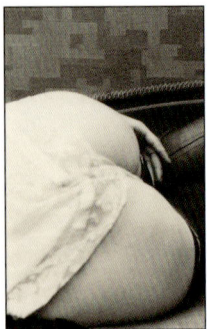

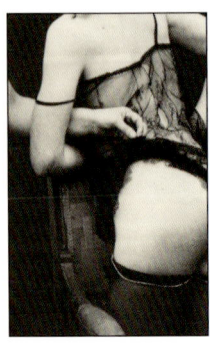

Lingerie, Opéra d'Antin Bookshop, the Madeleine Bookshop, Madeleine Library, the *Beauregard Bookshop*, the *Bonne Nouvelle Bookshop*, the *Boulevards Bookshop*, the *Tuileries Bookshop* and the *Colisée-Champs-Elysées Bookshop*. Some would disappear and others would appear, such as that at no. 11 rue Colisée. Some offered bilingual publications targeting the Anglo-Saxon clientele attracted to the Paris of the thirties, where the moral climate was still less prudish than in their own countries.

N° 350

———

c. 1935
Biederer Studio for Ostra Editions
Blank-backed postcard, 14 x 9 cm

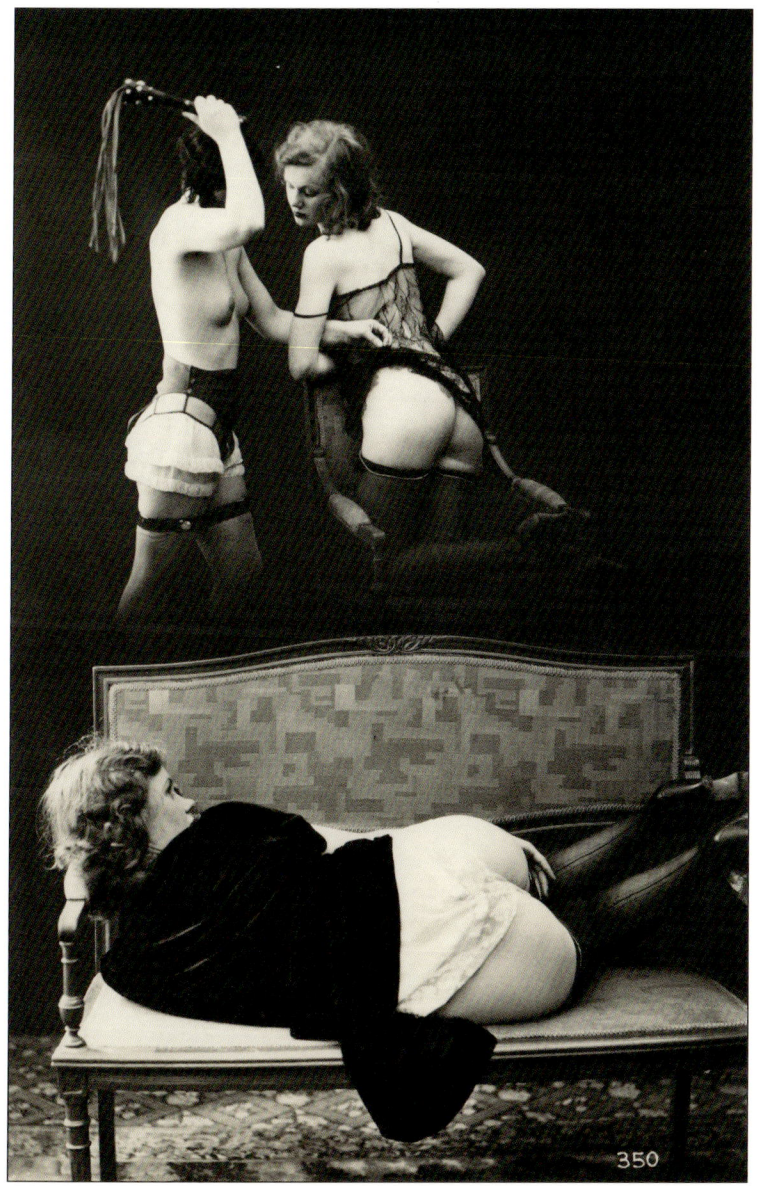

350

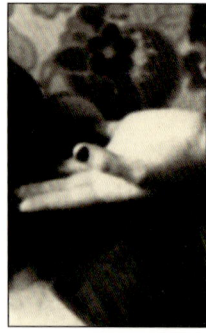

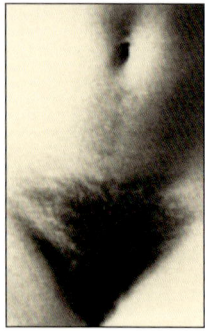

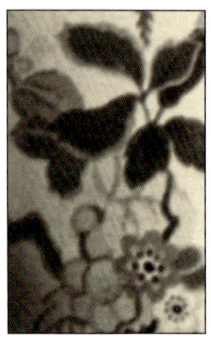

The Pictures of Mr. X

A part from the commercial production, there were also a number of amateur photographers. Some of these would regularly send photographs of their lady friends, mistresses or wives to the different magazines to be published. Among the thousands of erotic photographs examined, those of an anonymous photographer, who we will refer to as Mr. X, first attracts our attention because of their origins.

Untitled
––––––

c. 1935
Monsieur X
Gelatin silver print, 24 x 18 cm

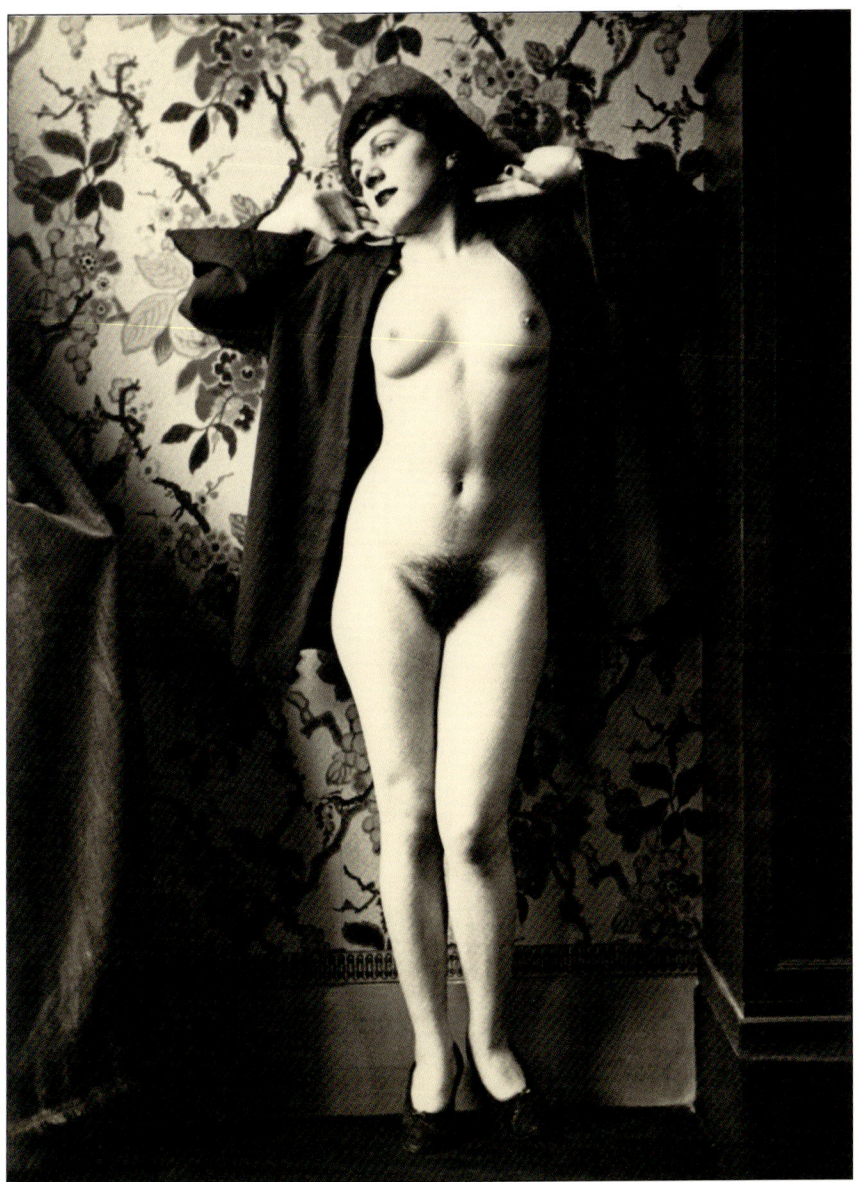

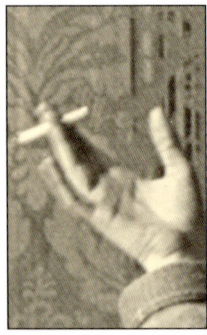

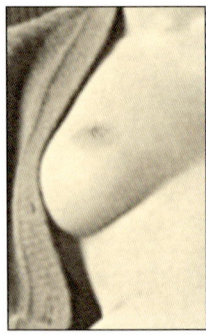

They cannot be found either in the albums or in the hiding places uncovered of collectors of this time. Not one could be found in the collections of great collectors such as Michel Simon or Paul Caron. There was a good reason for this, as Mr. X was an amateur photographer in the real sense of the word, who only took pictures for his own pleasure and not for commercial reasons.

Fortunately, because of his foresight, his collection was not destroyed by the family, as has happened so often elsewhere.

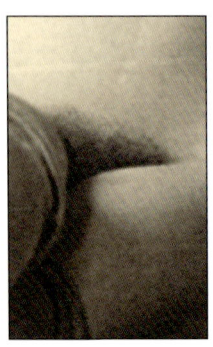

Untitled
————

c. 1935
Monsieur X
Gelatin silver print, 24 x 18 cm

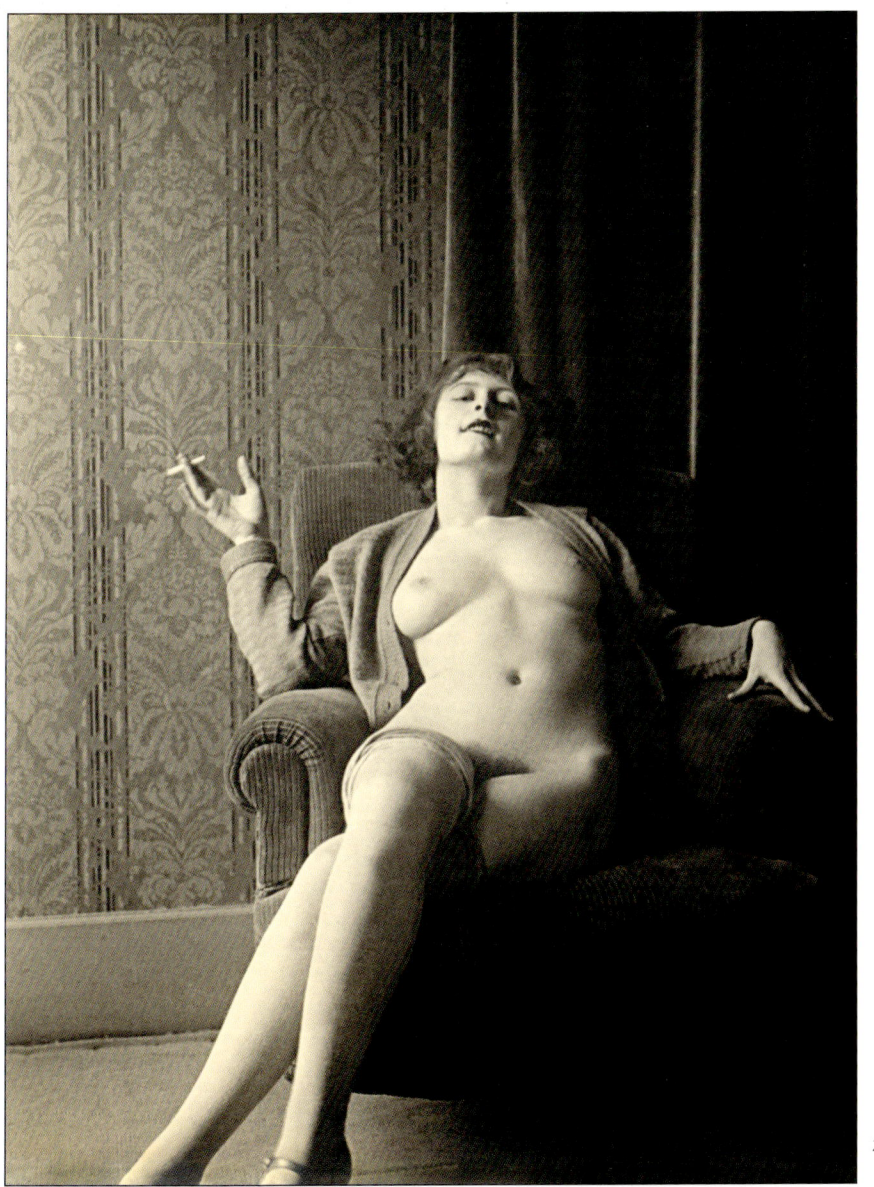

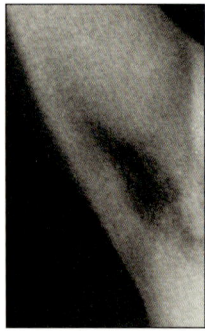

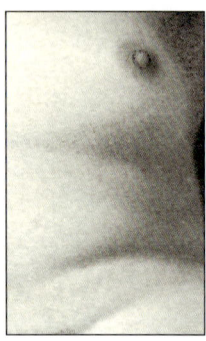

Twenty years or so ago, realising that he was getting on, this octogenarian decided to sell his entire photographic collection to a single Parisian bookshop that he had chosen for its taste for eroticism and its discretion. All the pictures feature nude or scantily dressed women, posing academically or in a very exhibitionistic manner. There are never any pictures of men. The very particular style of these pictures made it important to designate the author.

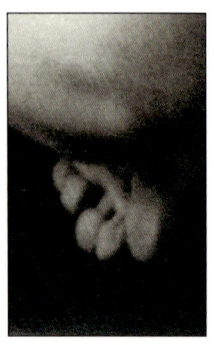

Untitled

c. 1935
Monsieur X
Gelatin silver print, 24 x 18 cm

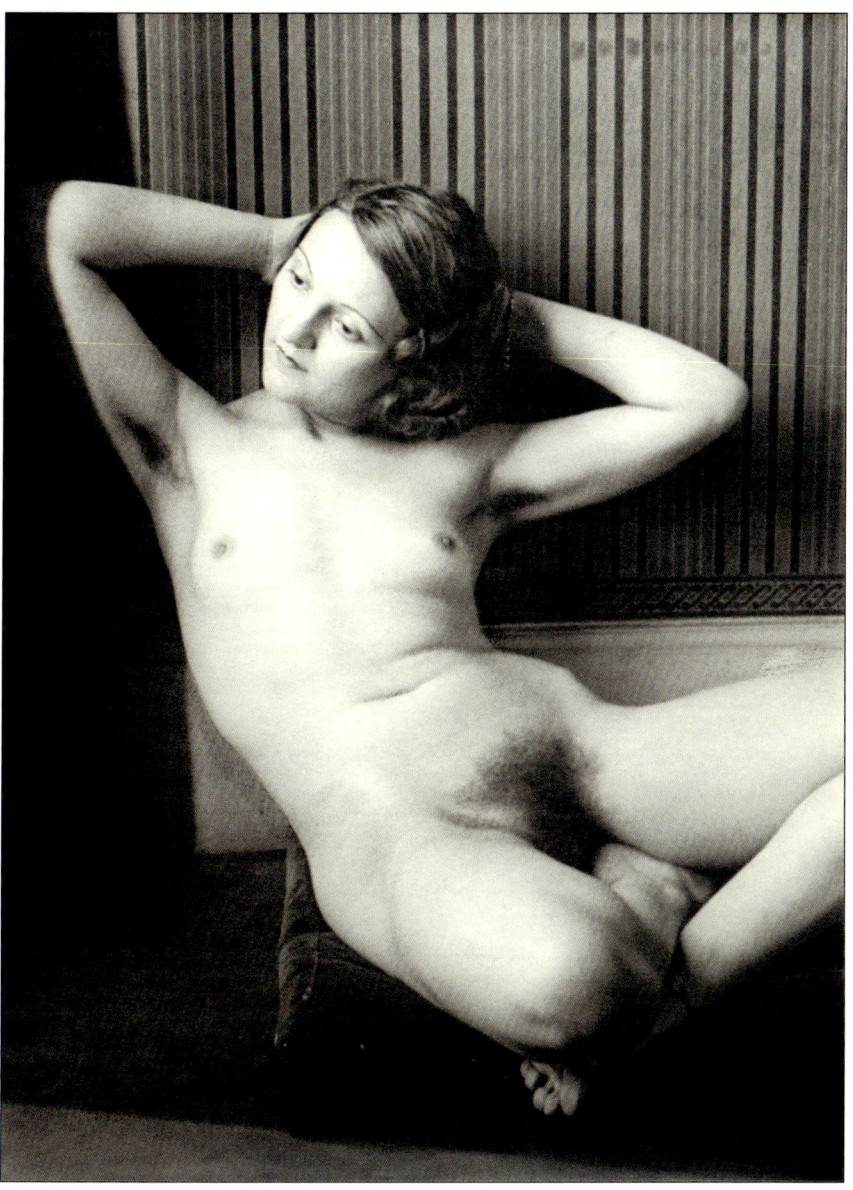

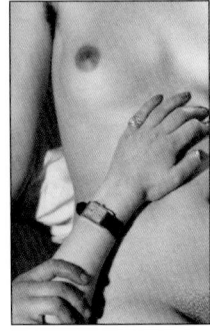

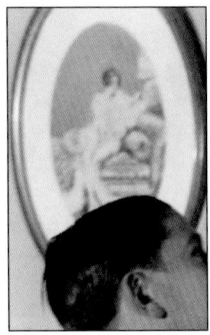

Thus, he became known as Mr. X for photography collectors and experts at auctions. The girls in the photographs are certainly not artists or photographers' models as might be expected, no more than the result of a chance meeting, where the girls agreed to strip before the camera. These girls are used to exposing themselves, to playing with their bodies, either by themselves or in groups. One can imagine that they lived and worked in the same

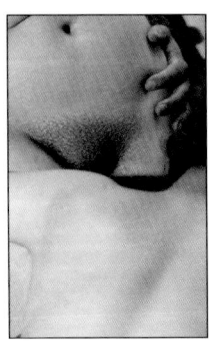

Untitled

c. 1935
Ostra Editions
Blank-backed postcard, 14 x 9 cm

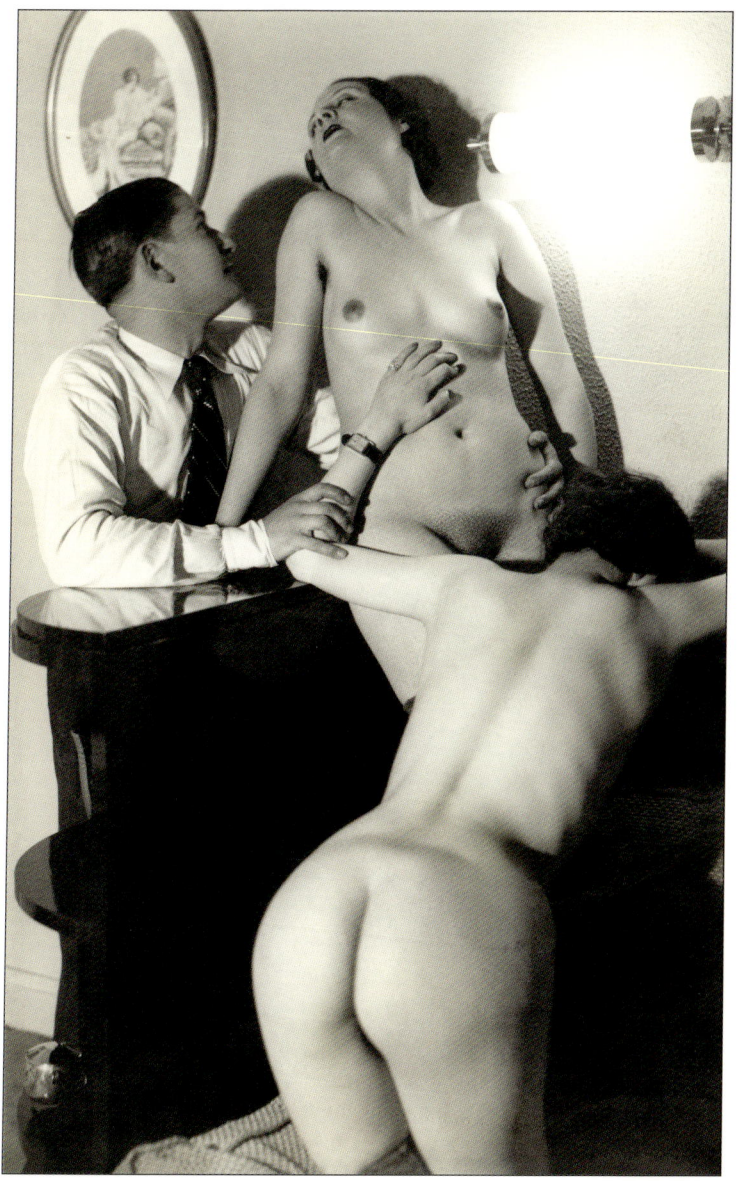

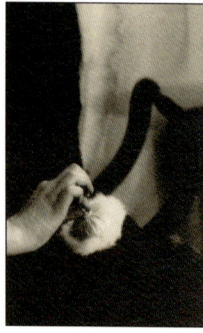

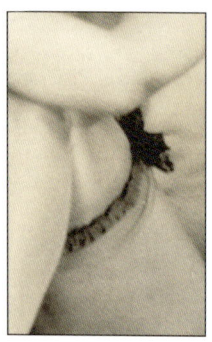

surroundings, in the same house, in which they sold their bodies. Moreover, the old fashioned interphones that sometimes feature on the walls of some bedrooms testify to the fact that these rooms are not in an apartment but in a hotel. A view taken from a balcony overlooking the Place Pigalle provides the proof; this is the world of Parisian prostitution, where Mr. X and his friend appear sometimes in the pictures, apparently moving about with ease and habit.

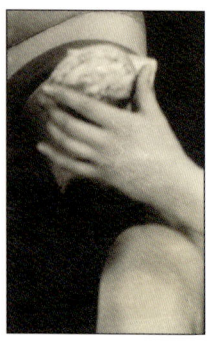

Untitled
———

c. 1935
Grundworth (?)
Gelatin silver print, 18 x 13 cm

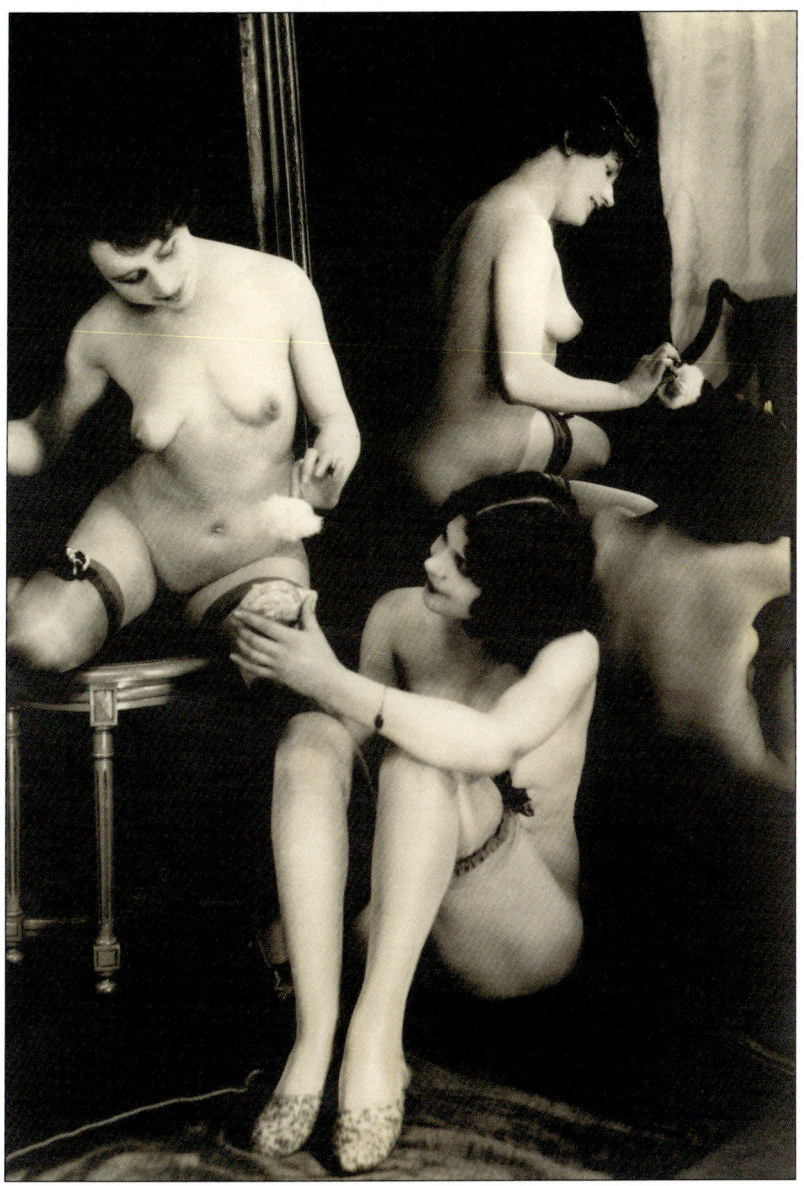

227

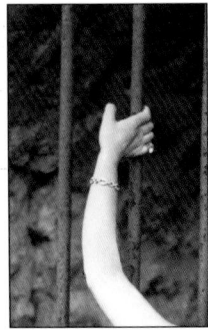

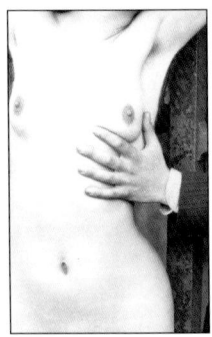

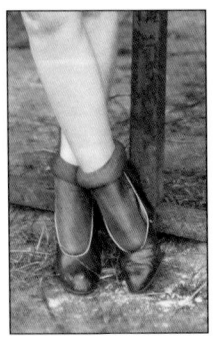

Mr. X is, in short, the French equivalent of E. J. Bellocq. This American photographer from the turn of the century, discovered by Lee Friedlander, and whose life was so well-illustrated by Louis Malle in his film *La Petite*, immortalised the girls from Storyville, the red light district of New Orleans. Mr. X officiated in the Pigalle district of the thirties with the same wit and happiness.

Untitled
———
c. 1935
Ostra Editions
Blank-backed postcard, 14 x 9 cm

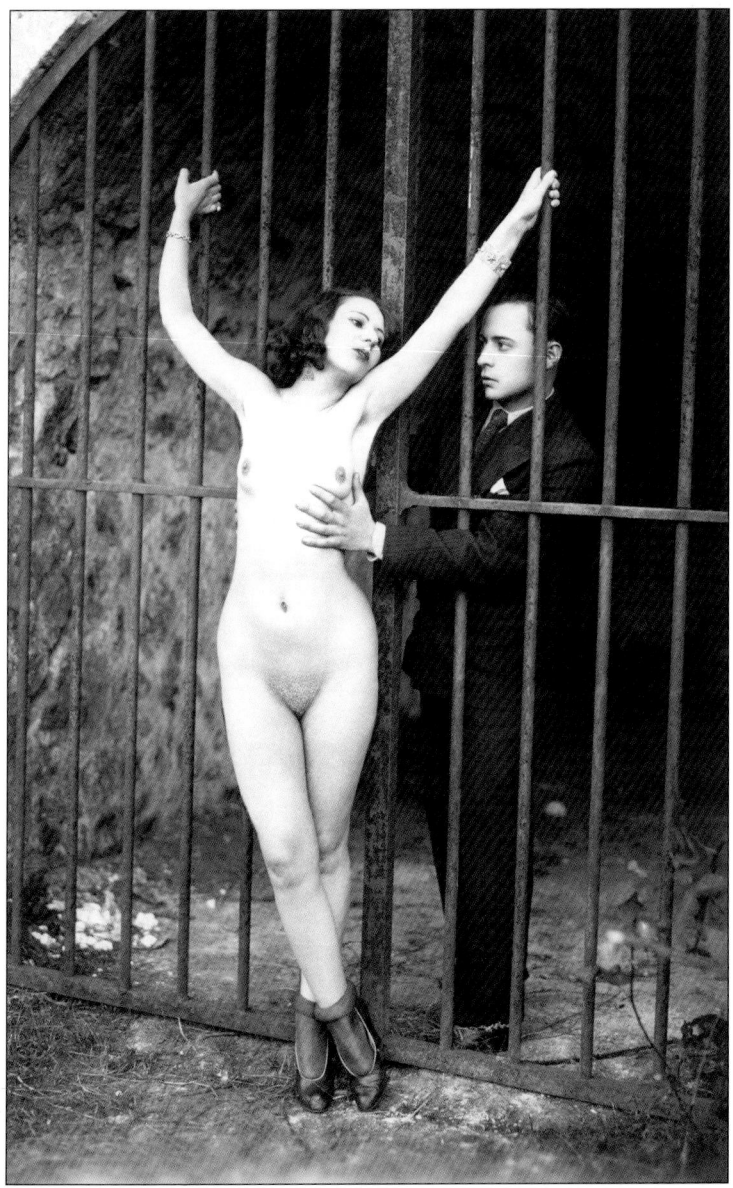

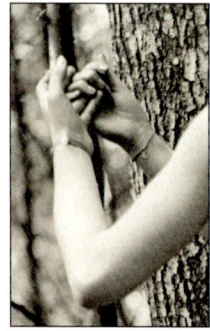

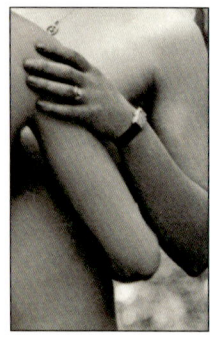

Conclusion

The year 1939 was marked by the declaration of war. The "Crazy Years" were buried forever, on both sides of the Rhine. In Paris, the inevitable advent of the "Popular Front" of 1936 was all that was needed to separate the French into two political factions. It was an infernal spiral that nothing and no one could check, since the bloody events which had taken place two years before, when the Right tried to take

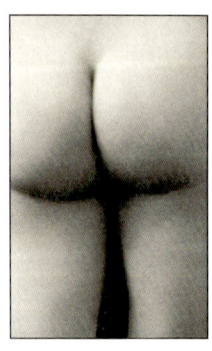

Untitled
_____

c. 1930
Ostra Editions (?)
Gelatin silver print, 18 x 13 cm

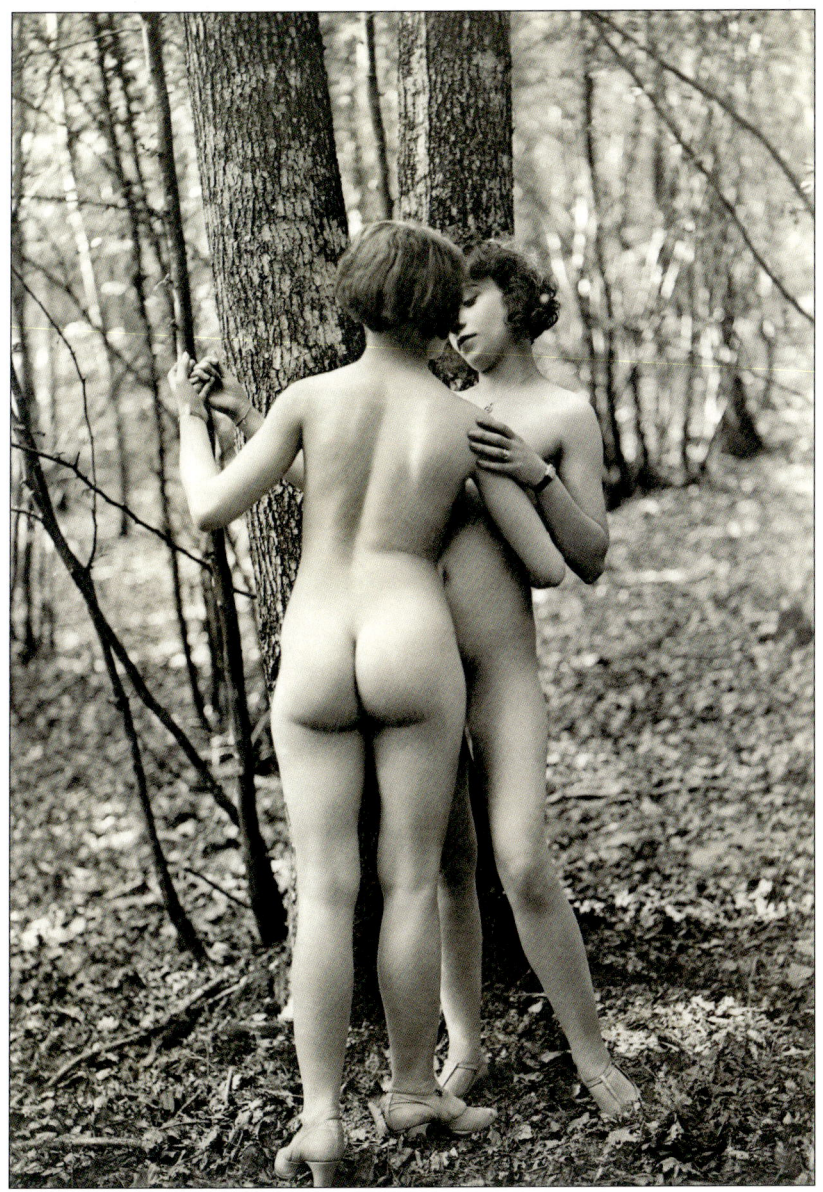

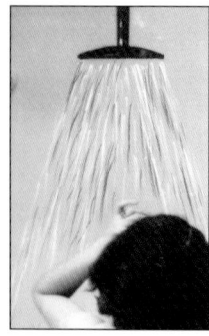

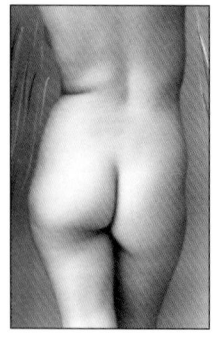

power by force, allowing the government of Daladier to promulgate decrees protecting "the family, the birth rate and the French race". These three adages would become "Work, Family, Country" under the Occupation and "National Revolution" government set up by Field Marshall Pétain. In Germany, the draconian conditions of the Treaty of Versailles crushed the people, clearing the path for the emergence of National Socialism. At the end of 1939, the Nazi invasion swept aside hastily prepared

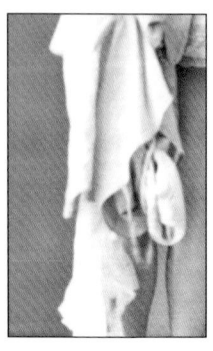

Untitled
―――――――

c. 1935
Biederer Studio for Ostra Editions
Gelatin silver print, 11 x 16 cm

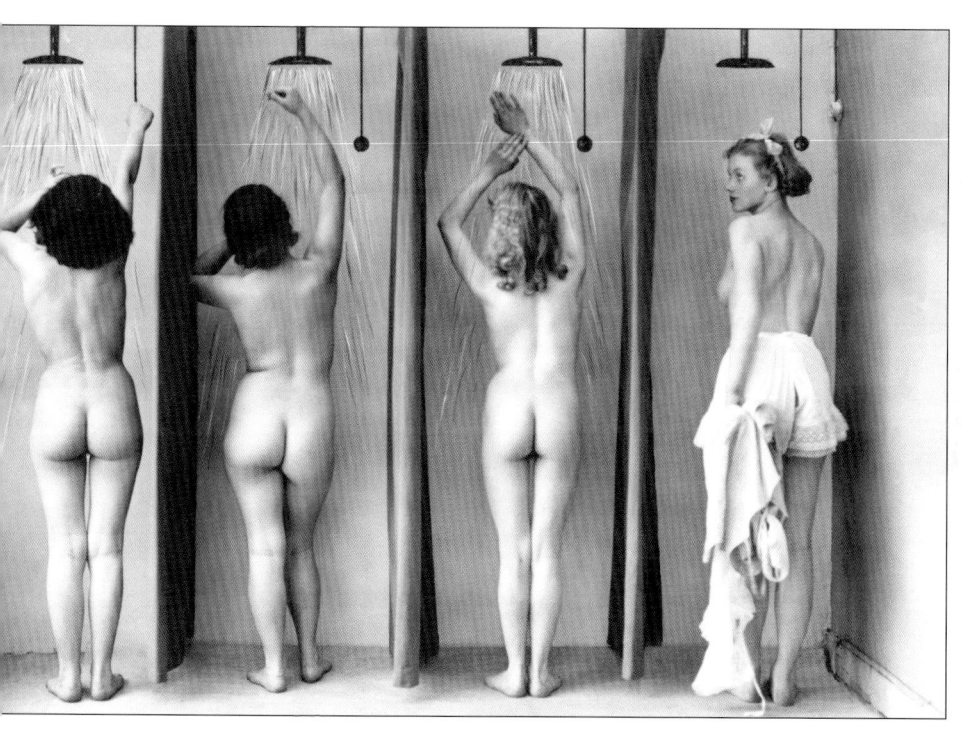

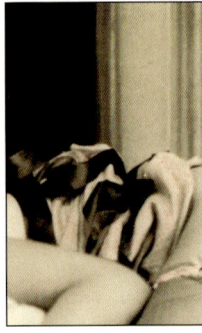

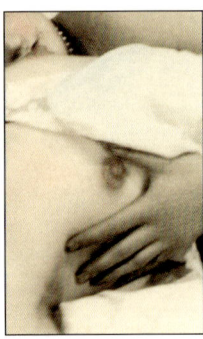

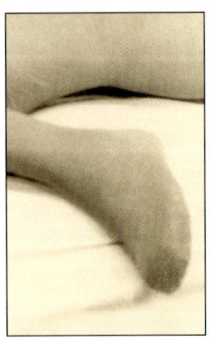

French defences during the first few weeks of the conflict, in what would be designated "this peculiar war".

By 1940, paper had become scarce. The little that was left was no longer used as a vehicle for the voluptuous images of Parisian women, but for the disgraceful propaganda of Vichy and the occupying forces. *Yva Richard* was still listed at no. 9 rue Pillet-Will under the laconic name *Linge* from 1941 to 1943, then disappeared forever from the directories.

Untitled

c. 1935
Grundworth (?)
Gelatin silver print, 13 x 18 cm

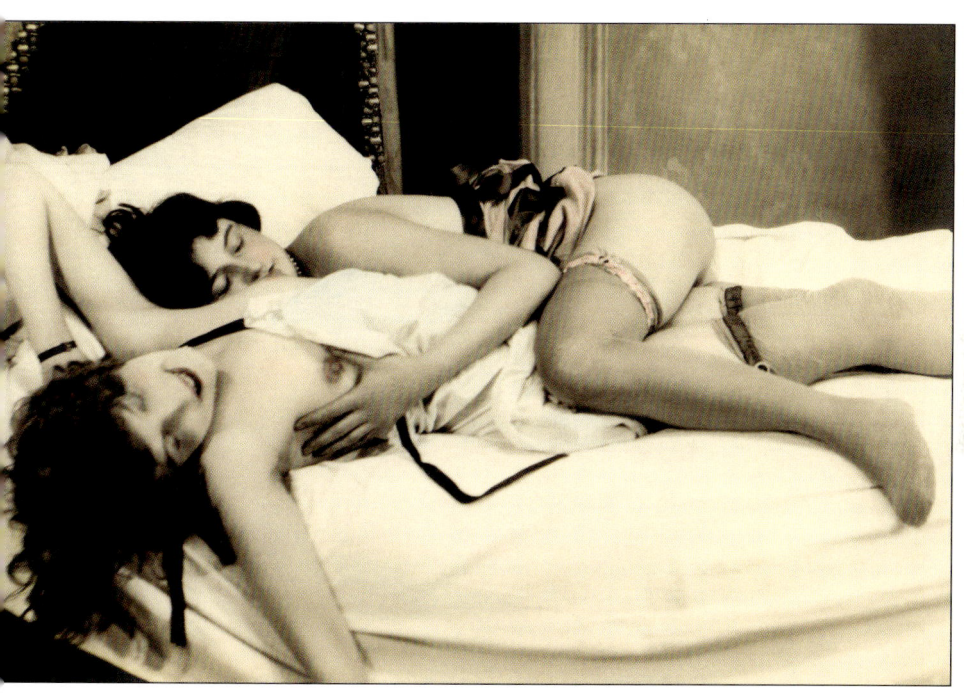

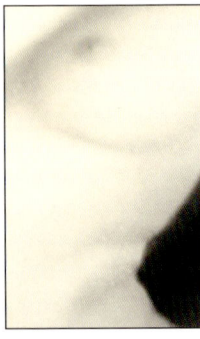

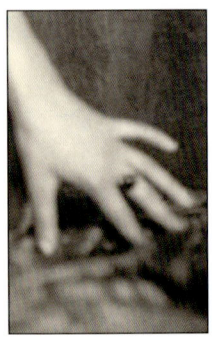

Behind this satirical name, a couple had fulfilled the dreams of lovers of debauchery for more than twenty years. It was a unique phenomenon, and no other similar enterprise would be able to unite with such success and grace the art and the pleasures of French eroticism. As far as the *New Bookshops* were concerned, they started to dwindle but did not disappear. By the time of the liberation of Paris in August 1944, the group still existed at no. 17 rue d'Antin, 37 rue Beauregard and at the *Colisée-Champs-Elysées Bookshop*, which housed the journal *Paris-Magazine*

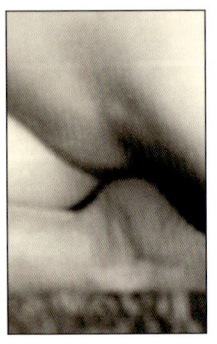

Untitled
———

c. 1935
Grundworth (?)
Gelatin silver print, 24 x 18 cm

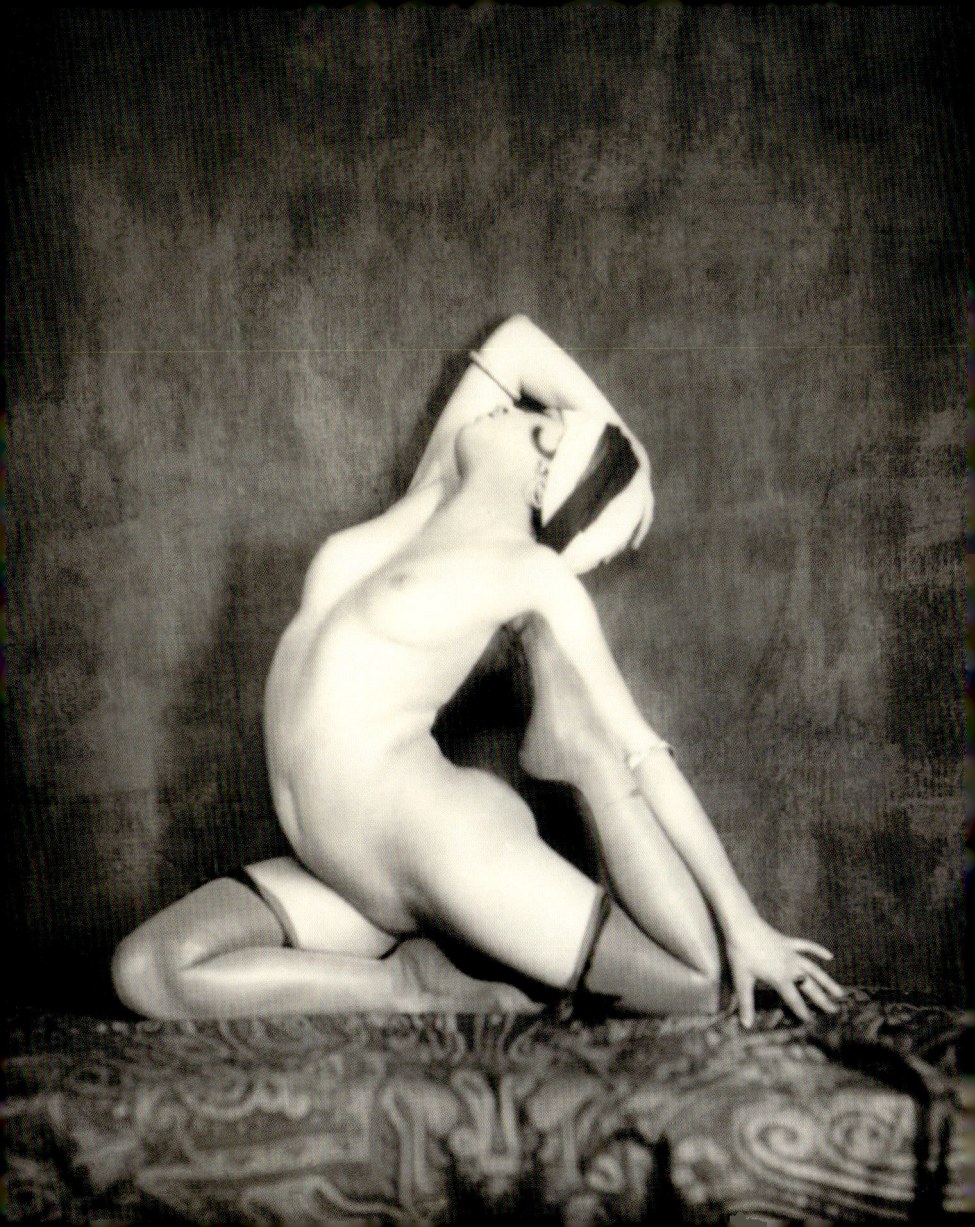

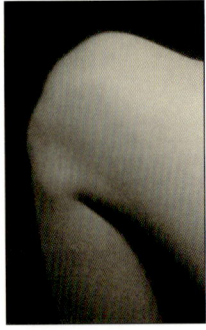

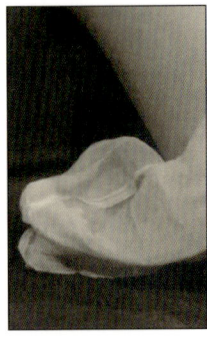

after the war for a few more years. The tailor *Williams* was listed at no. 4 rue du Ponceau, and the photographer *Biederer* at boulevard du Temple. In spite of the initial euphoria of the liberated France, nothing would be as before. After the horrors of 1914-1918, the laxest government of the time had allowed the explosion of the feeling of freedom which had led to the Crazy Years. However, after this war, nothing resembling this bygone era would take place, quite the contrary!

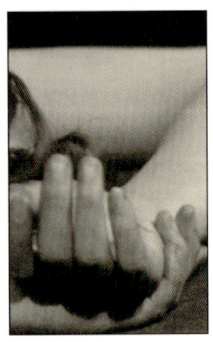

Untitled

c. 1935
Grundworth (?)
Gelatin silver print, 18 x 24 cm

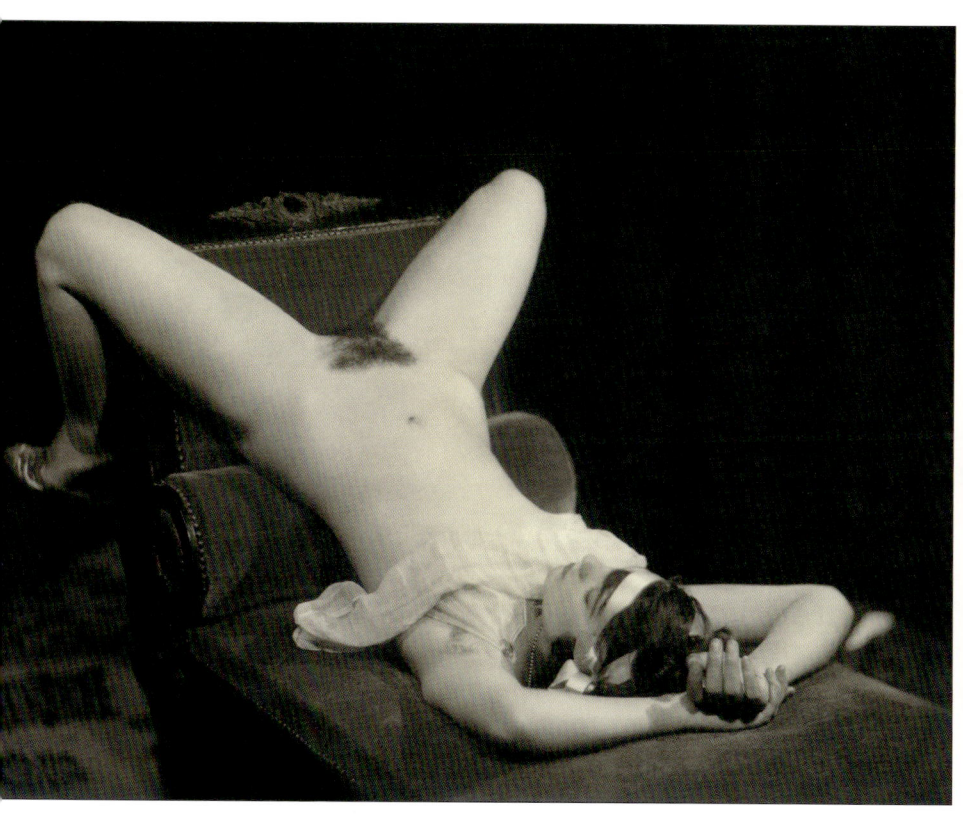

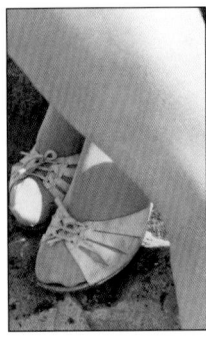

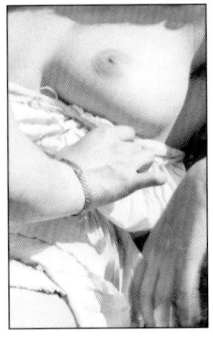

Yva Richard, *Diana-Slip*, *Mademoiselle Louisette* and all their friends disappeared, taking with them their world of fantasies, frivolities and transvestites. The world of prostitution had been in collusion with the occupying forces. Which ever way we look at it, they had taken too much advantage of the situation, and enjoyed themselves too much, whilst the rest of the French suffered in silence. A decree was passed, called the *Marthe Richard* law, which ordered the closure of the brothels, thus sending the girls onto the streets.

N° 713

———

c. 1935
Ostra Editions
Blank-backed postcard, 14 x 9 cm

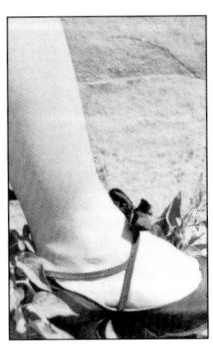

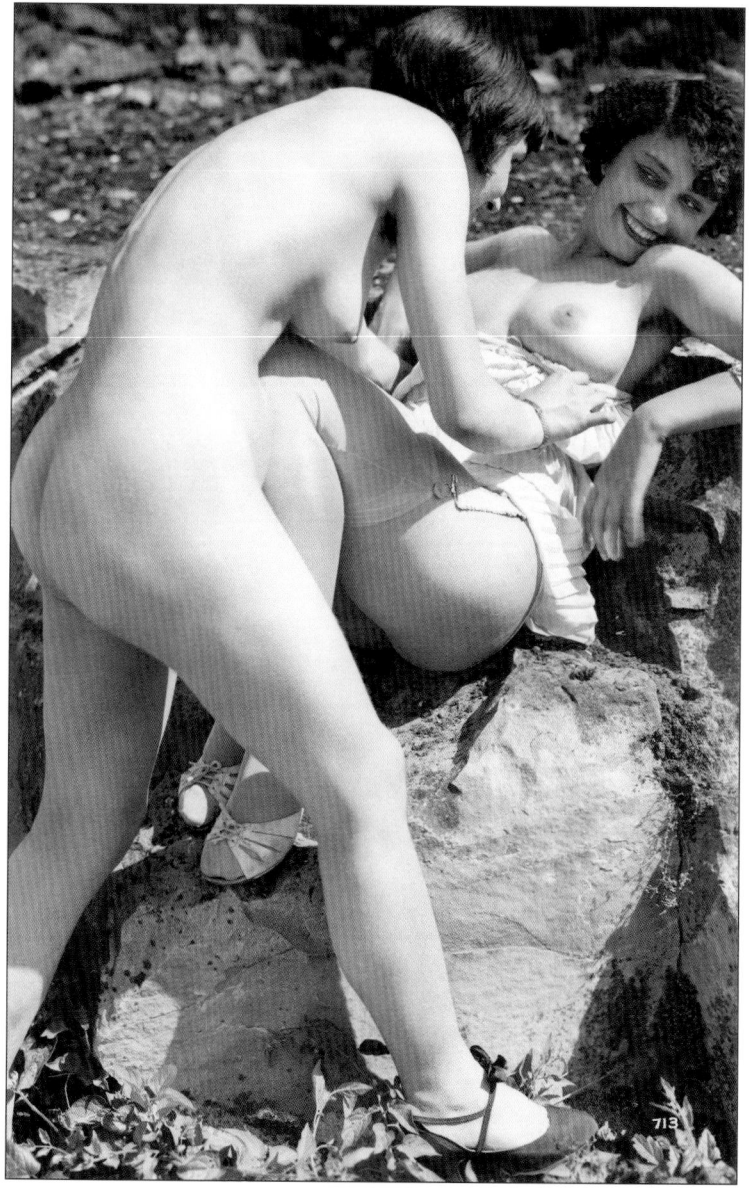

713

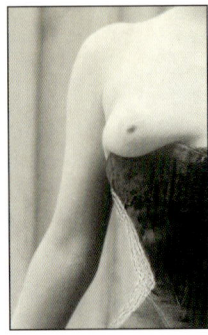

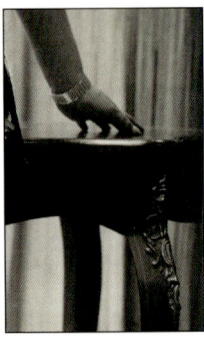

The censor conserved the stifling repression imposed by Pétain and any form of nudity was prohibited. As if that was not enough, in the fifties, works from the thirties were condemned by the courts, under the simple pretext that, although totally old fashioned, the themes used were spanking and domination. Amusements that had been tolerated and practised without any complaints from followers were now prohibited. Had the French authorities mistaken licentious games for Nazi abominations?

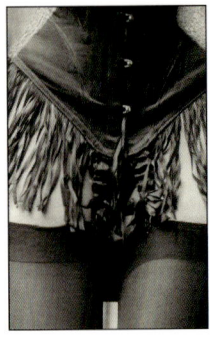

Excessive Corset
———————

c. 1935
Yva Richard
Gelatin silver print, 14 x 11.5 cm

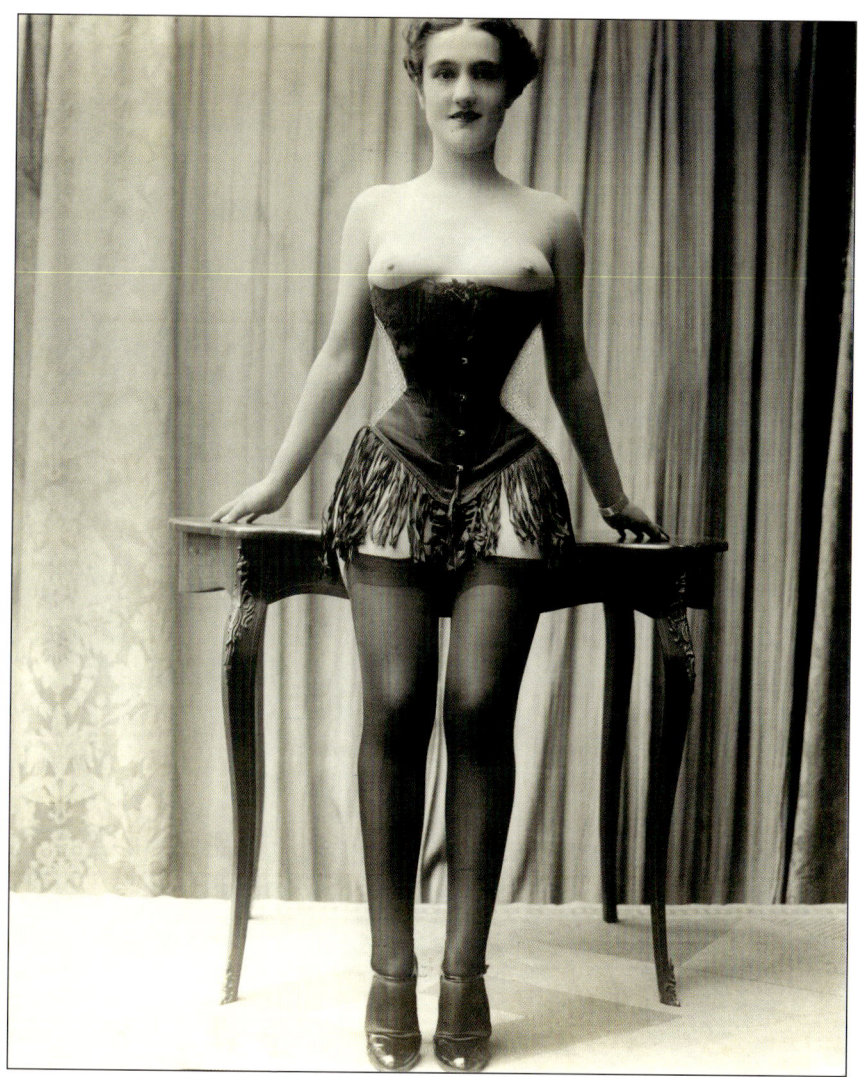

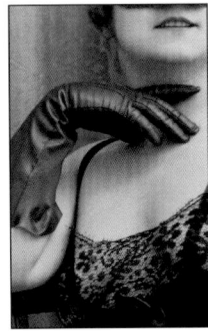

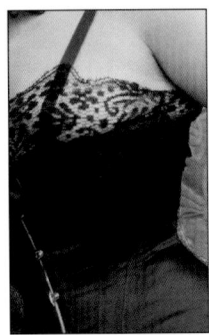

Had they confused republican tradition with the orthodoxy of obscure religions? The French were treated like little children, and henceforth, what they could see and hear was subject to censorship. It was the same as far as reading matter was concerned, and the works of the Marquis de Sade, André Pieyre de Mandiargues and many other masterpieces were wrenched from the cultural heritage which is the envy of the world. Then came the sixties and the utopia of 1968. Little by little the cold and academic eroticism of the

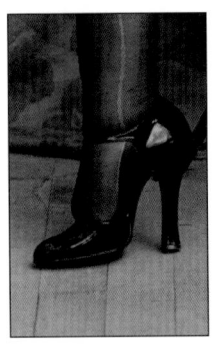

Thigh-high Stockings in Black Satin

c. 1935
Yva Richard
Gelatin silver print, 17 x 12 cm

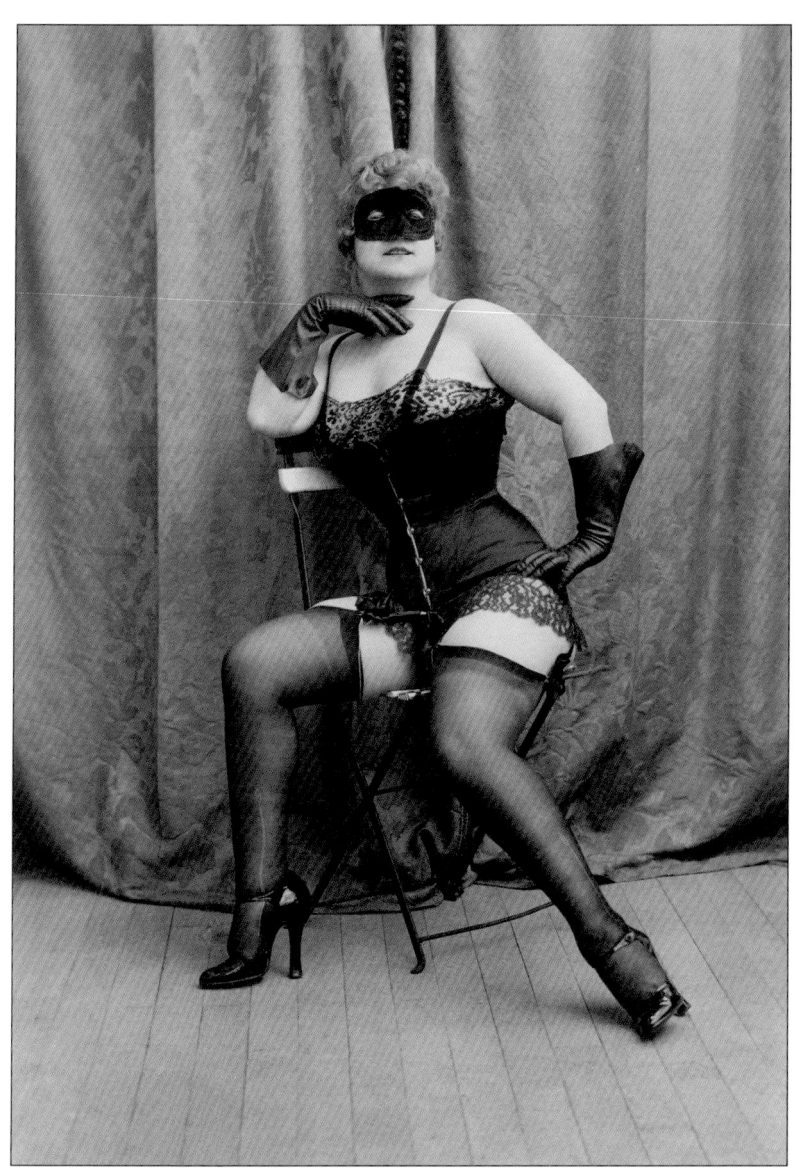

245

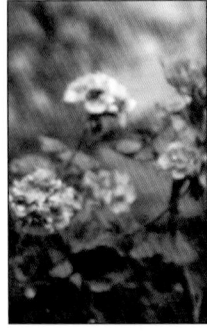

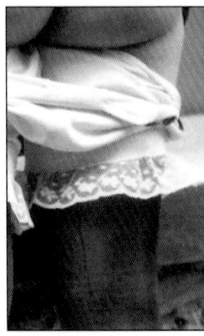

Scandinavian countries revived the Western world until we come to the contemporary period, where photography, as can be seen in the works of Pierre Molinier, Jan Saudek, Joël-Peter Witkin, Mapplethorpe and Gilles Berquet defy taboos and deal essentially with the suffering of sex, the fascination of violence and the anxiety of death - leaving no room for the voluptuous folly of our Crazy Years.

Oh nostalgia, when you take possession of our senses, there is no escape!

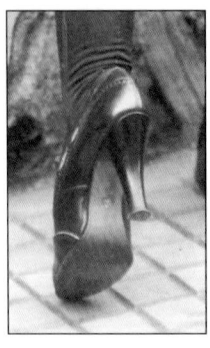

Untitled

c. 1937
Yva Richard
Gelatin silver print, 24.5 x 17 cm

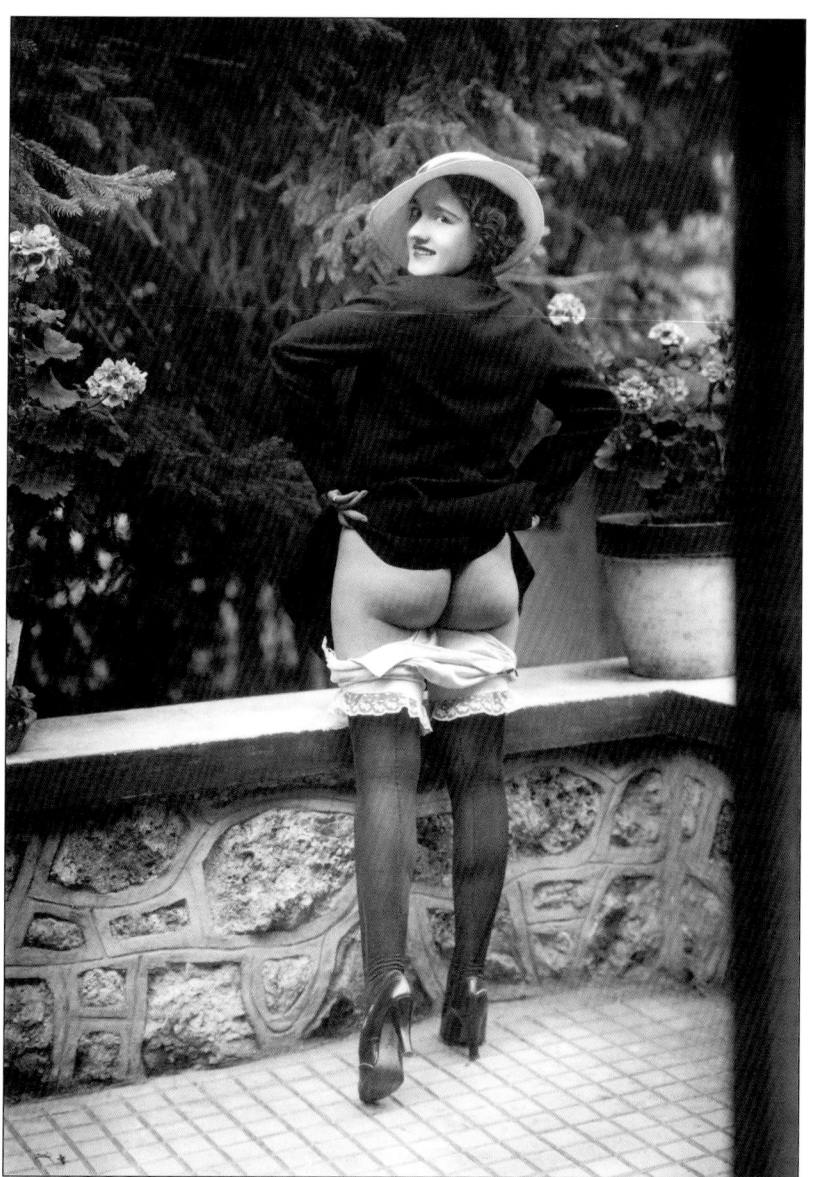

List of Illustrations

/ S

T

U